Douglas Genealogy

You are holding a reproduction of an original work that is in the public domain in the United States of America, and possibly other countries.You may freely copy and distribute this work as no entity (individual or corporate) has a copyright on the body of the work.This book may contain prior copyright references, and library stamps (as most of these works were scanned from library copies).These have been scanned and retained as part of the historical artifact.

This book may have occasional imperfections such as missing or blurred pages, poor pictures, errant marks, etc. that were either part of the original artifact, or were introduced by the scanning process. We believe this work is culturally important, and despite the imperfections, have elected to bring it back into print as part of our continuing commitment to the preservation of printed works worldwide. We appreciate your understanding of the imperfections in the preservation process, and hope you enjoy this valuable book.

THE DOUGLAS GENEALOGY.

THE DESCENDANTS OF

JOHN DOUGLAS

OF MIDDLEBOROUGH, MASSACHUSETTS, THE FIRST
OF THIS BRANCH IN AMERICA.

The Douglas Nobility of Scotland.

One generation passeth away and another
generation cometh. *Ecc. 1—4.*

—BY—
J. LUFKIN DOUGLAS.

MEMBER OF THE MAINE HISTORICAL SOCIETY.

BATH, MAINE.
SENTINEL AND TIMES PUBLISHING CO.
1890.

72.354

RECEIVED
JAN 28 1892
WIS. HISTORICAL SOC;

PREFACE.

The study of history is productive of much that is of a noble and elevating character. It is natural for all to desire to know something of the country whence his ancestors sprang, as well as of his native land; and is it not of vastly more interest for one to be able to tell who his ancestors were and something of the history of their struggles, progress and honors? It is a custom handed down to us from the patriarchs of old, who were very careful to preserve and cherish the memory of their departed. The children of Israel were charged to carry the bones of Joseph and have them deposited in the Holy Land. It is a duty we owe posterity to leave a record of the deeds of our generation.

From my earliest recollection I have desired to know who my ancestors were, where they lived and what they did. In 1867 I began this work, not thinking to extend it beyond the limits of my grandfather and his immediate descendants; but I became so interested in the subject that I concluded to continue the research still further. I had often heard my father relate the story of John, the ancestor of our branch in America, who was born in Scotland, and at the age of twelve years was kidnapped in London and brought to Boston and who subsequently married and settled in Middleboro, Mass. and was the father of three sons, Elijah, John and George. Elijah settled in Maine.

One hundred and twenty years had now elapsed since Elijah or his descendants had heard from his brothers or their posterity. I felt a natural desire to learn of their whereabouts. Through the kindness of the clerk of Middleboro, I was enabled to open a correspondence with the descendants of those two brothers scattered throughout nearly every state in New England.

I have devoted the greater part of two years to gathering and writing the matter for this work. Nearly the entire copy has been written three times and carefully corrected; yet in a work of this kind I am aware that accuracy is quite impossible. I have searched town and church records and have sought information in all ways possible.

Had this Genealogy been commenced twenty years earlier much information could have been obtained which has now been lost by the death of those who possessed it.

Many family records have either been lost or were never kept and in a few instances the writing was not legible and thus mistakes may have occurred. Still it affords me much satisfaction to be able to present this volume so completely to my numerous relatives.

In some families names have been transposed, parents sending them one way and children another. Thus Nancy Amanda has been changed to Amanda Nancy. I have endeavored in all cases to arrange names correctly and acceptably to all concerned.

In the matter of individual biography I have carefully examined all that has been received and have used what was deemed of interest to the reader, and would have been pleased to have inserted more had it been received.

The genealogical history of the Douglas Nobility was taken from the Peerage of Scotland, written in 1764 by Robert Douglas. There are many different records of the origin, name and history of the family, yet they all have their rise from the one source and it is reasonable to believe that this account is authentic.

PREFACE.

As to the correct way of spelling the name, I find in use Duglas, Douglas and Douglass. From all accounts of history, as well as of heraldry, the original way of spelling the name is generally spelled Douglas.

Every person has the privilege of spelling his name as he chooses. As far as known, I have written each name as it has been received. Previous to the fifth generation the name was Duglas or Douglas.

The coat-of-arms was obtained from Scotland through the heraldry office in New York and minutely compared with works on the subject and found to be the proper arms for all bearing the name, without regard to the branch to which they belong.

In my researches in this work, I have come across several branches of this great Douglas tree. The one known as the Stephen A. Douglas branch is numerous in Connecticut. Their genealogy has been published by Mr. Charles H. James Douglas of Providence, R. I. The Francis Douglas branch is to be found in Gardiner, Hallowell and that vicinity. A branch is also found in Gorham, Sebago and Windham.

The reader must know that much time and not a little money has been used in compiling this genealogy. It has been a labor of love and not one for gain, for if I realize enough to pay the expense I shall be satisfied.

In preparing this volume I have formed very many pleasant acquaintances among relatives whom I should not otherwise have met.

My sincere thanks are tendered to all who have in any way aided me in this undertaking.

J. LUFKIN DOUGLAS.

BATH, MAINE, April, 1890.

THE DOUGLAS NOBILITY.

THE FOLLOWING GENEALOGICAL HISTORY OF THE DOUGLAS NOBILITY OF SCOTLAND WAS TAKEN FROM ROBERT DOUGLAS PEERAGE OF SCOTLAND, WRITTEN A. D. 1764.

If a long train of illustrious ancestors distinguished by the highest titles and connected with the most august and noble families in Europe, can make any name remarkable and great, there is no subject that can plead a higher claim than the Douglas; but it is the least part of the glory of this family that it has been honored with alliances by marriage into the first rank of nobility in Scotland, England and France. Having matched eleven times with the royal house of Scotland, and once with that of England. They were more distinguished for their virtue and merit than by their titles; and the luster of their actions outshown the splendor of their birth. Hence we see them leading the van of our armies in Scotland, supporting by their valor the kingdom of France, tottering on the head of Charles VII, when reduced to the last extremity by the bravery of the English; with many other acts of military glory that have made this family renowned through all Europe.

The traditional account of the origin of this noble family, transmitted to us by historians is as follows:

In the year of our Lord 770, in the reign of Solvathious, king of Scots, one Donald Bane of the Western Isles, having invaded the Scotch territories, and routed the royal army, a man of rank and figure came seasonably with his friends and followers to the king's assistance; he renewed the battle and obtained a complete victory over the invader. The king being desirous to see the man, who had done him so signal a piece of service, he was pointed out to him by his color or complexion, in these words of the old Gallic or Cettic language SHOLTO DU GLAS or GLASH in English, "Behold that black or swarthy colored man," from which he was named Sholto the Douglas. The king royally rewarded his great services, and gave him a grant of several lands and large possessions in the country of Lanark, which were called Douglas; and from hence came the sirname of the family.

This Sholto is said to have left two sons.

2 I. Hugh, ancestor of the Douglases in Scotland.

3 II. William, progenitor of the Scoti Douglasi in Italy when he settled. He married the daughter of

Antonio Spetino, a lady of one of the most honorable families in that country.

4 WILLIAM De DOUGLAS,

said to be lineally descended from the above named Sholto, who was created lord or dominus de Douglas by king Malcolm Canmore at a conventus procerum held in Forfar A. D. 1057: He lived after the year 1100 and left issue two sons:

5 I. Sir John de Douglas.
6 .II. Sir William of Glendoning of whom the Douglases of Strabrock and Pompherston are descended

5 SIR JOHN second Lord of DOUGLAS

succeeded in his father's lifetime, was designed of Douglas & Burn; lands which lie in the Shier of Selkirk, and were long in the possession of the family of Douglas. He was a man of great note in the reign of king David I. and dying about the year 1145, was succeeded by his son

7 SIR WILLIAM third Lord of DOUGLAS.

He is found witnessing characters by king David I. and Jocelin bishop of Glasgow between the year 1174 and 1199. He married Margaret, daughter of Eriskinus de Kerdal by whom he had six sons and one daughter.

Children :—

8 I. Archibald Lord of Douglas born about 1160; married Margaret Crawford.
9 II. Bricius de Douglas, who was bred to the church before the year 1203 was made Bishop of Murray.—He died 1222.
10 III. Alexander de Douglas was sheriff of Elgin.
11 IV. Henry de Douglas.
12. V. Hugo de Douglas.
13 VI. Friskinus de Douglas.
14 VII. Margaret married Kieth Grant Marshal of the kingdom.

8 ARCHIBALD fourth Lord of DOUGLAS,

eldest son of William third Lord of Douglas. He settled on the family estate, and married Margaret, daughter of Sir John Crawford, which gave him large possessions in addition to what he inherited from his father. He died about 1240.

CHILDREN :—
15 I. SIR WILLIAM his heir.
16 II. SIR ANDREW ancestor of the Earl Morton.

15 SIR WILLIAM fifth Lord of DOUGLAS.

He is said to have married Martha the sister of the Earl of Carrick. He appears in 1255 as one of the Scottish partisans of King Henry III of England. He died A. D. 1276.

CHILDREN :—
17 I. HUGH his heir.
18 II. WILLIAM who succeeded his brother.

17 HUGH sixth Lord of DOUGLAS

married Margaret, daughter of Patrick and sister of Hugh, lords of Abernethy; and dying without issue about 1286, was succeeded by his brother, William.

18 WILLIAM seventh Lord of DOUGLAS.

He married Elizabeth, daughter of Alexander, sixth lord high stewart of Scotland. On account of his great boldness and valor, he was called William the Hardy. He was among the first men of rank who joined Sir William Wallace, in his rising against the English in 1297. In 1295 he was governor of Berwick. He owned lands in one English and in seven Scottish counties.

He was the only man of rank in Scotland that could never be prevailed upon to submit to a prince who had no right or title to the kingdom, but what force gave him. He died a prisoner at the castle of York, England A. D. 1303.

CHILDREN:—

19 I.   JAMES LORD OF DOUGLAS.
20 II. HUGH DE DOUGLAS.
21 III. ARCHIBALD DE DOUGLAS.

19   JAMES eighth Lord of DOUGLAS, son of William the Hardy, who was distinguished by the name of Good Sir James, and by all our historians is allowed to have been one of the greatest heroes of his time. He joined king Robert Bruce as soon as he began to assert his title to the crown, and assisted at his coronation in 1306. He was at the battle of Bannockburn where he had no small glory gained against the English that day. By a charter from king Robert, he obtained possession of all the lands and town of Douglas dated at Berwick, April 11, 1329.

King Robert, finding himself drawing near his end, and unable to undertake a journey to the Holy Land to perform a certain vow he had made, requested his friend, Sir James Douglas that at his death he would have his heart embalmed and put in a silver casket, and that he should cary it to Jerusalem and bury it near our Saviour's sepulcher. Sir James executed the arduous task though it cost him his life; for which the family got added to its arms argent a man's heart gules, ensigned with an imperial crown.

He was in seventy battles and was victorious in all but thirteen, leaving the name of "the Black Douglas;"

—so he was called from his swarthy complexion—as a word of fear by which the English mothers stilled their children.

<blockquote>
"Hush ye, hush ye, little pet ye,
Hush ye, hush ye, do not fret ye,
The Black Douglas shall not get ye."
</blockquote>

He was killed in Spain August 31, 1331, and was buried in the church of Saint Bride in Scotland.

[Some historians say that Sir James was slain by the Moors before reaching the Holy Land. All agree that he was killed in Spain A. D. August, 31, 1331.]

20   HUGH ninth Lord of DOUGLAS,

second son of William the Hardy, was never married; but resigned his lands in favour of his nephew William, afterwards Earl of Douglas.

21   ARCHIBALD Lord of GALLOWAY,

third son of William the Hardy, was a man of great bravery and courage which he gave many proofs in engagements with the English. He was a faithful friend of king David Bruce. He was appointed governor of Scotland in king David's absence, and at last lost his life in the service of his country A. D. 1333. He married a daughter of John Cummings.

CHILDREN :—

    22 I. WILLIAM, afterwards Earl of Douglas.
    23 II. ELEANORA, who married Alexander Earl of Carrick.—

22   WILLIAM first Earl of DOUGLAS

was also Earl of Marr. He was the only son of Archibald Lord of Galloway. In 1357 he was created Earl of Douglas. It is said that he disputed the succession to the Scottish crown with Robert II. but this seems to be a mistake, for he was a great friend of Robert II, and obtained his daughter in marriage with his son and performed many noble acts in his country's service in that king's reign. He married (1) Margaret, daughter of Donald, sister and heiress of Thomas, Earl of Marr, by whom he had

    24 I. JAMES Earl of Douglas.
    25 II. LADY ISABELLA DOUGLAS countess of Marr.
    By (2) wife Lady Margaret Dunbas.
    26 III. ARCHIBALD.
    By (3) wife Lady Margaret Stewart daughter of king Robert II. countess of Angus and dowage of Marr.

27 GEORGE DOUGLAS,

who succeeded to the Earldom of Angus upon his mother's resignation, ancestor of the Earl of Angus Marquisses and Duke of Douglas.

24 JAMES second Earl of DOUGLAS

was also Earl of Marr. He invaded England and was met by the Percies. He fell at the battle of Otterburn July, 31, 1388. He married Isabella Stewart daughter of king Robert II. They had only one son child, who died in infancy.

26 ARCHIBALD third Earl of DOUGLAS

and Lord of Galloway, was son of William first Earl of Douglas and Margaret Dunbar. He died in 1400. He married Jean, daughter and heiress of Thomas Murray Lord of Bothwell.

    CHILDREN:—

    28 I. ARCHIBALD fourth Earl of Douglas.
    29 II. LADY MARJORY who married David, prince of Scotland.
    30 III. WILLIAM Lord of Nithsdale married Egidia, daughter of king Robert II.

26 ARCHIBALD fourth Earl of DOUGLAS,

Lord of Bothwel, Galloway and Annadale, son of Archibald and Jean (Murray) Douglas. He defended the castle at Edinburgh against king Henry and the English army. He lost his life at the battle of Vonoil A. D. 1424. He married Margaret Stewart daughter of king Robert III.

CHILDREN:

31 I. ARCHIBALD fifth Earl of Douglas.
32 II. JAMES Earl of Abercorn.
33 III. LADY MARGARET married William Earl of Orkney.
34 IV. LADY ELIZABETH married John Stewart Earl of Bucan.
35 V. LADY HELEN married Alexander Louden of Hotton.
36 VI. LADY MARY.

31 ARCHIBALD fifth Lord of DOUGLAS,

Lord of Bothwel and Galloway and marshal of France. In 1424, he was sent ambassador to England with others to treat about king James's ransom which they happily accomplished, and returned to Scotland with their royal master the same year. He died A. D. 1439 and was buried in the church of Douglas, where his tomb yet remains inscribed with his high titles of Duke of Tourain, Earl of Douglas, and Lord of Galloway. He married Lady Eupheme Graham.

CHILDREN:

37 I. WILLIAM 38 David.
39 II. LADY MARGARET called the fair maid of Galloway. She married (1) William, (2) James, Earls of Douglas, (3) John Earl of Athole.

37 WILLIAM sixth Earl of DOUGLAS,

third Duke of Turenne a boy of sixteen. His power and foreign possessions made him an object of fear to the Scottish crown, and having been invited to an entertainment in the castle of Edinburgh, he was assassinated with his brother A. D. 1440. He and his brother being unmarried the estate devolved upon their uncle James, Earl of Abercorn.

32 JAMES seventh Earl of DOUGLAS,

fourth Duke of Turenne, married Beatrix daughter of Robert, Duke of Albany, Gov. of Scotland. He died A. D. 1453.

CHILDREN:—

40 I. WILLIAM eighth Earl of Douglas.
41 II. JAMES.
42 III. ARCHIBALD Earl of Murray.
43 IV. HUGH, 44 JAMES, 45 HENRY.
46 V. LADY MARGARET married James Douglas, Earl of Morton.
47 VI. LADY BEATRIX.
48 VII. LADY JANE.
49 VIII. LADY ELIZABETH.

40 WILLIAM eighth Earl of DOUGLAS,

fifth Duke of Turenne, son of James and Beatrix Douglas, was long in great favour with King James II., but afterwards lost the royal vavom and appears to have entered into a league with the Earl of Crawford and others of the nobility, against the King, by whom he was stabbed to the heart and died instantly at Sterling Castle, February 2, 1452. He married his cousin Margaret, daughter of Alexander, fifth Earl of Douglas. Leaving no children he was succeeded by his brother James.

JAMES ninth Earl of DOUGLAS,

and sixth Duke of Turenne. In 1454, he made open

war against King James II., as the murderer of his brother and kinsman, the sixth and eighth Earls of Douglas. The issue seemed doubtful for a time, but the Hamiltons and others being gained over to the king's side. Douglas fled to England. The castles of Douglases were dismantled, and the earldom of Douglas came to an end by forfeiture after an existance of ninty-eight years during which it had been held by no fewer than nine lords. The last Earl lived many years in England and was made a Knight of the Garter. He died in the abbey of Lindores, April 15, 1488. The male line of the first and second sons of William first Earl of Douglas thus ended.

GEORGE DOUGLAS first Earl of ANGUS

was the son of William first Earl of Douglas and Lady Margaret Stewart, countess and heiress of Angus. He was put in possession of his mother's estate and honors very young by her resignation in parliament of the earldom of Angus. He married May 24, 1397, Lady Mary Stewart, daughter of King Robert III. He accompanied his cousin the Earl of Douglas to the battle of Hamilton where he was taken prisoner in 1402, and died in England of the plague the following year.

CHILDREN :—

50 I.   WILLIAM Earl of Angus
51 II. SIR. GEORGE.
52 III. LADY ELIZABESH married Divid Hay of Lockarret.

50 WILLIAM DOUGLAS, second Earl of ANGUS.

He had the chief command of the army at the battle of Piperdain where the Scots obtained a complete victory over the English commander by the brave Percy, in 1436. He married Elizabeth, daughter of William Hay. He died A. D. 1437.

THEIR CHILD:—

53 I. JAMES Earl of Angus.

JAMES DOUGLAS third Earl of ANGUS

married Mary Stewart, daughter of King James I., and dying without issue, the estate and honors devolved upon his uncle George.

51 GEORGE DOUGLAS, fourth Earl of ANGUS,

son of George, first Earl of Angus and Lady Margaret Stewart. He was appointed one of the govenors of King James III., which office he discharged with honor. He had the chief command of the king's forces, during the ninth Earl of Douglas' rebellion, which he suppressed A. D. 1455, by which he obtained their old inheritance of Douglasdale. He married Elizabeth, daughter of Sir Andrew Sibbald.

CHILDREN :—

54 I. ARCHIBALD fifth Earl of Angus.
55 II. GEORGE.
56 III. LADY ANNIE married Wm. Lord Graham.
57 IV. LADY ELIZABETH married Sir Robert Graham.
58 V. LADY ISABEL married Sir Alexander Ramsay.

He died A. D. 1463, and was succeeded by his eldest son.

54 ARCHIBALD DOUGLAS fifth Earl of ANGUS,

was commonly called the great Earl. After filling the highest offices in the state and adding largely to the family possessions retired to the priority of Canons in Galloway where he died A. D. 1514. He married Elizabeth, daughter of Robert Boyd Lord High Chancelor of Scotland.

CHILDREN:—

59 I. GEORGE Master of Angus.
60 II. SIR WILLIAM DOUGLAS.
61 III. GAVIN DOUGLAS Bishop of Dunkeld.
62 IV. LADY MAJORY married Earl of Glencairn.
63 V. LADY ELIZABETH.
64 VI. LADY JANAT.
65 VII. SIR ARCHIBALD.

59 GEORGE DOUGLAS, Master of ANGUS,

son of Archibald, fifth Earl of Angus. He was in great favor with King James IV. He married Elizabeth, daughter of John Lord Drummond.

CHILDREN:—

66 I. ARCHIBALD sixth Earl of Angus.
67 II. SIR GEORGE.
68 III. WILLIAM.
69 IV. ELIZABETH married John Lord Yester, ancestor of the Marquis of Tweeddale.
70 V. JANET.
71 VI. MARGARET married Sir James Douglas ancestor of the Duke of Queenberry.
72 VII. ALISON, 73 JEAN, 14 ISABEL.

He died on the field of Flowden with his royal master Sept. 9, 1513.

66 ARCHIBALD DOUGLAS sixth Earl of ANGUS,

sun of George, Master of Angus was made Knight by King Henry II., of France. He married Margaret, daughter of King Henry VII., sister of

King Henry VIII. of England, and widow of King James IV., of Scotland.

CHILDREN:—

73   I.   JAMES, Master of Angus who died young.
74   II. LADY MARGARET DOUGLAS who married Matthew Earl of Lennox and was mother of Henry Lord Darnly, who was the husband of Mary, Queen of Scotts and father of King James VI.

So of this Earl of Angus, not only the royal family of Great Britain, but most of the crowned heads of Europe are descended. He died at the castle of Tantallon A. D. 1556.

67   SIR GEORGE DOUGLAS,

son of George, Master of Angus married Elizabeth, daughter and heiress of David Douglas.

CHILDREN:—

75   I.   DAVID, afterwards Earl of Angus II. JAMES married III. LADY ELIZABETH DOUGLAS, daughter of James Douglas third Earl of Morton. He succeeded to the earldom of Morton by intail, and was rejent of Scotland, vide title Morton.
76   IV. ELIZABETH.
77   V.   MARY.
78   SIR GEORGE was killed at the Battle of Pinkie.

75   DAVID DOUGLAS, seventh Earl of ANGUS,

son of Sir George and Elizabeth Douglas, married Margaret, daughter of Sir John Hamilton of Clydesdale.

CHILDREN:—

79   I.   ARCHIBALD eighth Earl of Angus.
80   LADY MARGARET married 1st Sir Walter Scott, 2nd Francis Stewart Earl of Bothwell.
81   II. LADY ELIZABETH married John lord Maxwell. The earl died 1588, and was succeeded by his son.

79 ARCHIBALD DOUGLAS eighth Earl of ANGUS, called the good earl. He married 1st Lady Margaret Earskine, 2nd Lady Margaret Lesley, daughter of George, Earl of Rothes, and dying without any surviving issue A. D. 1588; the male line of George Master of Angus thus ended, and the estate and honors devolved upon next heir male, Sir William Douglas.

WILLIAM DOUGLAS ninth Earl of ANGUS, son of Sir William Douglas. He was strongly attached to the interest of Queen Mary. In 1591, he obtained from King James VI., a charter confirming all the ancient privileges of the family of Douglas viz; the first vote in parliament of leading the vanguard in battle and to carry the crown at coronation to him and his heir-male. He married Giles, daughter of Sir Robert Graham.

CHILDREN:—

82	I.	WILLIAM Earl of Angus.
83	II.	SIR ROBERT DOUGLAS.
84	III.	GARVIN.
85	IV.	JOHN.
86	V.	ARCHIBALD.
87	VI.	MARGARET.
88	VII.	SARAH.
89	VIII.	ELIZABETH.
90	IX.	JEAN.

He died A. D. 1591, and was succeeded by his eldest son.

82 WILLIAM DOUGLAS tenth Earl of ANGUS, son of William Douglas, married Elizabeth, daughter of Lord Oliphant. He was a man of great learing and knowledge.

CHILDREN:—

91 I. WILLIAM eleventh Earl of Angus.
92 II. JAMES.
93 III. SIR FRANCIS.
94 IV. LADY MARY.
95 V. LADY MARGARET.

He died A. D. 1616.

WILLIAM DOUGLAS, eleventh Earl of ANGUS, was created first marquis of Douglas by King Charles I., in 1633. He married 1st Margaret, daughter of Claud Hamilton.

CHILDREN by first wife:—

96 I. ARCHIBALD.
97 II. LORD JAMES.
98 III. MARGARET married Earl of Stirling.
99 IV. LADY JEAN
100 V. LADY GRIZEL.

He married (2) Lady Mary Gordan.

CHILDREN by (2) marriage:—

101 VI. WILLIAM Earl of Selkirk afterwards Duke of Hamilton Vide title Hamilton.
102 VII. LORD JAMES.
103 VIII. LADY HENRIET.
104 IX. LADY CATHERINE.
105 X. LADY ISABEL married William duke of Queensberry.
106 XI. LADY JEAN.
107 XII. LADY LUCY.
108 XIII. LADY MARY

He died 1660.

96 ALEXANDER Earl of ANGUS, son and apparant heir of William, marquis of Douglas.

He married 1st Annie Stewart, daughter of Esme duke of Lennex.

CHILD by first wife:—

109 I. JAMES afterwards marquis of Douglas.

Two daughters who perished at sea in a voyage to France.

He married (2) Lady Jean, daughter of David Earl of Memys, by whom he had a son.

110 II. ARCHIBALD Earl of Forfair.
111 III. LADY MARGARET married Alexander viscount of Kingston.

109 JAMES DOUGLAS, son of ARCHIBALD

was the second Marquis of Douglas. He married (1) Barbara Earskine.

CHILDREN:—

112 I. JAMES Earl of Angus. He married (2) Lady Mary Kerr, daughter of Robert Marquis of Lothian.

CHILDREN by (2) marriage:—

113 II. ARCHIBALD Duke of Douglas.
114 III. LADY JANE DOUGLAS married Sir John Stewart. Said to have twins, 115 ARCHIBALD and 116 SHOLTO.

The Marquis died A. D. 1700, and was succeeded by his son.

113 ARCHIBALD DOUGLAS, third MARQUIS.

was created Duke of Douglas by Queen Annie, April 18, 1703. He married Margaret, eldest daughter of James Douglas, but died without issue, July 21, 1761.

Archibald Stewart: the only surviving son of his sister, Lady Jean or Jane was served heir to his uncle Archibald Duke of Douglas on Sept. 9, 1761, and is now designed ARCHIBALD DOUGLAS OF DOUGLAS ESQ. The Duke dying without issue made the title of duke became extinct; but that of marquis of Douglas &c., devolved upon his grace the present Duke of Hamilton, his undoubted heir-male; he being lineally descended of William, Earl of Selkirk eldest son of the second marriage of William first Marquis of Douglas. The Duke of Hamilton was accordingly upon the 1st of Dec. A. D. 1761, served and restored heir-male to the said Archibald, Duke of Douglas, and is now designed George, James, Duke of Hamilton, and Brandon Marquis of Douglas, Earl of Angus &c., &c.

Vide title of Hamilton.

DOUGLAS COAT-OF-ARMS.

EXPLANATION OF THE DOUGLAS ARMS.

The orignal Douglas arms was a blue shield with three stars. The imperial heart was added to commemorate King Robert Bruce's dying request to the good Sir James Douglas, that he should cause his heart to be taken out and embalmed and placed in a silver casket and that Douglas should carry it to the Holy Land and have it buried near the sepulchre of our Savior.

The three STARS which the Douglases bear in common with the Murries seem to denote the descent of both from one ancestor. They are the heraldic way of showing a spear rowell denoting that the dignity of Knighthood has been conferred upon the wearer for fidelity.

The HELMET is common to all arms, but differ in position, in material and shape, according to the rank of the wearer a Baronet has his full front blue. The one the Douglas arms is a simple esquire or gentleman.

The CAP of Maintenance or the cap of triumph, is as historical as the cap of liberty, and like the latter has a Roman origin. It was carried before the Roman generals in their entry into the capital, after their return from a successful war. It is turned up with esmine.

The LAMBREGUIN or SCROLL around the top of the shield belongs to the ornamental part of Heraldry and is common to all arms, and had its origin in the fact that in the times of the Tournaments crusades they formed a cloak around the helmet or head piece, but in time the cloak got cut up into shreads and rags by the battle axes of the combatants, and now in modern days they form them into leaf-like scrolls.

The SALAMANDER denotes that the family has flourished amidst difficulties, trials and persecutions, that it stands out from and amidst the flames of adversity and distruction triumphant.

The TORTOIS or band which is above the helmet should be WHITE and BLUE to correspond with the color of the arms. It used to be in olden times a roll of ribbons and was used to bind the crest to the helmet but in later years it has lost its primitive shape and character.

THE MOTTO.

JAMAIS ARRIERE, "Never behind" alludes to the peculiar precedence inherent in their earldom of Angus.

COLOR.

The two colors in the Douglas arms are blue for fidelity, and white for purity. White represents silver.

EXPLANATIONS.

A consecutive numbering runs through the whole book, so far as the name of DOUGLAS is concerned, beginning with JOHN DOUGLAS, the original emigrant of this branch of the great family

This numbering is found on the left hand of the page, before the name of each individual in the series of his record descendants as a child.

Thus, are found ten children of JOHN DOUGLAS, numbered from 108 to 118 inclusive.

This mark, † immediately following a consecutive number denotes that a distinct and additional notice of the person to whom that number belongs is reserved for a separate and subsequent paragraph. The place where this occurs may be found by looking for the same consecutive number like this 114: immediately preceding the name to which it belongs. Thus, Isaac Douglas, whose consecutive number is 114, is afterwards found as the head of a family.

Only one consecutive number belongs to an individual.

By means of this, and several indexes at the end of the volume, any person and his ancestry and posterity are easily found.

If there be occasion to mention an individual elsewhere, his place in the series is indicated by his consecutive number in brackets: thus [311].

A small figure after a name and just above the line. thus, Samuel Douglas [4] denotes the generation in which the individual belongs, and serves in part to distinguish him from others of the same name.

The name at the head, or parent of each separate family, is found at the beginning of the notice of such family printed in CAPITALS. It is found convenient to insert immediately after the parent's name, the name of his or her American progenitors, thus: BENJAMIN DOUGLAS [4] (JOB,[3] ELIJAH,[2] JOHN [1]).

The families are arranged in the order of seniority, as they occur in the second generation.

When a town is mentioned without naming the state, Maine is to be understood, unless the place be universally known.

When a woman's name occurs in this wise Mary (Braley) Douglas, Braley is her maiden name and Douglas the one acquired by marriage.

To find the name of an individual recorded in this volume: Suppose it to be John Douglas, the eldest son of Cornelius Douglas. The name of John Douglas is of frequent occurence in this book. This John was born in 1768. Find the name of John in among the Christain names of the Douglases in index 1, preceded by 1768 the year of his birth, and following is the consecutive number 34, which you will find in the proper place in the body of the work.

First Generation in America, of the Descendants of John Douglas of Middleborough, Plymouth County, Massachusetts.

FIRST GENERATION.

1 JOHN[1] DOUGLAS was born in Scotland about the year 1695. His father was a wealthy and influential man, possessing a large tract of land, and renting a number of houses. John had an uncle, a merchant living in London, who wished his nephew to go and live with him, promising to make him his heir, as he had no children of his own. To this his father would not consent; but the boy, then twelve years of age, was so well pleased with his uncle's generous offer, that he ran away with the intention of going to him. On reaching London he could not find his uncle; so he strolled down about the wharves, as a little boy would naturally do. There lay in port a man-of-war nearly ready for sea. The boy attracted the notice of the crew who, taking advantage of his being alone and unprotected, pressed him on board the ship and concealed him till they were well out to sea. The vessel was bound for Boston, and arrived there in due time. John was sold or put out to a man till he should become of age, in a consideration of a sum of money required to pay his passage. Whom he

lived with or how he fared during the remainder of his minority is not known. Neither is it known that his father ever knew what became of his lost son. We next hear of John in Middleborough, Plymouth County, Mass., where about A. D. 1719, he married Eunice Rattleaf (or Ratliffe) of that town. They settled on a farm he bought of John Bennett, Jr., containing thirty-seven acres, for the sum of thirty pounds. The farm was situated in the Township of Middleborough, Mass., being in the 134th lot in the third allotment in the purchase known as the sixteen shilling purchase. The deed bearing the date of May 27, 1739. They always resided on this farm, where they died at an advanced age, and were buried in the town graveyard.

The children of John and Eunice (Rattleleaf) Douglas born in Middleborough, Mass., were:

2 I. †Elijah² born about 1720; married 1st, Phebe Taylor; 2nd, Elizabeth Estes.

3 II. †John² born about 1722; married Mary Braley.

4 III. †George² born about 1724 or 5; married Patience Caswell.

SECOND GENERATION.

2. Elijah¹ Douglas (John 1) eldest son of John and Eunice (Rattleleaf) Douglas, was born in Middleborough, Mass., about A. D. 1720; married, first, April 27, 1742, Phebe Taylor Married by Benjamin Ruggles, Esq. They settled in his native town. They had born unto them three sons and two daughters. His wife, the eldest son and two daughters died and in the year 1751, he, with his surviving sons, bid adieu to the land of their birth, to find a home in the wilds of the district of Maine.

They pursued their journey east as far as Falmouth where it appears they remained a short time. The same year he bought in company with Benjamin Winslow, one-half of New Damariscove Island, (now either Haskell or Bailey's Island) lying in Casco Bay, in the Township of North Yarmouth (now Harpswell,) for the sum of seventy-six pounds thirteen shillings and four pence, lawful money. The Island was purchased of Jonathan Preble, of Georgetown. The deed bears date of January 30, O. S. 1750-51, recorded in the Register of Deeds Office in York County, Book 29, page 90.

He married (2) Elizabeth, daughter of Edward and Patience Estes, born in Hanover, Plymouth County, Mass., April 7, 1731. At the time of their marriage she was residing with her parents at North Yarmouth (now Harpswell). They settled on a farm of forty three acres, which he bought of Mary Hais, the estate of Richard Hais, deceased, situated on Merryconeag Neck, (now Harpswell Neck.)

The deed was granted July 5, 1757. There has been added to the farm sixty acres of land; and the old log house which stood near what is known as Hais' Brook, in which were born unto them five sons and three daughters, has given place to two successive framed houses, which were built on the main road. The farm is now owned and occupied by Henry Merryman. Elijah did a large business in chopping and shipping cord wood from Birch Island to Boston. Tradition informs us that he was a great worker and a very powerful man with the axe; that on one occasion, having been disappointed in his help, and wishing to complete the loading of the vessel, he chopped seven cords of wood in one day. In 1775, he removed to the Township of Royallsborough (now Durham,) where he bought and settled on the farm known as the John Plummer farm; where traces of the cellar where his old house stood, are still to be seen.

He owned all the land now included in the farms owned by Thomas Philbrook, John Plummer and Alexander Ewing. He also owned other farms, and was quite forehanded for those days. He was the first of the name that joined the society of Friends, having united with them at Falmouth, June 29, 1754, and continued a member for many years; but was subsequently disowned, on account of his going to law with a member of the society, contrary to their discipline. He weighed two hundred pounds and was five feet ten inches in heighth; of large muscular frame, and possessed all the characteristics of his Scottish ancestry. He was totally blind ten years previous to his death.

He passed the latter part of his days in the family of his son Joseph where he died in the year 1814, aged 94 years, and was buried near the Friend's meeting house, in Durham.

Children of Elijah, by first wife Phebe:—

5 I. MARTIN,[3] born in Middleborough, Mass., May 2, 1744. There is no further record of him and it is probable he died young.

6 II. † DANIEL,[3] born in Middleborough, 1747; married Sabry Russell.

7 III. † CORNELIEUS,[3] born in Middleborough Sept, 12, 1749; married (1) Ann Estes (2) Lydia Buffum.

Children by second wife Lydia:—

8 IV. † JOSEPH,[3] born in North Yarmouth, (now Harpswell,) April 8, 1753; married Mary McFall.

9 V. † JOB,[3] born in North Yarmouth, Oct. 9th 1754; married (1) Mercy Booker (2) Mary (McKenney) Campbell.

10 VI. † ISRAEL,[3] born in North Yarmouth, July 17th 1756; married Mary Rodick.

11 VII. † SARAH,[3] born in North Yarmouth, June 13th 1759; married Benjamin Doughty.

12 VIII. † PATIENCE,[3] born in North Yarmouth, March 24, 1761. She had two daughters. No further record of her has been found.

13 IX. † MARY,[3] born in North Yarmouth, July 10, 1763; married Daniel Booker.

14 X. † ELIJAH,[3] born in Harpswell, June 23, 1768; married Jenney Grant.

15 XI. † JOHN,[3] born in Harpswell, Nov. 8, 1774; married (1) Sarah Booker (2) Catherine (Briry) Booker.

3 JOHN[2] DOUGLAS, (John[1]) brother of the preceeding and son of John and Eunice (Rattleleaf) Douglas, was born in Middleboro, Mass., about A. D. 1722. About the year 1751, he married Mary Braley, and settled in his native town, on a farm situated near what is known as the Beech Woods. He bought the said farm of Mark Haskell, a tanner, for twenty-seven pounds of old tenor. The farm consisted of one-half part of the eighty-sixth lot of land in the third allotment of the sixteen shilling purchase. The deed bears date of February 10th, 1746. At the breaking out of the Revolutionary War, he volunteered his services in his country's defence. He was in the battle of Bunker Hill. Sometime during the early part of the war he was taken sick with the camp disorder, from which he never recovered. He died at his home in Middleborough, and was buried in the grave-yard in that town. After his death his widow lived with her son John, at Plymouth, Mass., where she died about 1788, and was buried in the grave-yard at Half Way Pond.

Their children all born in Middleborough, Mass. were:—

16 I. † JOHN,³ born March 11th 1752; married Lydia Southworth.

17 II. EPHRIAM,³ born about 1754; unmarried, died in the Revolutionary war 1777.

18 III. † MARY,³ born about 1757; married Libbeas Simmons.

19 IV. † ELIZABETH,³ born in the year 1760; married Ephriam Reynolds.

20 V. SARAH,³ born about 1763. It is reported by some persons that she was married; but to whom or where, or any further record of her has not been received.

21 VI. † PHEBE,³ born about 1767; married Roland Homes

22 VII. † ELISHA,³ born June 12th 1771; married (1) Celia Oskin (2) Hannah Russell.

4 GEORGE² DOUGLAS, (John¹) brother of the preceeding and son of John and Eunice (Rattleleaf) Douglas, was born in Middleborough, Mass., about 1725; married Prudence Caswell. He always resided in his native town on the Beech Wood road. He was a successful farmer, and a man respected for his integrity, and high moral character. He died at his homestead April 13th 1793. His wife died March 14th 1794. They were interred in their family graveyard.

Their children born in Middleborough, Mass., were:—

23 I. PRUDENCE,³ born about 1760; married Enoch Swift of Wareham, Mass. He was a farmer and shoemaker. They had no children. She died January 15th 1835.

24 II. † GEORGE,³ born August 26th 1762; married Patience Savery.

25 III. † NOAH,³ born about 1764; Married Mary Seakel.

26 IV. † SELAH,³ born about 1767; married David Niles.

27 V. JOTHAM,³ born about 1770.

THIRD GENERATION.

6 Daniel[3] Douglas, (Elijah[2] John,[1]) son of Elijah and Phebe (Taylor) Douglas, was born in Middleborough, Mass., 1747; married June 9th 1779, Sabry Russell of Duxbury, Mass. He settled in the town of Brunswick on a farm situated on what is known as Kincaid Hill, on the road leading from Brunswick village to the Friend's meeting house in Durham.

In 1797, he removed on a farm near Ring's Corner in the town of North Yarmouth, (now Freeport,) where he built a log house in which he and family lived many years; and then he built him a framed house. This, however, was not plastered during his lifetime. When a young man, while assisting at the raising of a frame for a building, he fell, striking upon his face and putting out both of his eyes. This accident occurred previous to his marriage, depriving him of the pleasure of seeing his wife and children. The old gentleman and his wife were in the practice of visiting among their friends with a cow, they called old Brindle, harnessed to a sled for a team. He was not a professor of religion, though a very good and kind man, and upright in all his dealings. The date of his or his wife's death is not known.

He was buried in the grave-yard near Friends' meeting house in Durham.

Their children all born in Brunswick were:—

28 I. † Cornelius,[4] born Sept. 19th 1780; married Hannah Whittemore.

29 II. † Nabby,[4] born 1782; married James Welch.

30 III. † Annie,[4] born 1784; married Samuel Grouse or Groves.

31 IV. † SALVANA[4] born 1789; married Zachariah Allen.
32 V. † PHEBE[4] born 1792; married Samuel Grouse.
33 VI. † DANIEL[4] born August 1796; married Sarah Bailey.

7 CORNELIUS[3] DOUGLAS, (Elijah,[2] John,[1]) brother of the preceeding and son of Elijah and Phebe (Taylor) Douglas, was born in Middleborough, Mass., Sept. 12, 1749. His mother died when he was an infant, and when only two years old his father together with himself and brother Daniel, removed to the town of Falmouth, Maine, where they remained a short time, then removed and settled on Merryconeag, now Harpswell Neck, which at that time was a wild and comparatively unsettled tract of land belonging to the town of North Yarmouth. In those early days of the history of Harpswell, there was but little cleared land for mowing fields, consequently, the farmers found it necessary to obtain fodder for their stock in other localities. Cornelius, in company with several young men, went into the interior about twenty-five miles in search of grass. They found a small tract of land clear of timber, where the beavers had formally built a dam across a small stream overflowing several acres. The dam had been partially torn away by hauling masts over it which drained the meadow, causing the wild grass to grow in great abundance. These young men cut and stacked a supply of this; then retracing their steps, guided only by spotted trees, they returned home reaching there late in autumn. They then provided themselves with the necessary articles for camp life, drove their father's cattle to their newly discovered territory, where they built a rude camp for themselves and a hovel for the cattle. They spent their time in tending the stock and making baskets; thus the winter passed quite pleasantly. It was by

these frequent visits to the back woods, that Cornelius chose his future home. At the early age of eighteen he married, Nov. 10, 1767, Ann, daughter of Edward and Patience Estes, (a sister of his step-mother,) born in Hanover, Mass., March 14, 1735. He resided in Harpswell until 1773, when he bought one hundred acres of wild land of the proprietors of the Pejepscot purchase for the sum of twenty-six pounds thirteen shillings and four pence, lawful money. His land was situated in the township of Royallborough, (now Durham.) The deed was given by Belcher Noyes Esq., of Boston, agent for the proprietors, Dec. 10, 1776. Upon this farm he built the fifth log house in the township. It was situated upon a little hillock some distance from where the highway now is. There are traces of the house still to be seen. His wife died Jan. 28, 1790. June 23, 1791, he married (2) Lydia, daughter of Joshua and Elizabeth Buffum, of Berwick. They had born unto them four sons and three daughters. The youngest daughter occupied the old homestead till her death. The old log house, after doing good service was taken down, and a framed one built nearer the road. And a few years since this was rebuilt still nearer the road, and in a more modern style. Cornelius was an acceptable member of the society of Friends and universally esteemed by the community where he resided. He died at his homestead June 20, 1821. His wife survived him a few years and died August 31, 1837. They were buried in the Friends' graveyard at South Durham.

The following marriage certificate of Cornelieus Douglas and Annie Estes was copied verbatim from the original and shows the form of marriage used by the Society of Friends:

Whareas Cornalas Duglas of Harpswell in the County of Cumberland, son of Elijah Duglas and Phebe his wife, and Ann Estis, Daughter of Edward Estes and Patience his wife, both of the aforesd town And County and Provence of the Massachuserts baye, in new-england, and having declared their intentions of taking Eich other in marage, before two publick meeting of the people, Called quakers, in Harpswill and falmouth according to Good order used amongst them, and Proceeding therein after Delibarate Consideration they also appearing Clear of all others, And having Consent of Parents and Relatives Concerend, were approved by sd meeting. Now these are to certify all whom it may concearn, that for eccomplishing their sd intentions, this 10th day of the 11th month called november, annodomi seventeen hundred sixty seven, they the sd Cornalas Duglas and Ann Estes appeared in a publick assembly of the afoursaid people. And others met together att their publick meeting house att Harpswell, afoursaid. And he, the said Cornalas Duglas, in a solom maner, taking the said Ann Estes by the Hand Did openly Declared as follows, friends I Desire you to be my witnesses, that I take this friend, Ann Estis to be my wife, promising through the Lord's assistance, to be unto Her a true and Loving Husband until it Shall pleas the Lord by Death to sepperate us. And then and their in the said assembly, the said ann Estis did in like manner Declare as followeth: friends, I Desire you to be my witnesses, that I take this friend, Cornalas Duglas, to be my Husband, promising through the Lord's assistance, to be unto him A true and Loving wife, until it Shall pleas the Lord by Death to sepperate us. And as a further conformation theirof, the said Cornalas Duglas and ann Estis did then and, by these Presents, set their hands, she according to Custom assuming the name of her Husband.

               Cornalas Duglas.
               Ann Duglas.

And we, whose names are hearunto subscribed, being present at the Solomnizing of said marriage and in manner afoursaid, as witnesses, have allso to these Presents Subscribed our names, the Daye and year above writen.

Josua Babb,	Elijah Duglas,
Nathaniel Pinkham,	Patience Estes,
Roger toothaker,	Lemuel Jones,
gideon toothaker,	John Barker,
Thankful Jones,	John Barker Jr.,
Sarah Pinkham,	Elizabeth Duglas,
Elenaor Hais,	Wait Jones,
Mary Hais,	Sarah Estes,
Bety Weber,	Elenor Estes,
Abagail Rodex,	Meray Jones,
catherine Pinkham,	Rachel Jones,

          Sarah Pinkham.

Children by first wife.

34 I. † John,⁴ born in Harpswell, Sept 8th, 1768; married Judith Collins.

35 II. † Edward,⁴ born in Harpswell, June 30th, 1770; married Esther Collins.

36 III. † Phebe,⁴ born in Harpswell, Nov. 12th, 1772; married Ebenezer Austin.

37 IV. Joseph,⁴ born in Royalsborough, (now Durham,) Aug. 1st, 1774, died June 6th, 1782.

Children by second wife Lydia.

38 V. † Anna,⁴ born in Durham, July 15th, 1792; married Samuel Goddard.

39 VI. Joseph,⁴ born in Durham, May 28th. 1793, unmarried. While attending the Academy at Hebron, he went into the river to bathe and was drowned, August 27th, 1814.

40 VII. † Joshua,⁴ born in Durham, Sept. 8, 1794, married (1) Jane Adams (2) Lucy Beal.

41 VIII † David,⁴ born in Durham, July 16th, 1796; married (1) Hannah Davis (2) Chloe Davis.

42 IX. † Cornelieus,⁴ born in Durham, June 12th, 1798; married Phebe Nichols.

43 X. † Lydia,⁴ born in Durham, Dec. 28th, 1799; married George W. Morse.

44 XI. † Patience,⁴ born in Durham, Feb. 15th, 1803; married Benjamin Davis.

8 Joseph³ Douglas, (Elijah,² John,¹ brother of the preceeding and son of Elijah and Elizabeth (Estes) Douglas, born in North Yarmouth, (now Harpswell,) April 8th, 1753, married, September 4th, 1773, Mary McFall, born Dec. 31, 1851. In 1781, he bought of Stephen Chase one hundred acres of wild land, situated in the township of Royalsborough, (now the town of Durham,) for which he paid the sum of two hundred and thirteen pounds, six shillings and eighteen pence, lawful * money. The deed was given

---
* The depreciation of the currency in the days of Revolution war, made it necessary to pay large sums of money for land as well as for all articles in use.

Nov. 20th, 1781. The lot was known in the first division of one hundred acre lots as No. 5 and 12; as the road passed through the farm, one-half in No. 5 and one-half in No. 12. On this lot he built a log house, which was of necessity the style of dwellings in use by the pioneer of Maine. In building his house he invited the neighbors to assist him, who laid up the walls in a half day; they supposing they where giving their labor, but Joseph insisted upon paying each one, which he did. Several successive houses have been erected upon this homestead farm and it has changed owners many times; it is now owned and occupied by Mr. Albert Booker, whose grandmother was a sister of the subject of this notice.

As a farmer, Joseph was successful. He marketed his produce at Brunswick Village, and by his frequent visits to that place made the acquaintance of the president of Bowdoin College, who became much interested in the young man. One day the students thought to have some sport with the young countryman, as he was dressed in his course homespun suit, his pants several inches too short which gave him a verdant appearance. They ridiculed and laughed at him for some time while the young farmer quietly bore all their insults and jeers; then with his ready wit and great flow of language silenced his opponents.

He was a powerful preacher in the Society of Friends, and much of his time and energies were devoted to the cause of Christ. Though his education was very limited yet he possessed natural ability which together with his deep piety made him a noble and useful man of his day. He made numerous religious visits to different states holding meetings among friends and others with wonderful results. His last sickness was short but severe, during which he often conversed with friends and relatives in regard to his readiness and the prospect of the great change which awaited him. He said, "I have not from the first of my sickness seen the least thing to hinder my change. I see no cloud in my way." To his wife he said, "Thou wilt have many afflictions to pass through but keep under the power of truth and it will make way for thee as it has done for me." At another time he said, "Oh! that I may be preserved in patience to wait my change, I have no desire to stay. The prospect looks so clear in respect to my going. I have peace—sweet peace indeed." He often expressed deep solicitude for his children, that they might be kept from the sins of the world. He departed this life December 22nd, 1821, and was buried in the Friends' burrying ground at South Durham.

His widow died later than 1832.

His Children were:—

45 I. ELIJAH,[4] born in Royallsborough, (now Durham,) June 24th, 1775; died young.

46 II. † DAVID,[4] born in Royallsborough, July 11th, 1779; married Waite Hawkes.

47 III. MOSES,[4] born in Royallsborough, July 28th, 1784. His intentions of marriage with Isabel Eaton was published in Brunswick, Dec. 20th, 1823, though he never married.

48 IV. ELIZABETH,[4] born in Royallsborough, May 20th, 1786; unmarried, lived at home with her parents where she died.

49 V. RACHAEL,[4] born in Durham, June 29th, 1788; married Hanson Hussey of Albion, where they resided and died. they had

three children, (50) Joseph (Hussey) (51) Jacob (Hussey,) both died about the age of 25 years; and one daughter name unknown died young.

52 VI. REBECCA,[4] born in Durham, May 29th, 1790, unmarried. She owned a small tract of land in Durham Some years previous to her death, she was afflicted with a white swelling on her leg, which caused amputation of the limb necessary. The doctor, who performed the surgical operation, took her land for his pay, or it was sold and the money paid him. The land has since gone by the name of the Bacay lot.

She lived with her nephew, Nathan Douglas where she died.

9 JOB[3] DOUGLAS, (Elijah,[2] John,[1]) brother of the preceeding and son of Elijah and Elizabeth (Estes) Douglas, was born in North Yarmouth, (now Harpswell,) October 9th, 1754; married June 3rd, 1776, Mercy Booker of his native town. He settled on a farm in North Yarmouth, (now Freeport,) near Ring's Corner, that he bought of his father. The agreement was that he should pay one hundred dollars annually until the farm was paid for, but owing to his having a very large family, he was unable to do more than support it.

May 1818, his wife died, and in 1819, he married (2) Mary (McKenney) Campbell, who was born in Georgetown. She owned a farm in Bowdoin, where she took her husband and the younger portion of his family. They subsequently sold their farm and bought one at West Bowdoin, where his (2) wife died. After her death, then an aged man without any means of support, his son Benjamin took him to his home and cared for him during the remainder of his life. He died March 15th, 1843, and was buried in the graveyard on Lichfield Plains.

Their Children were:—

53 I. † JOSEPH,⁴ born in North Yarmouth. (now Freeport,) Oct. 10th, 1776; married Elizabeth Sawyer.

54 II. † SAMUEL,⁴ born in North Yarmouth, Aug. 8th, 1778 ; married (1) Sarah Preble (2) Sarah Stevens.

55 III. † JAMES,⁴ born in North Yarmouth, July 1st, 1780 ; married Eliza M. Banks.

56 IV. ELIZABETH.⁴ born in North Yarmouth, Aug. 8th, 1782 ; married Thomas Preble, of Bowdoinham, where they lived and died — no children.

57 V. MERCY.⁴ born in North Yarmouth, March 14th, 1784, unmarried, died 1806.

58 VI. † ELIJAH,⁴ born in North. Yarmouth, Feb. 12th, 1786; married Sally Davis.

59 VII. † JOB,⁴ born in North Yarmouth, Nov. 27th, 1787; married Margaret Brown.

60 VIII † BENJAMIN,⁴ born in Freeport, Dec. 16th, 1789; married Betsey Porter.

61 IX MARY,⁴ born in Freeport, June 16th 1792 ; unmarried, died 1810.

62 X. MIRAM,⁴ born in Freeport, April 20th, 1794; unmarried, died at her brother Benjamin's.

63 XI † ISRAEL,⁴ born in Freeport, May 28th, 1796; married Patience Sylvester.

64 XII. SARAH,⁴ born in Freeport, January, 11th, 1798 ; married Robert Blanchard, of Bowdoinham, where they settled. She died Sept. 1829. One child (65) Harriet Ann (Blanchard) born 1825, m. —— Gould.

66 XIII † HANNAH,⁴ born in Freeport about 1800; married Mathew Campbell.

67 XIV. † RUTH,⁴ born in Freeport about 1802; married Joseph Forbus.

68 XV. ESTHER,⁴ born in Freeport, 1804;, married (1) David Gatchell; settled in Litchfield. In 1858, her husband died, she then removed to Bowdoin. In 1860, she married (2) Isaiah Emery. No children.

10 ISRAEL³ DOUGLAS, (Elijah,² John,¹) brother of the preceeding and son of Elijah and Elizabeth

(Estes) Douglas, was born in North Yarmouth, (now Harpswell,) July 17th, 1756; married Mary, daughter of John Rodick. He was a farmer and had one-half of his father's homestead in Harpswell, where he always resided and died.

Their children born in Harpswell were:—

69 I. THOMAS,[4] born Dec. 6th, 1777; married a lady who resided in the eastern part of the state. After living together a few years, for some cause they separated. He died July 2nd, 1827; one child, (70) James.

71 II. † PATIENCE,[4] born April 3rd, 1781; married James Rod:ck.

72 III. † DAVID,[4] born January 22nd, 1783; married Sally Merrymen.

73 IV. WILLIAM,[4] born June 19th, 1784; unmarried, died June 1810.

74 V. JENNEY,[4] born Dec. 17th, 1785; married Wanton Stover. She died Sept. 1807. Two children, (75) Simeon (Stover,) (76) Davis (Stover.)

77 VI † GEORGE,[4] born May 15th, 1787; married (1) Betsey Merryman, (2) Mary Merryman.

78 VII. HANNAH,[4] born Nov. 19th, 1790; died April 1807.

79 VIII. MARY,[4] born Jan. 9th, 1793; died Dec. 1806.

80 IX. HUGH,[4] born March 10th, 1796; died Aug. 1810.

11 SARAH[3] DOUGLAS, (Elijah,[3] John,[1]) sister of the preceeding and daughter of Elijah and Elizabeth (Estes) Douglas, was born in North Yarmouth, (now Harpswell,) June 13th, 1759; married Benjamin Doughty of Brunswick, where they resided. The date of her death or any further record of them has not been received.

Their children born in Brunswick were:—

HANNAH (DOUGHTY) m. Isaac Allen, resided and died in Freeport.

81   I.   JAMES (DOUGHTY.)
82   II. DAVID (DOUGHTY.)
83   III. BENJAMIN (DOUGHTY.)
84   IV. ICHABARD (DOUGHTY.)
85   V.   MARY (DOUGHTY) married William Hunt.
86   VI. PHEBE (DOUGHTY) married Daniel Tompson, of Brunswick.
87   VII. JEDIDIAH (DOUGHTY.)

12   MARY[3] DOUGLAS, (Elijah,[2] John,[1]) sister of the preceeding and daughter of Elijah and Elizabeth (Estes) Douglas, was born in North Yarmouth, (now Harpswell,) July 10th, 1763; married by Brigadier Thompson at Brunswick, May 15th, 1782, Daniel Booker, of her native town, born Feb. 25th, 1760. He setted in Harpswell. About 1795, he removed on a farm in the town of Bowdoin, where they passed the remainder of their days. She died Jan. 30th, 1844.

Their children were:—

88   I.   JAMES (BOOKER) born in Harpswell, Sept. 15th, 1783; married (1) Patience Dinslow, (2) Lydia Gatchell, a successful farmer residing in Durham.

89   II. ELIZABETH (BOOKER) born in Harpswell, Nov. 7th, 1785: died young.

90   III. MARY (BOOKER) born in Harpswell, Feb. 12th, 1789; married Dr. Simon Baker, residing in Durham.

91   IV. HANNAH (BOOKER) born in Harpswell, Sept. 16th, 1791: unmarried; died April 28th, 1870.

92   V.   DANIEL (BOOKER) born in Harpswell, April 19th, 1794; m. 1st, —— Hewey; resided in Topsham.

93   VI. ELIZABETH (BOOKER) born in Bowdoin, June 30th, 1796; married Joseph Beal, residing in Dover.

94   VII. MERCY (BOOKER) born in Bowdoin, Aug. 28th, 1799; married Abraham Whittemore; resided in Lisbon. She died April 15th, 1825.

95   VIII. PATIENCE (BOOKER) born July 10th, 1802; married Thomas Mann, residing at Gardiner.

96 IX. MIRAM (BOOKER) born in Bowdoin, Feb. 20th 1806; married Alfred Cox, residing in Bowdoin.

97 X. ISRAEL (BOOKER) born in Bowdoin, Nov. 6th, 1309; married Louisa Perrington.

13 ELIJAH³ DOUGLAS (Elijah,² John,¹) brother of the preceeding and son of Elijah and Elizabeth (Estes) Douglas, was born in Harpswell, June 23rd, 1768; married Oct. 1787, Jenny, daugter of Abraham Grant of Freeport. He remained on the homestead farm, which was left him by his father. He sold this farm for $1200, and bought two islands opposite Bucksport. He was unfortunate in his business affairs, and in old age he found his little property entirely consumed. He spent the last years of his life with Nathan Douglas in Brunswick. From the day on which he went there to live until his death he never left the farm. He worked what he could on the farm and the remainder of his support was furnished by his son, Capt. Samuel. He was a man of very few words and was extremely old. He died October 1849, and was buried in the Friends' grave-yard at South Durham.

Their children born in Harpswell were:—

98 I. † SAMUEL,⁴ born June 16th, 1788; married Esther Bartal.

99 II. † SUSANNA,⁴ born Feb. 27th, 1790; married Simeon Wheeler.

100 III. JOHN,⁴ born June 23rd, 1792; unmarried; died 1817.

101 IV. † WILLIAM,⁴ born Jan. 12th, 1795; marrried Mary Sennett.

102 V. † JENNEY,⁴ born Feb. 6th, 1797; married Mathew Simpson.

103 VI. † MARY,⁴ born June 13th, 1799; married John Field.

104　VII. Israel, born July 6th, 1802; married a lady in Bangor where he settled. He died there 1854.
105　VIII. † Elizabeth,⁴ born Sept. 29th, 1804; married Henry French.
106　IX. † Isaac,⁴ born Dec. 31st, 1806; married (1) Mary Pinkham (2) Phebe (Quinum) Morse.
107　X. † Elmira,⁴ born Dec. 14th, 1809; married —— Hobs of Falmouth.

14 John³ Douglas, (Elijah,² John,¹) brother of the preceeding and son of Elijah and Elizabeth (Estes) Douglas, was born in Harpswell, November 8th, 1774; married (1) August 5th, 1796, Sarah Booker, (2) Catherine (Briry) Booker. He settled on a part of his father's farm in Durham, which was willed to him by his father. In 1820, he sold this farm and bought one near the Androscoggin River in the same town, where he resided until a few years previous to his death. His last days were passed with his son Waitstell at Brunswick, where he died October 18th, 1853, and was buried in the grave-yard near his home in Durham.

The children by (1) wife born in Durham were;—

108　I. Polly,⁴ born May 16th, 1797; died same day.
109　II. Elizabeth,⁴ born June 18th, 1798; died April 5th, 1814.
110　III. † Hugh,⁴ born Aug. 19, 1800; married Julia A. Goddard.
111　IV. John,⁴ born March 21st, 1803; unmarried. At the age of 17 years, he fell upon a cart stake causing death Sept. 1820.
112　V. Joanna, born Aug. 20th, 1805, died 1808.
113　VI. † Nancy B.⁴ born Feb. 6th, 1808; married John B. Douglas, (311.)
114　VII. † Isaac,⁴ born Feb. 7th, 1811; married Abigail K. Webber.

115 VIII. SALLEY,[4] born Jan. 30, 1814.

Children by second wife:—

116 IX. ENOS,[4] born Sept. 2, 1816; married Nov. 1842, Nancy M. Jordan. She died in Durham; one child, Thomas. 117. Married (2) wife Sept. 1795, Mrs. Hannah (Fass) Hanscomb, residing in Lewiston.

118 X. † WAITSTILL[4] WEBBER, born Nov. 1, 1818; married Jane Day.

The following lines were taken from the Rising Sun, a paper published at Little River, Lisbon, composed on the death of John Douglas, (No. 111,) who received a mortal wound in his side by falling on the stake of a cart, while assisting in hauling in hay, Aug. 24, 1820, which terminated his life in 17 days.

> I pray the Lord direct my pen,
>   While I address the sons of men ;
> I pray excuse what you find wrong,
>   I now begin my mournful song.
>
> A youth of late in Durham dwelt,
>   The pangs of death, alas, he's felt ;
> That awful scene he's passed through,
>   Which must be passed by me and you.
>
> August the twenty-fourth 'twas found,
>   He had received a dreadful wound :
> Which so alarmed his loving friends
>   That for a surgeon they did send.
>
> But no relief could he him give,
>   He was not long on earth to live :
> It was God's will that he should go
>   And leave this world of care below.
>
> September tenth on Sabbath day
>   The spirit left this breathless clay ;
> In Jesus Christ he put his trust,
>   In hopes to live among the just.

> O, paren's dear, pray kiss the rod,
>   Consider it is the hand of God,
> Which has bereft thee of thy son,
>   'Tis but the will of God that's done.
>
> We must resign to God and say
>   That He has given and took away.
> He made and lent him unto you,
>   God is almighty, just and true.
>
> God visits thee with many woes,
>   And trials great we may suppose;
> Pray to the Lord that he will give
>   Thee patience whilst thou here doest live.
>
> To brothers kind and sisters dear,
>   You're left to drop a pitying tear;
> But let those fountains cease to flow,
>   Set not your hearts on things below.
>
> Your brother now is dead and gone.
>   And unto you he cannot return:
> Unite and live in peace and love.
>   And serve the Lord that reigns above.

15 JOHN[3] DOUGLAS, (John,[2] John,[1]) son of John and Mary (Braley) Douglas, was born in Middleborough, Mass., March 11, 1752; married, 1776, Lydia Southworth, born June 12, 1759. Early in life he fitted himself for a school-teacher. He taught a district school in his native town fifteen winters in succession. Soon after the breaking out of the Revolutionary war, he went to Boston and volunteered his services in the army. He was an Orderly Sergeant, which office he held until the end of his enlistment. He was paid off in continental money, which will be remembered was nearly worthless. He had to pay sixty dollars of it for a gallon of molasses, and one hundred dollars for a pound of tea. He was afterwards drafted, but not wishing to serve longer in the war, he gave a cow to a

man to go as his substitute. About the year 1786, he moved to Plymouth, Mass., and settled in the neighborhood known as the Halfway Pond. There were but few inhabitants there at that time, and no schools within several miles. He was the first man who interceded and raised money to start a school; and all that could be collected was thirteen dollars. For this sum he taught a school during the winter months of that year. After the death of his father, he removed to the old homestead, which was given him in consideration of his taking care of his mother during the remainder of her life; also to have the care and support of his youngest brother and sister until they became of age. In 1804, he removed to Clyden, N. H., where he resided three years, then removed back to Plymouth, where he lived until his death. He was a worthy member of the Baptist church, and was much respected by those who knew him, for his genial disposition and integrity; so honest and upright was he in all his dealings, that he was called "John the Baptist." He died in the year 1827, and was interred in the graveyard near the Halfway Pond.

Their children were:—

119 I. REBECCA,[4] born in Middleborough, Mass., Sept. 20, 1777 · died Sept. 6, 1778.

120 II. † EPHRAIM,[4] born in Middleborough, Nov. 22, 1778; married Deborah Haskins.

121 III. LYDIA,[4] born in Middleborough, Dec. 24, 1780; died 1785.

122 IV. † JOHN,[4] born in Middleborough, Aug. 3, 1782; married (1) Mehitable Elliot (2) Iantha Howard.

123 V. EARL,[4] born in Middleborough, Nov. 13, 1784; married Mary Reynolds (146).

124 VI. † WARREN,[4] born in Middleborough, Sept. 20, 1786; married Rhoda Thrasher.

125 VII. † Lucy,⁴ born in Middleborough. Sept. 9, 1788 ; married Joseph Bates.
126 VIII. † George,⁴ born in Plymouth, Mass., Jan. 21, 1792 ; married Eliza Nightengale.
127 IX. † Joshua,⁴ born in Plymouth, Jan. 25, 1794 ; married Mary S. Pierce.
128 X. Southworth,⁴ born in Plymouth, Aug. 1, 1796 ; died July 1807.
129 XI. † Lydia,⁴ born in Plymouth, Jan. 16, 1799 ; married Prince Manter.
130 XII. † Elijah,⁴ born in Plymouth, May 24, 1801 ; married Louisa Freeman.
131 XIII. Sarah, born in Crydon, N. H., March 24, 1805 ; unmarried ; died May. 1822.

16 Mary² Douglas, (John,² John,¹) sister of the preceding, and a daughter of John and Mary (Braley) Douglas, was born in Middleborough, Mass., about 1757; married Libbeas Simmons. He was a farmer, and resided in Troy, Maine, where they died.

Their children, probably born in Troy, were:—

132 I. Elijah (Simmons) born —— married Ruth Russell.
133 II. Betsey (Simmons) born —— married David Vickey.
134 III. Thaddeas (Simmons) born —— ; died young.
135 IV. Mary (Simmons) born —— married Jere Mitchell.
136 V. Persilla (Simmons) born —— married Joseph Mitchell.
137 VI. James (Simmons) born —— married Hannah Buzzard.
138 VII. Sarah (Simmons) born —— married David Reynolds.
139 VIII. Judath (Simmons) born —— married Wm. McCauslin.
140 IX. Libbeas (Simmons) born —— married Esther Kelsey.
141 X. Lydia (Simmons) born —— married James Parker.

17 Elizabeth³ Douglas, (John,² John,¹) sister of the preceding, and daughter of John and Mary (Braley) Douglas, was born in Middleborough, Mass., 1760; married Ephraim Reynolds, of Augusta, Maine,

where they settled. In 1815 or 16, they removed to Warsaw, Wyoming County, New York. They were six weeks on the road. They hired a house to live in a short time, then Mr. Reynolds bought a farm in Gainesville, New York, where he moved his family. He subsequently sold this farm to Earl Douglas, (his wife's brother) and his son Jacob, in consideration of he and his wife being supported during their lives. The deed was given January 1819.

Their children born in Augusta were:—

142 I. TRYPHENA (REYNOLDS) born 1780; married William Boyington. She died Nov. 1838.

143 II. EPHRAIM (REYONLDS) born ——; married Phebe Reynolds. He resided in Gainesville, New York.

144 III. ELIZABETH (REYNOLDS) born ——; married Ephraim Reynolds. (cousin.)

145 IV. DANIEL (REYNOLDS) born —— married Sarah Simmons of Ohio. He has not been heard from for many years.

146 V. MARY (REYNOLDS) born —— married Earl Douglas (her cousin.) No. (123.)

147 VI. ROGER (REYNOLDS) born Oct. 1791; unmarried; died Sept. 22, 1853.

148 VII. PHEBE (REYNOLDS) born 1794; unmarried; died at Gainesvill, N. Y., 1818.

149 VIII. HANNAH (REYNOLDS) born March 22, 1797; married March 22, 1820, Rufus Jewett, of Warsaw, Wyoming Co., N. Y. She died Dec. 19, 1856.

150 IX. JACOB (REYNOLDS) born 1802; married about 1824, Betsey Tompson. After living together several years for some reason they separated, and never again lived together.

151 X JOHN (REYNOLDS.)

152 XI. LYDIA (REYNOLDS.)

18 PHEBE[3] DOUGLAS, (John,[2] John,[1]) sister of the preceeding and daughter of John and Mary (Braley) Douglas, born in Middleborough, Mass.,

about 1767; married Roland Homes of Plymouth, Mass. They settled in Troy, Maine, where she died.

There children were:—

153 I. ELISHA (HOMES.)
154 II. MARY (HOMES.)
155 III. SAMUEL (HOMES.)

19 ELISHA³ DOUGLAS, (John,² John,¹) brother of the preceeding and son of John and Mary (Braley) Douglas, was born in Middleborough, Mass., June 12, 1771; married (1) Celia Oskin, (2) Hannah Russell. His mother died when he was quite young, and he lived with his brother John until old enough to earn a living for himself. He settled in his native town where he resided until 1800, at which time his wife died and the following year he married his second wife, and moved to Troy, Maine. In 1810, he removed to Winterport; and the same year to Monroe. He was quite a thrifty farmer. He also devoted some of his time to hunting. In 1814, when the English invaded Hampden, Elisha was called out with the militia, who were in charge of General Blake, to oppose the enemy. The army was brought into line, and Gen. Blake rode in front, and forbade their firing until they received orders. By this time the British had landed. Elisha chose his ground and commenced action; firing a number of rounds before he was discovered. When the enemy saw the smoke they fired and wounded him in the arm, by which cause it was ever afterwards stiff, and he received a pension for his disability. In 1830 or 31, he removed to Burnham, where he died in the year 1851. His (2) wife died Feb. 1868.

Their children were:—

156 I. † ABSALOM,[4] born in Middleborough, Mass, Nov. 27, 1795,; married Realfy Caswell.

157 II. MARIAM,[4] born in Middleborough, Oct. 1, 1797; married —— Mirick.

158 III. † CELIA,[4] born in Middleborough, Jan. 13, 1799; married John Michols.

Children by second wife:—

159 IV. † HANNAH,[4] born in Troy, Me., Dec. 20, 1802; married Isaac Jordan.

160 V. † RUTH,[4] born in Troy, Oct. 21, 1804; married Collins Pattee.

161 VI. † LUCY,[4] born in Troy, June 3, 1808; married S. Emery Jewell.

162 VII. † ELIZABETH,[4] born in Monroe. May 21, 1810; married Nathaniel Hooton.

163 VIII. † HIRAM R,[4] born in Monroe, Apr. 27, 1812; married Fanny Trambly.

164 IX. PHEBE, born in Monroe, Oct. 8, 1814; married (1) Asa Runnels, who died in the (165) War of '61, 1 child, Lucy, (Runnels) born July 29, 1833; M. Edwin Gilmore. who died 1873; —(2) 1860, John Pushaw, resided in Burnham. Mrs. Phebe Pushaw died Sept. 1873.

166 X. MAHALAH, born in Monroe, Feb. 19, 1817, and died the same day.

20 GEORGE[3] DOUGLAS, (George,[2] John,[1]) son of George and Prudence (Caswell,) Douglas, was born in Middleborough, Plymouth Co., Mass., August 26, 1762; married Dec. 5, 1790, Patience Savery, of Wareham, Mass. He settled on a farm in his native town. In the year of 1801, he removed to Brookfield, and in 1804 to Rochester, Mass., where he was successfully engaged in farming until his death, which occurred March 10, 1843. His wife died Dec. 11, 1863.

Their children born in Middleboro, Mass., were:—

167 I. † BARNABAS NYE,[4] born Nov. 11, 1791; married Phebe N. Swift.

168 II. † BETSEY,[4] born July 14, 1793; married Nathaniel King.

21 NOAH[3] DOUGLAS, (George,[2] John,[1]) brother of the preceeding, and son of George and Prudence (Caswell) Douglas, was born in Middleborough, Mass., about 1764; married Mary Seekel, of Taunton. He settled on a farm in Middleborough. He resided for a short time at New Bedford, where he died.

Their children born in Middleborough, were:—

169 I ELIAS,[4] born about 1792. He was a mason by trade; unmarried; died at Russells Hills Dartmouth, Mass.

170 II. † NOAH,[4] born about 1794; married Rachel Maxfield, of Dartmouth.

171 III. † GEORGE,[4] born Feb. 20, 1796; married (1) Hannah Churchill, (2) Alsaider Pierce.

172 IV. ALLEN,[4] born 1799. When thirteen years of age, he was drowned at Lakeville.

173 V † MARY,[4] born —— married Job White.

174 VI. NANCY,[4] born —— died unmarried.

175 VII. PRUDENCE,[4] born —— married Willard Gray, of Little Compton, R. I., farmer; no children; resided in New Bedford, where he died.

176 VIII. KERZIAH,[4] born —— unmarried. She resides at New Bedford.

177 IX. HARRIET,[4] born —— married Henry T. Sherman. They resided at Acushnet, Mass., where they died. No issue.

22 SELAH[3] DOUGLAS, (George,[2] John,[1]) sister of the preceeding, and daughter of George and Prudence (Caswell) Douglas, born in Middleborough, Mass., about the year 1767; married David Niles of Freetown, Mass., where they settled on a farm.

No further record of the family received.

Their children were:—

178 I. JOTHAM, (Niles) ⎫ born in Freetown where they
               Twins ⎬
179 II. DAVID (Niles) ⎭ both died young.

FOURTH GENERATION.

23 CORNELIUS[4] DOUGLAS, (Daniel,[3] Elijah,[2] John,[1]) eldest son of Daniel and Sabry (Russell) Douglas, was born either in Brunswick or Durham, September 19, 1780; married about 1801, Hannah Whittemore, of Cape Cod. He settled in Litchfield, in that portion of the town known as Litchfield Neck. He always followed farming as a livelihood, and was an honest and upright citizen, and very industrious; but was quite unfortunate in acquiring a sufficient supply of this world's goods to maintain him through life, and in his old age he came to want. He passed his last days in the alms house in Litchfield, where he died A. D., 1833.

His children born in Litchfield were:—

180 I. † ABNER,[5] born August 28, 1802; married (1) Abigail Allen, (2) Elmira (Morrill) Douglas.

181 II. LEVI,[5] born January 14, 1804; marreed Elmira Morrill; died March 1, 1850; children died in infancy.

182 III. RACHAEL,[5] born August 7, 1806; married ———. Resided at Patucket, Mass., no further record received.

183 IV. HIRAM,[5] born January 15, 1809; married December 3, 1834, Nancy Nye, resides at Hallowell. One child, Wm. A. born in H. August 15, 1837; died there September 26, 1837.

185 V. † LEMUEL,[5] born April 12, 1812; married Olive B. Berry.

186 VI. MAHALA,[5] born August 11, 1819; died August 1844; unmarried.

187 VII. † MARY A.[5] born February 25, 1821; married Moses H. Arthor.

188 VIII. SEWALL,[5] born March 6, 1823; unmarried. He served in the Rebellion of '61.

24 NABBY[4] DOUGLAS, (Daniel,[3] Elijah,[2] John,[1]) sister of the preceding, and daughter of Daniel and Sabry (Russell) Douglas, was born in Brunswick, 1782; married July 21, 1804, James Welch, of Brunswick. Their last place of residence was Durham, where they died.

Their children were :—

189 I. NANCY (WELCH) born in Brunswick; married Joel Richardson, resided in Durham.

190 II. JOHN (WELCH.)

191 III. SARAH BAILEY (WELCH.)

192 IV. SABRINA RUSSELL (WELCH.)

193 V. ESTHER C. (WELCH)

194 VI. JAMES (WELCH) married Charlotte Patridge. He resides in Durham.

25 ANNIE[4] DOUGLAS, (Daniel,[3] Elijah,[2] John,[1]) sister of the preceding, born in Brunswick, 1784; married 1804, William Groves, of Brunswick. He owned one-half of his wife's father's farm in Freeport, where they

settled and resided for several years. In 1829, he sold his part of the farm to his wife's brother Daniel, and removed to the town of Mercer, where they lived and died.

Their children born in Freeport were:—

195 I. Lucy (Groves) born in 1805; married Amasa Gould, of Belgrade.
196 II. John (Groves) born July 6, 1807; married a lady of one of the Western States.
197 III. Mary Ann (Groves) born May, 1810; married —— Clark, of Mercer.
198 IV. Mikel (Groves) born February 3, 1812.
199 V. Delenda (Groves) born October 20, 1813.

26 Sylvania[4] Douglas (Daniel,[3] Elijah,[2] John,[1]) sister of the preceding and daugter of Daniel and Sabry (Russell) Douglas, was born in Brunswick 1789; married 1810, Zachariah Allen; resided and died in Durham.

Their children born in Durham were:—

200 I. Phebe (Allen) born August 10, 1811.
201 II. Joseph B. (Allen) born Sept. 16, 1814; married Sept. 1842.
202 III. Daniel D. (Allen) born April 19, 1817; married December 3, 1843.
203 IV. Mary (Allen) born May 28, 1819.
204 V. Levi D. (Allen) born March 4, 1821.

27 Phebe[4] Douglas, (Daniel,[3] Elijah,[2] John,[1]) Sister of the preceding, and daughter of Daniel and Sabry (Russell) Douglas, was born in Brunswick about A. D., 1792; married February 9, 1809, Samuel Groves,* of Brunswick. He settled on a farm in Litchfield; removed to Brunswick and resided on the road

---
*His name is on the town records of Brunswick Grows, though h's children spell their name Groves.

leading to Bath, where she died December 10, 1849. He died June 1858.

Their children born in Litchfield were:—

205 I. MARY ANN (GROVES) born January 1, 1810; married 1833, Joseph H. Town; resides West Gardiner.

206 II. SAMUEL (GROVES) born October 3. 1812; married (1) Elizabeth Campbell, (2) Salley Merrills; resides in Manchester.

207 III. PERMELIA (GROVES) born October 17, 1815; married 1838, Daniel Town. She had five husbands. Her last residence, was at Salem, Mass., where she died 1870.

208 IV. OLIVER (GROVES) born October 5, 1817. He was killed while at work sinking a well in 1835.

209 V. SARAH S. (GROVES) born February 22, 1819; married 1838, Benjamin Curtis. She had three husbands; resided at Bath where she died 1867.

210 VI. HENRY W. (GROVES) born April 11, 1821; married 1845, Abigail Grows; resides in Brunswick.

211 VII. RUFUS (GROVES) born February 7, 1824; married 1847, M. Stilkey. They reside at Brunswick.

212 VIII. AURILLA (GROVES) Twins born July 14, married 1844, Thos. C. Jones.
213 IX. ISABEL married 1848, Edwin Brown, of West Bath.

214 X. GEORGE W. (GROVES) born October 31, 1830; married 1851, Lucy Ann Lake; resides in Durham.

215 XI. PHEBE (GROVES) born May 3, 1833; married March 1850, James Williams; resides in Lockford, California.

28 DANIEL[4] DOUGLAS, (Daniel,[3] Elijah,[2] John,[1]) brother of the preceding and son of Daniel and Sabry (Russell) Douglas, was born in Brunswick, August 1796. He was eighteen months old when his father moved to Freeport. He married Sarah Bailey. He inherited one-half of his father's homestead where he lived and took care of his parents. The old log house in which they had lived for a quarter of a century, he replaced with a framed one. This, however, was not plastered for many years. He died at his home March

NOTE.—The record of the births of the family of Daniel (4) were taken from the records of the town of Freeport, as there was no family record to be found, and are doubtless correct.

30, 1864, and was buried in the Friends' grave-yard at So. Durham, where a grave-stone marks his resting place. His wife died September 29, 1858.

Their children born in Freeport were:—

216   I. ANNIE BAILEY[5] born October 18, 1818; married August 1851, Jeremiah Dolley. They have no children; resides on a small farm in Durham, in what is known as the Osgood neighborhood.

217   II. CATHERINE[3] A. born August 6, 1820; died February 15, 1840.

218   III. † DIANNA DILLINGHAM[5] born May 23, 1822; married Ezra Jordan Hoit.

219   IV. DANIEL ROBERT[5] born June 5, 1824; unmarried, ship carpenter. He owned the old homestead, after the death of his father; but subsequently sold it and made his home with; his sister Dolley. He fell dead in the road in Durham 1887.

220   V. AMOS BAILEY[5] born February 28 1827; unmarried died September 7, 1860.

29   JOHN[4] DOUGLAS, (Cornelius,[3] Elijah,[2] John,[1]) eldest son of Cornelius and Ann (Estes) Douglas, was born in Harpswell. September 8, 1768; married March 14, 1791, Judith, daughter of Samuel and Hannah Collins. He lived on a farm near his brother Edward, on the road leading from Brunswick Village to the Friends' meeting house in Durham. He and his wife were members of the Society of Friends, and much esteemed by those who knew them. He died at his home in Brunswick, June 17, 1820. At this early date there was no road from his home to the Friends meeting-house and four men carried the corpse through the woods to the grave-yard near Friends meeting-house where he was buried. His widow removed to Durham where she died in 1841.

Their children born in Brunswick were:—

221   I. ISRAEL,[5] born January 25, 1792; unmarried. He was

a young man of promise, and had acquired a good education, but alas, his hopes were suddenly blasted. While quite young in years he was attacked with rheumatism, and so severe was this disease that he was unable to even feed himself. For many years he was confined to his bed. A traveling quack doctor came along and made his parents believe that he could cure him; but his medicine made him worse and he soon died about 1833. The doctor gave him saltpetre which caused his death. His mother took his death hard, though he had been a great sufferer.

 222 II. † HANNAH, born about 1794; married 1815, Abner Eaton.

 223 III. † ABIJAH,^{5} born June 25, 1796; married Phebe Estes.

 224 IV. † PHEBE,^{5} born July 7, 1798; married Thomas Jones.

 225 V. † RHODA,^{5} born April 30, 1800; married December 6, 1821, Thomas Coombs.

 30 EDWARD^4 DOUGLAS, (Cornelius,^{3} Elijah,^{2} John,^{1}) brother of the preceding, was born in Harpswell, June 30, 1770. His early years were passed on his father's farm where he acquired the habit of industry and perseverance which ever characterized him in life. April 29, 1794, he bought of Samuel Thompson, of Topsham, thirty-three and one-third acres of unimproved land, for which he paid the sum of twenty-two pounds, two shillings and three pence, lawful money. This parcel of land was situated in the township of Brunswick, on the Freeport line, commencing with the standing trees. He cleared a few acres the first year, which he planted with corn, and harvested one hundred bushels of shelled corn. He hired a girl for one dollar per week to do the husking. He built no buildings on the place, and owned it but a few years, then sold it. He bought of Robert McManus one hundred acres of land in Brunswick, on which were a small clearing and a log house, for which he

paid five hundred dollars, lawful money. The deed was given June 26, 1798. It appears from record that he occupied this farm a year before the deed was given and during the spring made maple sugar. The first seed he put into the ground on this farm was a pint of apple seeds.

May 4, 1797, he married Esther, daughter of Samuel and Hannah Collins, born in Durham, February 17, 1770. Soon after their marriage they commenced house keeping in the log house on the farm. There were no roads in that part of the town, and he procured a pocket compass by which he ran out one by spotting trees. A petition was drawn up, signed, and presented to the County Commisioners who established a road which is still in use and known as the Durham road.

In 1801, he built a large two story house in place of the old log house, where he lived until his death. He was an active enterprising man and managed his business affairs judiciously. Although he never filled any public office, yet he did a great amount of business for others. He was distinguished in his day as a master carter, and his services were much employed by those having buildings and vessels to haul. He was a consistant and highly esteemed member of the Society of Friends and much respected by the community. He died while temporarily absent from home in the town of Vassalboro, April 18, 1823, and was buried in the Friends' grave-yard near Oak Grove Seminary.

September, 1823, all the buildings, fences and roads on his widow's farm were burned by the great fire that passed over that portion of the town. The boys built a camp in the field where they watched and harvested the little not destroyed by the fire.

The old family bible bought in 1823, and published in 1799, also the old-style eight-day clock, reaching from floor to ceiling, bought in 1808, for which sixty dollars was paid, (and still keeps good time) together with several deeds and their marriage certificate (Friends' style) were rescued from the flames, and are very carefully preserved as relics of "ye olden times" by her youngest son, Edward Franklin, who always lived at home and had the care of his mother. March 19, 1841, the widow with her son Edward Franklin, removed and settled in Dover, where she died.

Their children born in Brunswick, were:

226 I. † PAUL,[5] born March 18, 1798; married (1) Nancy Warren, (2) Emily Sawyer.

227 II. † HULDAH,[5] born Feb. 4, 1800; married Francis Harmon.

228 III. EUNICE,[5] born Aug. 2, 1802; married, (1) October 1828, Louy Harmon, of Durham; (2) Simon Bryor, of Dover, where they resided She died Jan. 9, 1865.

229 IV. † JOHN,[5] born July 30, 1804; married Charity P. Coombs.

230 V. † PHEBE,[5] born Aug. 31, 1807; married William P. Larrabee.

231 VI. † RUFUS,[5] born Aug 21, 1809; married Marilla S. Nickerson.

232 VII. † EDWARD FRANKLIN,[5] born Aug. 17. 1812; married Elvira C. Stoddard.

31 PHEBE[4] DOUGLAS, (Cornelius[3], Elijah[2], John[1],) sister of the preceding, and daughter of Cornelius and Anna (Estes) Douglas, was born Nov. 12, 1772; married, Jan. 24, 1793, Ebenezer Austen of Falmouth. They resided in Canada a number of years, then removed to Vassalboro.

No record of his death has been received. She died January 15, 1817.

Their children, all born in Canada except the oldest:

233   I.   ANNA (Austen) born in Falmouth, January 3, 1794; married John Estes, December 26, 1829, resided in China, Maine, where she died August 4, 1840.

234   II.   JOHN (Austen) born in Falmouth, November 8, 1795; married December 30, 1858, Adaline Cook; residence Calais, where he died April 2, 1875.

235   III.   DAVID (Austen) born in Canada October 10, 1797; unmarried; died in China, Maine, July 16, 1854.

236   IV.   CORNELIUS (Austen) born January 1, 1799; died July 1800.

237   V.   CORNELIUS (Austen) born January 6, 1801; unmarried. In his earliest days he was a successful school teacher. About the year 1850 he conceived the idea of inventing perpetual motion, devoting much of his time and energy upon the subject, but of course failed to accomplish his object. He died at his brother John's, in Calais, April 14, 1875.

238   VI.   LYDIA (Austen) born January 24, 1803; unmarried.

239   VII.   PHEBE DOUGLAS (Austen) born December 31, 1804; November 12, 1829 married Robert Knowles. They reside in New York.

240   VIII.   SUSANNA (Austen) born February 27, 1807; married (1) October 8, 1829, Stephen Estes; (2) John Estes, August 3, 1849.

241   IX.   ESTHER (Austen) born April 1, 1809; December 12, 1833, married Barnabas French; 2d marriage February 18, 1875, Danford Parmeter; reside in China, Maine.

242   X.   REBECCA (Austen) born September 23, 1811; March 23, 1831, married George Estes; resides in China.

38.   ANNA[4] DOUGLAS, (Cornelius[3], Elijah[2], John[1],) daughter of Cornelius and Lydia (Buffum) Douglas, was born in Durham, August 15, 1792. Married February 7, 1822, Samuel, son of Silas and Elizabeth (Kennard) Goddard, of Brunswick, where they settled on his father's homestead, where they always resided. She died Octo-

ber 4, 1840, and was buried in the Friends' graveyard at South Durham. He died October 23, 1873.

Their children born in Brunswick :

243   I.   IRA (Goddard) born August 10, 1826; married December 31, 1857, Hannah M. Beal. Shoemaker and farmer; resides in Durham.

244   II.   SILAS (Goddard) born December 29, 1827; married (1) November 29, 1855, Amy P. Bailey, daughter of Joseph Bailey, of Freeport; died June 21, 1867. (2) Lydia B., daughter of Lemuel and Maria Jones, of Brunswick. He is a farmer and plow manufacturer. Resides on the old homestead farm and had the care of his father until his death.

245   III.   LYDIA ANN (Goddard) born February 21, 1830; married May 29, 1856, Amiel Eben Phelps. They reside at Worcester, Mass.

246   IV.   PATIENCE DOUGLAS (Goddard) born May 9, 1833; married November 11, 1855, Rev. Isaac A. Field; resided in Phipsburg till 1886, when they removed to Worcester, Mass.

247   V.   SALOME JANE (Goddard) born January 23, 1835; married September 21, 1868, Augustus F. Cox, boot and shoe manufacturer at Portland, where they reside.

40.   JOSHUA[4] DOUGLAS, (Cornelius[3], Elijah[2], John[1],) brother of the preceding and son of Cornelius and Lydia (Buffum) Douglas, was born in Royallsborough, now Durham, September 8, 1794. His boyhood days were spent with his parents, laboring on the farm during the summer months and attending school winters. The advantages for acquiring an education were necessarily limited; still by perseverance and good attention to his studies during the few weeks of school, he obtained a fair business education for those days. When twenty years of age he took a violent cold which so prostrated him, that for more than a year he was able to do but little labor. On recovering somewhat from his illness he hired the homestead farm of Andrew Adams for one year, boarding in his family,

HOMESTEAD OF JOSHUA DOUGLAS, DURHAM, MAINE.

where he made the acquaintance of Jane, daughter of Andrew and Ruth (Lufkin) Adams, born in Royallsborough, now Durham, October 22, 1794; whom he married at the Friends' meetinghouse in Durham, June 11, 1818.

He bought a farm of fifty acres in Brunswick, of Gideon Toothaker, for which he paid the sum of seven hundred dollars. The deed was given April 11, 1817. September, 1823, he lost one thousand dollars worth of property by the great fire, which burnt nearly everything before it for a mile in width and five miles in length; his barn, well filled with hay and grain, wood, chopped in the woods, and all his fences were swept away by the conflagration. The following year he sold the farm and bought Andrew Adams' homestead, situated near Plummer's Mill, in Durham, where he resided until 1835, at which time he sold out to Henry Plummer, and bought a farm of one hundred acres, of Caleb Jones, lying on the Androscoggin River, in Durham, where he resided till his death. His wife died February 24, 1838. August 29, 1839, he married for his second wife, Lucy, daughter of Jonathan and Lucy Beal, of Durham.

Much of his life was spent in poor health; at one time he was unable to do any labor for two years. While Providence seemed to frown upon him in depriving him of property and health, God's bountiful grace was wonderfully bestowed upon him, and through all his trials and adversities he was patient and resigned to the good Shepherd, who careth for his flock.

His parents were members of the society of Friends, and their discipline provides that when both parents are members of the society, their children are also members, by birth-right, which was the privilege of the subject of this memorial.

When a boy only fourteen years of age, while alone in the barn, he was feelingly impressed with the great power and love of God, which filled his young heart with joy. He was plainly shown that there was a place of misery as well as a place of happiness and bliss. Though like Samuel, he did not know it was the voice of God speaking to him. Not heeding this impression he soon lost sight of it entirely, though always a moral and upright man, and constant in attendance at church.

When about thirty years of age he was stricken under powerful conviction of his sins and the need of pardon. So keenly was his mind exercised that often in the silent watches of the night he would retire to some secluded place and pour out his desire to God in prayer, that He would have mercy on his soul. Frequently, while in the field about his daily work, he would put up a silent prayer to Him, who only could forgive sins. He soon felt it his duty to call his family together and read a portion of scripture. This was a great cross; but like the psalmist, he thought "Have I been so long time pleading for mercy and am I unwilling to bear this cross?" The following morning he gathered his little family around him and read a chapter in the Bible, which so affected him that his heart was broken into tenderness. Tears of penitence coursed down his cheeks; humbled thus, he was willing to fall upon his knees and implore God's forgiveness. When he arose, all was light about him; the great Deliverer had spoken peace to his captive soul and set it free.

So punctual was he in the observance of his family devotions, that no hurry in business or haste to reach the

cars ever caused him to neglect this means of grace.
Soon after his conversion he commenced to exhort in
meeting and felt a deep interest for the salvation of souls.
He made the journey with horse and carriage to New-
port, R. I., twice to attend yearly meeting.

He frequently accompanied Thomas Jones, a minister
among Friends, on religious visits through different States.
November 21, 1854, he was recommended as a minister
by the Society of Friends. He labored zealously for the
Master at home in his own meeting, as well as in different
States and in Canada, holding meetings among his own
society and others, with good results.

June, 1869, while at work in his cellar, he was attacked with a severe cold from which he never recovered.
For eleven years he suffered patiently, perfectly resigned
to the will of his Heavenly Master. He was never heard
to murmur or complain. It was pleasant to visit his sick
room and converse with him. During the protracted
years of his sickness many travelling Friend ministers
called on him and would talk with him and engage in
prayer. At one time he said "I don't expect to be here
long but it is well; it looks peaceful."

His companion was untiring in her efforts to do all
she could to comfort him. He had a strong constitution
which caused him to endure great pain and suffering, and
thus he lived year after year.

January 21, 1881, as the sun was sinking behind the
western horizon and all was hushed to silence and awe
in his home, his spirit quietly left its tenement of clay
and was wafted by angels to its rest with Jesus.

The funeral took place at Friends meeting house in
Durham. A short sermon was preached by Nathan Douglas [276] from these words, "All the days of my appointed

time will I wait till my change come."—Job 14;14. Remarks were made by several Friend ministers, also by Rev. Geo. Plummer, of Lisbon Falls. He was buried in the cemetery near Friends' meeting house at South Durham. An appropriate head stone marks his last earthly resting place. In 1888 his body was disinterred and buried in the cemetery near his old homestead.

Children by [1] wife Jane:

248 I. †Joseph,[5] born in Brunswick, March 24, 1819; married Ann G. Beal.

249 II. †Eliza Jane,[5] born in Brunswick, February 23, 1822; married James Goddard.

250 III. †George,[5] born in Durham, May 11, 1824 ; married Elizabeth A. Prescott.

251 IV. †John,[5] born in Durham, February 26, 1828; married Ann Maria Hamblin.

252 V. †Charles,[5] born in Durham, August 24, 1830; married Annie E. Fisher.

253 VI. †Joshua Lufkin,[5] born in Durham, April 17, 1833; married Helen L. Harvey.

Child by [2] wife Lucy.

254 VII. †William Henry,[5] born in Durham, October 13, 1847; married Ella H. Rolfe; (2) Mrs. Eliza B. (Tibbetts) Clason.

41. David[4] Douglas, (Cornelius[3], Elijah[2], John[1]), brother of the preceding and son of Cornelius and Lydia (Buffum) Douglas, was born at the old homestead in Durham, July 16, 1796. His boyhood days were passed with his father on the farm summers, and at school a few weeks during the winter months. When about twenty-one years of age he went to sea, which business he continued to follow a few years, during which time nothing worthy of note occurred. About the age of twenty-three he married Hannah, daughter of Walter and Hannah

Davis, born in Brunswick, July 17, 1795. He settled on a farm bordering on China Neck in the town of China; here he resided but a few years and then removed to his native place in Durham, to live with his parents through their remaining years.

Subsequently his youngest sister married and took his place as care-taker of their mother. In 1824 or 1825 he with his family removed to North Vassalboro, where he worked in a tannery for a man by the name of Southworth, until in assisting in taking down a building which fell and he with it, breaking one of his arms and five ribs, which laid him by over seven months. During his illness his wife died leaving him with four small children, the youngest dying soon after at the age of eleven months. He married for his second wife, January 21, 1829, a cousin of his first wife, Chloe Davis.

About this time he bought a farm in Fairfield of his wife's father, residing in the same house where she was born. In this house they had born unto them five children, two of them dying in infancy. In the spring of 1840, he exchanged farms with a man by the name of Ward, situated in Palmyra, where he soon removed. Soon after his second marriage he and his wife made a profession of religion and joined the society of Friends, of which they remained worthy members to the close of life. About the year 1842 he was appointed an elder in that society. He was many times called upon to fill important positions in civil as well as religious life; he was often chosen arbitrator in the settlement of difficulties He served his town as selectman one or more years. All these positions he faithfully filled; he was very hospitable at his home and it was a pleasure for him to entertain all Christians without regard to sect. In 1859 or '60, he with his wife and youngest son and his family removed and settled in Bloomington, Clinton County, Ohio, where he and his son opened a variety store. His health which had been failing for several years now gave way, and he died at his residence in Ohio, December 3, 1863, having lived to see all his children who are living married. He was six feet two inches in height, well proportioned, of large, muscular frame, capable of great endurance physically, of strong intellectual powers and a very retentive memory. He died a triumphant death, having known his robes being washed and made white in the blood of the Lamb.

His dying words were "I am going, but I am perfectly happy in Jesus." His wife Chloe, who had been a most devoted, loving wife and a faithful, praying mother, survived him several years. She died May 22, 1881, in her eighty-first year and was buried by the side of her companion, in Bloomington, Ohio.

Children by first wife:

255 I. LYDIA ANN,[5] born in China, September 10, 1820; unmarried; died in Vassalboro, July 10, 1841.

256 II. HANNAH,[5] born in Durham, May 20, 1822; married March 16, 1853, Joseph Lane.

257 One child. HENRY DOUGLAS (Lane) born May 30, 1858.

258 III. EUNICE,[5] born in Durham, March 4, 1824; married October 23, 1848, Joseph Winslow, born May 9, 1824. They reside in St. Albans. She is an eminent ministress in the Society of Friends and a woman of much worth. Her labors in the ministry are everywhere well received.

259 IV. JOHN HENRY,[5] born in Vassalborough, January 6, 1826; died November 26, 1827. Children by second wife.

260 V. †JOHN HENRY,[5] born in Fairfield, November 27, 1832; married Mariam Carter.

261 VI. †ROBERT WALTER,[5] born in Fairfield, November 11, 1834; married Margaret A. Clifford.

CORNELIUS DOUGLAS.

262 VII. DAVID CORNELIUS,[5] born in Fairfield, January 5, 1840; died in St. Albans, October 5th, 1843.

Two daughters born in Fairfield, died in infancy.

42. CORNELIUS[4] DOUGLAS, (Cornelius,[3] Elijah,[2] John[1]) brother of the preceding, was born in Durham, June 12, 1798; married January 27, 1820, Phebe, daughter of John and Abigail (Frye) Nichols, of Berwick, born there September 10, 1799. He settled on the old homestead where he remained one year, and in April, 1821, he removed and settled on a farm that he bought of Caleb Nichols, in the town of Winslow, where he resided three years. Then he went and lived one year on a farm in Vassalboro, known as the Austen farm ; then removed back to his farm in Winslow where he resided until he removed to the State of Ohio. In 1831, he was recommended to the work of the ministry in the society of Friends by Vassalboro monthly meeting. His first religious visit was made in 1832 to the families of Friends and others in the vicinity of Durham monthly meeting. This visit brought him back to his native town and to mingle for a few days with those he had associated with in his youthful days.

The practice of visiting and holding religious exercises in Friends' families used to be quite prevalent. In 1841, he visited and held religious meetings in the western part of New England, New York, Philadelphia, Ohio and a general visit within the limits of Indiana yearly meeting of Friends. In 1845, he again made a religious visit to the States of Ohio and Indiana, also to Baltimore and Philadelphia. In the autumn of 1846, he with his wife and youngest daughter removed to Springfield, Clinton County, Ohio. The following year they removed to Richmond, Indiana, where he took charge of a Friends'

Boarding School, for six months. In 1850 he visited Kansas and held meetings among some of the tribes of Indians. The same year he removed his family to Kansas and superintended the Shawne Indian Mission School, which position he occupied two years, giving good satisfaction.

We have mentioned only a few of his many religious visits, in all of which he was well received and in eternity many will remember his faithful labors for the truth. In all his travels of thousand of miles, he never received a dollar of remuneration; choosing to be as Paul said "chargeable to no man." He owned a nice farm a few miles out of the village of Wilmington, Ohio, which afforded him a handsome revenue. By his extremely prudent habits and industry he laid by a handsome fortune.

In 1855 he attended Friends' Yearly Meeting at Plainville, Indiana, and while absent from home took a severe cold and it was with great difficulty that he reached his home, where he lingered only a few days. He died August 7, 1885, and was buried in the cemetery at Bloomington, Ohio. His wife died November 7, 1886, and was buried by the side of her husband.

Their children:

263 I. †John Nichols,[5] born in Durham, November 15, 1820; married Sarah T. Jones.

264 II. †Lydia,[5] born in Winslow, February 26, 1824; married Nathan C. Bailey.

265 III. †Mary,[5] born in Winslow, August 26, 1835; married (1) Dr. E. F. Everest; (2) Philip P. Harner.

43. Lydia[4] Douglas, (Cornelius,[3] Elijah,[2] John,[1]) sister of the preceding and daughter of Cornelius and Lydia (Buffum) Douglas, was born in Durham, December 28, 1799; married November 15, 1827, George W.

Morse, born January 10, 1802. He was a farmer. They resided in Bowdoinham, where she died November 29, 1843, and was buried in Friends' burying ground at South Durham. He died November 29, 1871.

Their children born in Bowdoinham :

266 I. GEORGE NELSON (Morse), born April 4, 1832; unmarried; the latter part of his days was passed in ill health. He died quite suddenly at his father's house December 27, 1860.

267 II. AUGUSTUS FRANKLIN (Morse) born February 24, 1835; married May 24, 1865, Sarah E. Gray. He is a photographer; resides at Hallowell; he keeps store there at the present time.

44 PATIENCE[4] DOUGLAS, (Cornelius,[3] Elijah,[2] John[1]) youngest daughter of Cornelius and Lydia (Buffum) Douglas, born in Durham, February 15, 1803; married December 31, 1829, Benjamin, son of Benjamin and Dorcas (Wharff) Davis, of Pownal, born April 16, 1803. He was a very honest and upright man, a kind husband and an affectionate father. He died very suddenly October 21, 1862, while at work for a neighbor. He bought the old Douglas homestead in Durham, where they resided, and where she was born and where she lived till her death, April 24, 1887.

Their children born in Durham :

268 I. DORCAS WHARFF (Davis) born August 13, 1831; married January 11, 1849, Joseph Tuttle; resided at Pownal. She died December 27, 1888.

269 II. MARGARET SNOW (Davis), born August 31, 1833; unmarried; died of consumption December 16, 1854.

270 III. JOSEPH HENRY (Davis), born October 2, 1835; married (1) November 24, 1864, Hattie W. Richardson, of Brunswick; (2) Julia Ann Day, of his native town. He now owns and occupies the old homestead and had the care of his mother till her death. He is a carriage manufacturer and has served his town as select man several years, and is at present time chairman of the Board.

271 IV. LYDIA ELLEN (Davis) born November 28, 1837, married June 17, 1858, Samuel Webber, of Guilford, where they reside on a farm.

272 V. WILLIAM PENN (Davis), born May 15, 1841; married, April 16, 1865, Louisa Day of Durham. He owns a small farm in Durham where he resides, and works farming and blacksmithing. They have two children.

273 VI. BENJAMIN FRANKLIN (Davis), born December 5, 1843; married, September 8, 1867, Augusta E. Record, born January 18, 1844. He was a shoemaker, resided at Freeport Corner, where he died September 30, 1880. His widow died later.

46 DAVID[4] DOUGLAS, (Joseph,[3] Elijah,[2] John,[1]) son of Joseph and Mary (McFall) Douglas, born in the township of Royallsborough, now Durham, August 11, 1779; married August 24, 1805, at Friends' meeting-house in Windham, Waite Hawkes, daughter of Nathaniel and Mercy (Jones) Hawkes, born July 3, 1772.

He acquired a liberal education for the opportunities afforded in those days, and was an active business man. He taught several district schools, in his own and adjoining towns. He was clerk of Friends' monthly meeting at Durham for many years. In 1806 he bought a farm in Harlem, now the town of China, but we do not learn that he ever moved on to it. In 1808 he bought one-half of his grandfather's farm in Durham, for which he paid the sum of two hundred dollars. It was that half of Elijah Douglas' homestead now owned by Thomas Philbrook, where he resided several years laboring on his farm and making bricks.

In 1809 he bought a farm in Brunswick of Caleb Estes, for which he paid nine hundred dollars. On this farm he had a windmill where he ground corn. The farm is now owned by James H. Cox. He lived at one time in a schoolhouse that stood near his father's farm, which was afterwards owned by Jesse Crosman. About 1816, he removed to Windham; 1829, returned to Durham; 1834 or '85 removed again to Windham where he died.

Their children:

274 I. †MERCY,[5] born in Durham January 26, 1808; married Mark Knight.

275 II. †MARY,[5] born in Durham March 10, 1810; married, (1) February 29, 1856, Mark Knight of Windham, where they resided and where he died; (2) May 28, 1870, Robert Goddard of Brunswick where they reside. She had no children.

276 III. †NATHAN,[5] born in Brunswick January 18, 1812; married Lucy Day.

277 IV †EUNICE,[5] born in Brunswick October 27, 1813; married George P. Day.

278 V. †JOSEPH,[5] born in Windham April 21, 1817; married, (1) Phebe Jones; (2) Mary J. Cook.

53 JOSEPH[4] DOUGLAS. (Job,[3] Elijah,[2] John,[1]) son of Job and Mercy (Booker) Douglas, born in North Yarmouth, now Freeport, October 10, 1776: married —— 1800, Elizabeth, daughter of Stephen and Sarah Sawyer of Durham. He settled first on Litchfield Neck, then at Five Islands in Georgetown, where he remained a few years, then removed to Winnegance in the town of Phipsburg. He subsequently removed to Bath. His last place of residence was at Hallowell, where he died about the year 1843.

Their children:

279 IX. †JAMES,[5] born in Durham September 1, 1800; married Elmira Burgess.

280 II. JOB,[5] born in Litchfield June 21, 1802; married Rachel Blaisdell of Phipsburg. He was an exhorter and intended to enter the ministry, had his life been spared him. He died at Hallowell a few years after his marriage. One child.

281 ELIZABETH[6].

282 III. SARAH,[5] born in Litchfield November 25, 1804; unmarried; died 1824.

283 IV. †Theodates,⁵ born in Litchfield February 11, 1807; married her cousin Samuel Douglass.

284 V. †Joseph,⁵ born in Litchfield January 11, 1809; married his cousin Mercy Douglass.

285 VI. Mary,⁵ born in Litchfield June 18, 1810; died August 19, 1810.

286 VII. Mary 2d,⁵ born in Litchfield August 18, 1811; died 1833; unmarried.

287 VIII. †Hannah Elizabeth,⁵ born in Litchfield April 5, 1814; married Abraham Douglas (293).

288 IX. Peter,⁵ born in Litchfield April 18, 1816; unmarried; October, 1841, he shipped as cook on board the schooner Tonky of Bath, Capt. Thomas D. Wakefield, master, bound for New Haven. When off Cape Cod they encountered a severe storm which drove the vessel ashore on the Cape. The Capt. and Peter perished on the wreck and Peter was buried near where the schooner went ashore.

54 Dr. Samuel⁴ Douglass, (Job,³ Elijah,² John,¹) brother of the preceding and son of Job and Mercy (Booker) Douglas, born in North Yarmouth, now Freeport, August 8, 1779; married, (1) Sarah, daughter of Abraham and Elizabeth (Welch) Preble. He settled in Litchfield where he resided many years. He was taken sick of consumption and his recovery was doubtful. While lingering with this disease he discovered a remedy that entirely restored his health. Encouraged by the good results which his medicine had upon himself, he devoted most of his time in the study and practice of medicine. September 15, 1817, he married (2) Sarah Stevens of Lewiston. In the year 1818 he removed to No. 4 Plantation (now Mexico) where he bought a lot of wild land of the agent of the Dixie's heirs, for which he was to pay one hundred dollars, which failing to do, in 1834 he sold the improvements which he had made on the farm for a horse and chaise. With his team he travelled all about

the State doctoring, mostly with roots and herbs, with some success. He died in Mexico in 1866.

His children by his first wife, born in Litchfield:

289 I. †BETSEY,[5] born January 27, 1802; married Abraham Preble.

290 II. THOMAS,[5] born October 17, 1804; unmarried; lost at sea about 1831.

291 III. †SAMUEL,[5] born March 15, 1806; married Theodates Douglas. (284).

292 IV. †MERCY,[5] born January 4, 1809; married Joseph Douglas. (284).

293 V. †ABRAHAM,[5] born May 10, 1814; married Hannah E. Douglas. (287).

294 VI. †GARDINER,[5] born October 11, 1812; married Asenath S. Orr.

295 VII. JOHN,[5] born July 31, 1814; married Roanna Nickerson of Topsham. He settled in Topsham, then removed to Bangor and worked at his trade, blacksmithing. Has not been heard from for many years: one child.

296 SARAH B.,[6] born in Bangor; married and resides in Brunswick.

Children by second wife, all born in Mexico, except the eldest:

297 VIII. †JOANNA,[5] born December 30, 1817; married John E. Roff.

298 IX. †MARIAM,[5] born July 10, 1819; married Stephen Ward.

299 X. JULIA ANN,[5] born April, 1821; died May, 1822.

300 XI. ELISHA,[5] born June 8, 1822; married Elvira Chamberlin. He died while in the war of 1861.

301 One child, Samuel.

301½ XII. SOLOMAN,[5] was born December 13, 1823; unmarried; was a shoemaker. While at work for Mr. L. Day in Brunswick, he had for a shop mate a noted infidel, who talked so much of his unbelief into him that he was heard to remark that he had as soon die now as at any time. Sunday, September 20, 1846, while the family was at church, young Solomon went to the barn and there hung himself with a rope halter. His remains were taken to Bowdoinham and buried in the village grave-yard.

302   XIII. NANCY,[5] born September 13, 1825; married February, 1843, Stephen Beckwith of Vermont.

Their children:

303   I. JULIA ANN (Beckwith), born January 10, 1844; died aged 21.

304. II. SARAH E., born 1846; died same year.

305   III. ETTA (Beckwith) born 1848; is dead.

306   XIV. JULIA,[5] born April 21, 1827; married James Ward; resided in Poultney, Vermont; no children; she died in 1858.

307   XV. IRENE,[5] born April 22, 1831; died December 7, 1832.

308   XVI. WILLIAM[5] BOOKER, born April 7, 1833; married, 1852, Sarah Eldridge. He was a mason by trade and resided at Dorchester, Mass. He died at Dover, N. H., January 1, 1857. He left a will, which was proved by the Probate Court in Sagadahoc County, and a part of his property was willed to his mother, as he died childless.

309   XVII. SARAH,[5] born February 1, 1835 and died in 1845.

55   JAMES[5] DOUGLASS, (Job,[3] Elijah,[2] John,[1]) brother of the preceding and son of Job and Mercy (Booker) Douglas, born in North Yarmouth, now Freeport, July 1, 1780; married, December 19, 1799, Eliza M. Banks, daughter of Philip Banks, born in Lewiston.

He settled in Freeport, where he resided a few years and then removed to Litchfield Neck. In 1806 he removed back to his native town and settled on a farm, which probably was a part of his grandfather's, of three hundred acres, situated on Prout's Gore in Freeport. He was living there at the breaking out of the war of 1812 and enlisted in the service for one year; served his time out and re-enlisted for the remainder of the war. At the close of the war he moved into a house on the farm of Edward Estes, nearly opposite the gate leading to the house of Hugh Gatchell, where he resided one year. His son, Nehemiah O., was born in that house. He removed from there to the Gore, which was in Durham or Freeport, where he built a house and passed the remainder of his days. He died July 2, 1821 and was buried on Daniel Douglas' farm. In 1851 his son, John B., had his remains disinterred and buried in the Pine Grove Cemetery at Lisbon Falls. His wife died and was buried by the side of her husband.

Their children:

310 I. LUCY, born in Freeport, 1801; married Sylvanious Harrington; children, Rubama M., George Bragdon, Joseph; died August, 1820.

311 II. †JOHN BANKS,[5] born in Litchfield April 1, 1803; married Nancy B. Douglass. (113).

312 III. †JAMES S.,[5] born in Freeport March 24, 1807; married Azubah Godwin.

313 IV. †WILLIAM BOOKER,[5] born in Freeport April 7, 1809; married Mary Duran.

314 V. ELIZA, born in Freeport, 1811; died young.

315 VI. LOUISA, born in Freeport 1812; married, 1st, Samuel Starbird; 2d, Solomon McKinney; one child, William Henry (Starbird.)

316 VII. †NEHEMIAH OWEN,[5] born in Durham, September 3, 1814; married, 1st, Jane Hall; 2d, Mrs. Lydia E. (Cole) Willis.

317 VIII. †PHILIP BANKS,[5] born in Durham, May 20, 1816; married Mary Ann Knight.

318 IX. RHODA, born in Durham, 1819; died in Freeport, March, 1821.

58 ELIJAH DOUGLASS, (Job,[3] Elijah,[2] John,[1]) brother of the preceding, was born in North Yarmouth, now Freeport, February 12, 1786; married, July 24, 1808, Sally Davis of Litchfield. The marriage ceremony was performed by John Neal, Esq. He settled on a farm in Freeport, near his father's homestead, where he died about 1814. His widow married (2) David Gatchell of Litchfield.

Their children, born in Freeport:

319 I. ELIJAH,[5] born about 1809; unmarried. The summer he was twenty-five years old he hired out on a farm in the eastern part of the State. After he was done work for the farmer, and with his summer's wages in his pocket, he started for his home in Freeport, and was never seen or heard from afterwards and it is probable that he was murdered.

320 II. ABIGAIL,[5] born in 1811; married Isaac Sawyer; settled in Pittston.

321 One child, Elijah (Sawyer).

322 III. JANE,[5] born about 1813; married Reuben McClannel; settled in Gardiner.

323 One daughter, Lizzie (McClannel).

59. JOB[4] DOUGLASS, (Job,[3] Elijah,[2] John,[1]) son of Job and Mercy (Booker) Douglas, born in North Yarmouth, now Freeport, November 27, 1787; married Margaret Brown, a farmer and resided on Litchfield Neck. He was a devoted Christian and much respected by those who knew him. He died at his home in Gardiner, January 1, 1845. His widow died in Hallowell November, 1851.

Their children born in Litchfield, were:—

324 I. †CHARLES,[5] born in 1812; married Emeline Poor.

325 II. †ESTHER,[5] born in 1814; married Alexander Bubier.

326 III. †MARY ANN,[5] married William S. Gordon.

327 IV. AMASA,[5] born May 8, 1818; married, May 9, 1841, Huldah Sinclair. He is a farmer and lives in Manchester; no children.

328 V. JOHN,[5] born June 4, 1820; married, August, 1854, Octava Campbell; died in Hallowell; no children.

329 VI. †ALFRED,[5] born September 15, 1822; married Frances E. Nash.

330 VII. †SETH,[5] born April 14, 1825; married Mary J. Smith.

60. BENJAMIN[4] DOUGLASS, (Job,[3] Elijah,[2] John,[1]) brother of the preceding and son of Job and Mercy (Booker) Douglas, born in Freeport, December 16, 1789;

married, October, 5, 1815, Betsey, daughter of James and Hannah (Booker) Potter, born in Harpswell July 4, 1793. They were married by Sylvanus Waterman, Esq. He settled on a farm in Bowdoin that he bought of a Mr. Davis In 1818 he sold this farm and bought another, lying partly in Bowdoin and partly in Litchfield. He was a stone mason and did much of that work for his neighbors and townsmen. He was a devoted Christian, a good citizen and a man much respected. He died at his homestead July 13, 1871, and was buried in the grave-yard on Litchfield Plains. His wife died December 11, 1882, aged 89 years.

Their children born in Bowdoin were :—

331 I. †George,[5] twin, born August 7, 1816; married Rebecca Cook.

332 II. †Charles,[5] twin, born August 7, 1816; married Eunice Pratt.

333 III. Hannah[5] Elizabeth, born December 5, 1818; died November 6, 1819.

334 IV. †William,[5] born March 31, 1821; married Roxcilla Rodick.

335 V. Isaiah,[5] born August 13, 1823; married, September 1, 1853, Abbie, daughter of William and Rebecca Tarr, of Bowdoin. He is the only surviving child of the large family. He is a farmer and resides at the old homestead and supported his mother until her death. No children.

336 VI. †Benjamin Booker,[5] born December 10, 1825; married Rachel J. Bates.

337 VII. Sarah Jane,[5] born December 12, 1828; died Sept. 20, 1830.

338. VIII. Alonzo Simeon,[5] born February 14, 1833; unmarried; died at his father's December 12, 1863.

63. Israel[4] Douglass, (Job,[3] Elijah,[2] John,[1]) brother of the preceding and son of Job and Mercy (Booker) Douglass, born in Freeport, May 28, 1796; married

Patience Sylvester, of his native town. He was a farmer and resided in St. Albans, where he died.

Their children were:—

339 I. DULENCIN,⁵ born in Freeport; married ——Libby.
340 II. BARTON,⁵ born in Freeport.
341 III. BATHANA,⁵ born in St. Albans.
342 IV. SUSAN,⁵ born in St. Albans; died in Bangor.
343 V. ISRAEL,⁵ born in St. Albans.

No further records of this family were received.

66. HANNAH⁴ DOUGLASS, (Job,³ Elijah,² John,¹) sister of the preceding and daughter of Job and Mercy (Booker) Douglas, born in Freeport about 1800; married Mathew Campbell of Bowdoin, a son of her father's second wife. They settled on his father's homestead, which he afterwards sold and they removed to Litchfield, from thence to Anson, where she died.

Their children were:—

344 I. OCTAVA (Campbell) twin, born in Bowdoin; married John, son of Job Douglass, Jr.
345 II. LUCRETIA (Campbell) twin, born in Bowdoin.
346 III. ALFRED (Campbell) born ——
347 IV. WILLIAM (Campbell) born ——
348 V. JOHN (Campbell) born ——; married Mercy Forbus [356.]
349 VI. ALONZO (Campbell) born ——
350 VII. WARREN (Campbell) born; was drowned in Winthrop Pond.
351 VIII. REBECCA (Campbell) born ——

67. RUTH⁴ DOUGLASS, (Job,³ Elijah,² John,¹) daughter of Job and Mercy (Booker) Douglas, born in Freeport in 1802; married Joseph Forbus of Bowdoin; settled on his father's homestead, removing to Litchfield and to Manchester, where she died July, 1861.

Their children were:—

352   I.   MARY (Forbus) twin, born in Bowdoin; married George Young.

353   II.   MARTHA (Forbus) twin, born in Bowdoin; married Joseph Young.

354   III.   AXIE (Forbus) born in Bowdoin; married David Hall; resides in Monmouth.

355   IV.   MERCY (Forbus) born in Bowdoin; married John Campbell, [348]; resides at West Gardiner.

356   AMANDA (Forbus) born in Litchfield; married Henry Dustin; resides in Litchfield.

71. PATIENCE[4] DOUGLASS, (Israel,[3] Elijah,[2] John,[1]) daughter of Israel and Mary (Rodick) Douglas, born in Harpswell, April 3, 1781; married Capt. James Rodick; settled in Harpswell; removed to Freeport, where she died August, 1838.

Their children were:—

357   I.   ISRAEL (Rodick) born in Harpswell May 2, 1805; married, January 19, 1830, Lucinda Toothaker of Brunswick; farmer; resides in Freeport.

358   II.   DANIEL (Rodick) born in Harpswell October 16, 1815; married, September 16, 1849, Martha A. Firbush, mariner; resides in Freeport.

359   III.   JANE (Rodick) born April 5, 1817; married, November 15, 1835, Randall Brewer; resides in Freeport.

360   IV.   ELIZA J. (Rodick) born May 20, 1820; married, Dec. 15, 1836, Ard Brewer of Freeport; resides in Farmingdale.

361   V.   MARY (Rodick) born January 17, 1822; married, Oct. 20, 1846, Abner W. Royal, of Freeport; house joiner; resides at Richmond.

362   VI.   SOPHRONA (Rodick) born December 3, 1823; married, July 28, 1846, Andrew Gould of Freeport, where they reside. He is a mariner.

363   VII.   ROXILANA (Rodick) born August 15, 1825; married August 20, 1843, William Douglas, [334]

72. CAPT. DAVID[4] DOUGLASS, (Israel,[3] Elijah,[2] John,[1]) brother of the preceding and son of Israel and Mary

Rodick) Douglas, born in Harpswell January 22, 1783; married, October 3, 1803, Sally Merryman, born 1784.

Their children born in Harpswell:—

364 I. †CLARRISSA,⁵ born December 29, 1803; married Robert Merryman.

365 II. HARRISON,⁵ born August 15, 1805; died 1807.

366 III. †JANE,⁵ born June 15, 1809; married Nehemiah Curtis.

367 IV. MARY,⁵ born October 10, 1811; married John Steel; resided in Bowdoin; she is dead; one child, died young.

368 V. †DELIGHT,⁵ born June 30, 1813; married Samuel Longley.

77. GEORGE⁴ DOUGLASS (Israel,³ Elijah,² John,¹) son of Israel and Mary (Rodick) Douglas; was born in Harpswell May 15, 1787; married (1) Betsey Merryman. He was a farmer. Settled in his native town; removed to Litchfield where his (1) wife died. He married (2) Dec. 20, 1820, Mary Merryman, a sister of his first wife. He died January, 1821.

Children all by first wife, born in Litchfield; all dead.

369 I. WILLIAM,⁵ born October 27, 1812.

370 II. HANNAH,⁵ born October 15, 1814.

371 III. DAVID,⁵ born November 15, 1816.

372 IV. SARAH,⁵ born December 25, 1818.

78. ⋅ CAPT. SAMUEL⁴ DOUGLASS (Elijah,³ Elijah,² John¹) son of Elijah and Jenney (Grant) Douglas, was born in Harpswell June 16, 1788; married, November 19, 1813: Esther, daughter of William and Elizabeth Bartall of Freeport. He settled on his father's homestead, where he lived two years, and in 1815 removed on to the farm that he bought of David Tompson, (formerly the property of Col. John Reed) situated on Pleasant Point, on the bank of the Merrymeeting Bay, in Topsham. He followed the

sea for the greater part of the time until the year 1837. He was an active and industrious business man; was Treasurer and Collector of his town for several years. For many years previous to his death he was engaged in the fire insurance business. He was much respected by his many friends and neighbors. He died at his home in Topsham, July 29, 1868. His wife died July 28, 1874.

Their children were:—

373 I. OLIVER A.,[5] born in Harpswell July 12, 1815. He died at Topsham July 2, 1819.

374 II. PAULINE JANE,[5] born in Topsham April 11, 1818; resides on the homestead farm.

375 III. SAMUEL.[5] born in Topsham October 14, 1819; married, December 25, 1865, Isabella Rogers. He was a farmer and resided in his native town where he died June 10, 1888; one child.

376 MARY ISABELLA, born in Topsham October 26, 1866.

377 IV. WILLIAM B,[5] born in Topsham September 10, 1824; unmarried. Occupied the old homestead. He died at his home in Topsham July 10, 1881.

378 V. ESTHER ANN,[5] born in Topsham June 2, 1827; she married, June 19, 1886, Joseph Russel, of her native town, where they reside.

99. SUSANNA[4] DOUGLASS (Elijah,[3] Elijah,[2] John,[1]) daughter of Elijah and Jenney (Grant) Douglas; was born in Harpswell February 27, 1790; married, February 13, 1813, Simeon Wheeler of Harpswell. He was a farmer and settled in his native town. In 1828 he moved to Bucksport, where they resided a short time, and removed and settled in Orrington, where they passed the remainder of their days. Mrs. Wheeler died May 10, 1843; Mr. Wheeler died February 10, 1842.

Their children:—

379 I. LYDIA BUFFUM (Wheeler) born in Harpswell, October 1, 1814; married, February 22, 1834, Herman Smith, a farmer; resided in Orrington.

380 II. JOHN DOUGLAS (Wheeler) born in Harpswell October 26, 1816; married, November 25, 1841, Sarah Jones. House joiner; died in Bangor June 19, 1868.

381 III. DAVID PERRY (Wheeler) born in Harpswell June 8, 1819; died December 6, 1839.

382 IV. WILLIAM HENRY (Wheeler) born in Bucksport, Oct. 3, 1830; married, April 19, 1853, Eliza R. Pinhorn.

101. WILLIAM[4] DOUGLASS (Elijah,[3] Elijah,[2] John,[1]) brother of the preceding and son of Elijah and Jenny (Grant) Douglass; was born in Harpswell January 12, 1795; married, February 24, 1819, Mary Sennet of Harpswell, born there January 31, 1795. They settled in Harpswell. In 1825 he removed and settled on a farm in the town of Bucksport, where they have since resided. Mrs. Douglass died April 5, 1875. Mr. Douglass died at his home June 21, 1881.

Their children; two oldest born in Harpswell, the others born in Bucksport:—

383 I. JOHN,[5] born October 20, 1821; married, May 27, 1849, Mary R. Sennett. He was a master ship builder. He was a worthy member of Felicity Lodge, No. 19 of F. & A. M.; was its W. M. for the years 1874–5. He resided at Bucksport, where he died March 21, 1889.

384. One child. JAMES HOWARD, born in Bucksport October 17, 1850. He has been clerk for several years in a dry goods store, for G. L. Bradley. Was for a time in that business for himself. Married, February 1, 1882, Annie L. Smith. Now resides in Gardiner

385. One child, John Frederick Howard, born October 9, 1884.

386 II. †JULIA ANN,[5] born October 14, 1823; married Jotham R. Chipman.

387 III. †WILLIAM,[5] born April 12, 1825; married Thankful W. Hinks.

388 IV. ELIZA H.,[5] born December 25, 1827; married Jesse Atwood.

389 V. RICHARD O.,[5] born 1829. When three years of age he was left in the house alone for a few moments; when his mother returned she found him with his clothes on fire and so badly burned that he died in a short time.

390 VI. STEPHEN SENNETT,[5] born January 17, 1832; married Lucinda R. Everett. He was a farmer and resided at the old homestead and took care of his parents. He died May 8, 1877. She died March 3, 1888.

391 VII. DAVIS BENNETT,[5] born August 3, 1833; married June 10, 1865, Priscilla D. Atwood. He is a ship carpenter and resides in his native town. No children.

392 VIII. †MARY JANE,[5] born February 23, 1840; married October 18, 1858, William Williams.

102. JENNEY[4] DOUGLASS, (Elijah,[3] Elijah,[2] John,[1]) sister of the preceding, and daughter of Elijah and Jenney (Grant) Douglas, born in Harpswell, February 6, 1797; married Mathew Simpson, of Brunswick. They settled first in Harpswell, and subsequently removed to Bucksport. He followed the sea.

Their children:

393 I. LYDIA (Simpson[5]) born in Harpswell; married John Smith. They reside in Bucksport.

394 II. DANIEL (Simpson[5]) born in Bucksport; unmarried; resides in the West.

103. MARY[4] DOUGLASS, (Elijah,[3] Elijah,[2] John,[1]) sister of the preceding and daughter of Elijah and Jenney (Grant) Douglas, was born in Harpswell, June 13, 1799; married John Field, born October 18, 1800. He was a farmer and resided in Brunswick, where he died. Mrs. Douglass died there later.

Their children born in Brunswick:

395 I. ELMIRA J. (Field) born June 10, 1827; died of consumption February 17, 1857.

396 II. MARY ANN (Field) born January 2, 1829; married. William C. Chambers. Died April 21, 1854.

397 III. JULIETT (Field) born September 13, 1831; died April 16, 1850.

398 IV. ELIZA F. (Field) born July 19, 1833; married 1875 Daniel Drake.

399 V. ABIGAIL G. (Field) born July 5, 1835; died May 27, 1852.

400 VI. SUSAN M. (Field) born August 7, 1837; died August 27, 1858.

105. ELIZABETH[1] DOUGLASS, (Elijah,[3] Elijah,[2] John,[1]) sister of the preceding and daughter of Elijah and Jenney (Grant) Douglas, born in Harpswell September 29, 1804; married January 13. 1831, Henry French.

Their children:

401 I. WILLIAM (French) born February 9, 1833.
402 II. ELIZABETH A. (French) born January 5, 1835.
403 III. SAMUEL D. (French) born May 23, 1837.
404 IV. FANNIE M. (French) born January 28, 1842.
405 V. JEREMIAH (French) born April 15, 1844.
406 VI. CHARLES D. (French) born April 7, 1847.

106. ISAAC[4] DOUGLASS, (Elijah,[3] Elijah,[2] John,[1]) brother of the preceding, born in Harpswell, December 31, 1806; married (1) Mary Pinkham. He settled on Haskell's Island, where he resided five years. He then built him a house on a five acre lot situated on the lower part of Harpswell Neck. This land was his wife's portion left her by her father. His wife died May 16, 1867. October, 1869, he married (2) Mrs. Phebe (Quinum) Morse. He has followed fishing for a business ever since his boyhood days and has been very successful in his chosen pursuit.

Children by first wife born in Harpswell:

407 I. †JOHN WILLIAM,[5] born August 3, 1829; married Martha C. Randall.

408 II. †Daniel K.,[5] born December 16, 1830; married Deborah A. Randall.

409 III. Isaac Henry[5] born April 4, 1832; died May 13, 1852.

410 IV. George P.,[5] born March 24, 1834. Died in Harpswell.

411 V. Ambrose B.,[5] born April 29, 1839; died November 15, 1844.

412 VI. Albert,[5] born August 28, 1841; died September 6, 1843.

413 VII. Mary Ellen,[5] born October 28, 1843; died March 21, 1855.

414 VIII. Ambrose B.,[5] 2d, born October 2, 1846. He is insane and is in the Insane Hospital at Augusta.

415 IX. Oliver A.,[5] born October 8, 1848. Died in Harpswell.

110. Hugh[1] Douglass, (John,[3] Elijah,[2] John,[1]) son of John and Sarah (Booker) Douglass, born in Durham, August 19, 1800; married Julia Goddard, of Rumford. He was a blacksmith. Settled at Canton Village, where he resided until his death. He died of consumption March 21, 1836, and was buried in the graveyard at Canton Village.

Their children born in Canton:

416 I. William W.,[5] born —— died in infancy.

417 II. Sarah M.,[5] born —— died young.

114. Isaac[4] Douglass, (John,[3] Elijah,[2] John,[1]) brother of the preceding, born in Durham, February 7, 1811; married October 8, 1837, Abigail K., daughter of Edsell and Dorcas Webber, of Lisbon, born there May 12, 1817. They settled in Brunswick; removed to Harpswell 1847; subsequently removed onto his father's homestead farm in Durham, where he lived several years. He now resides at Lisbon Falls. He and his wife are much respected by a large circle of friends.

Their children:

418   I.   EDSELL AUGUSTUS,[5] born in Freeport, September 8, 1838.   Married January 10, 1878, Maria P. Bennett, of Durham.

419   II.   JOHN ANDREW,[5] born in Durham, December 10, 1844; died May 28, 1865, in Savannah, Ga.

420   III.   †ISAAC HUGH,[5] born in Harpswell, April 26, 1851; married April 26, 1879, Ella Martha Taylor, of Vassalboro. They reside at Lisbon Falls.

118.   WAITSTILL WEBBER[4] DOUGLASS, (John,[3] Elijah,[2] John,) son of John and Catherine (Briry) Booker Douglas, born in Durham, November 1, 1818. When seventeen years of age he was apprenticed to learn the house joiner's trade with his half brother, Daniel Booker, working at his trade summers and attending school during the winter term, until he was twenty-one years of age; at which time he went to Brunswick and worked at his trade five years. He married Jane, daughter of Isaiah and Deborah (Philbrook) Day, of Durham. He was in New Orleans several years, where he was engaged in taking contracts and superintending the erection of different kinds of buildings. He was employed one year as carpenter on board a ship which sailed on the Missisippi river. The vessel was wrecked on an island at the mouth of the river and he came near being drowned. When rescued he was brought to life only by using the utmost exertion. He settled in his native town, where he lived a few years, then removed to Brunswick Village. In the year 1864, he bought a farm of three hundred acres with good buildings thereon, of Capt. John Lombart, situated in the town of Wales, for which he paid the sum of six thousand and four hundred dollars. He resided on this farm until the summer of 1873, then removed temporarily to Walpole, Massachusetts, where he was engaged at his

trade. In the fall of 1875 he removed back on his farm. While engaged in business in the State of Massachusetts, he took cold, which caused a typhoid fever from which he died at his daughter's, in Walpole, Massachusetts, April 1, 1876. He was buried in Durham.

Their children are:

421 I. DEANNA,[5] born in Durham, January 17, 1842; married, March, 1872, Alden Moulton, of Green. They reside on her father's farm in Wales.

422 One child. Waitstill Douglass (Moulton) born March 17, 1873.

423 II. ORLANDO KELLOG,[5] born in Durham, August 30, 1846; married January 1, 1872, Cynthia R. Howe, of Waterville; settled in Walpole, Massachusetts.

424 III. GEORGE EMERY,[5] born in Brunswick April 28, 1850; married May 9, 1876, Ella B. Libby.

425 IV. JENNIE ELMER,[5] born in Brunswick, July 20, 1856; married, September, 1875, William McQuestion.

426 V. JOHN FRANKLIN,[5] born in Wales, April 23, 1858; died in Lewiston, March 2, 1880.

120. EPHRAIM[4] DOUGLASS, (John,[3] John,[2] John,[1]) son of John and Lydia (Southworth) Douglas, born in Middleboro, Massachusetts, November 22, 1778; married, 1801, Deborah Haskins. He volunteered in the War of 1812, and served under Gen. Brown; was in the Indian skirmish at Bridgwater, New York. He settled at Halfway Pond, Plymouth, Massachusetts; in 1804 he removed to Clydon, N. H. At length moved back to Plymouth, where he resided until his death, July 21, 1865. His wife died April 19, 1870. They were buried in the graveyard at Halfway Pond, in Plymouth, Massachusetts.

Their children:

427 I. MELENTHA,[5] born in Cryden, N. H., 1803, married Ira

Sanborne, of Grafton, N. H. Children, 1, Samuel; 2, Lois. Mrs. Sanborne is dead.

428   II. EPHRAIM,³ born in Cryden, March 17, 1808; unmarried; died on Staten Island about 1867.

429   III. DEBORAH,⁵ born in Grafton, N. H., February, 1810; married Robert Clark; settled in Middleborough, one child,

430   MARY CLARK.⁶

431   IV. JOSEPH,⁵ born in Grafton, February 25, 1812; married Rachel Nickerson. He was a mariner; settled in Plymouth, Massachusetts. where he died, June, 1865. His widow married (2) Ephriam Chabbock, one child.

432   JOSEPH,⁶ born 1858; died same year.

433   V. LYDIA,⁵ born in Grafton, April 30, 1817; married George W. Marsh.

434   VI. HANNAH,⁵ born in Grafton, November, 1819; married John Robinson, of Boston, where they settled.

435   VII. †ELIJAH,⁵ born in Plymouth, October 5, 1822; married Mehitable C. Douglass. [440]

436   VIII. †LUTHER,⁵ born in Plymouth, July 18, 1826; married (1) Lucy S. Gibbs, (2) Abbie J. (Dunham) Hamblin, (3) Mrs. Jane E. (Marsh) Allston.

122. JOHN DOUGLASS,⁴ (John,³ John,² John,¹) brother of the preceding, born in Middleborough, Plymouth County, Massachusetts, August 23, 1782; married (1) February 18, 1804, Mehitable, daughter of John and Mehitable Elliot. He resided in his native town until the age of five, at which time his father removed with his family to Plymouth, Massachusetts. He remained at home until 1802, then spent one year in the State of Maine. Soon after his marriage he settled in the town of Grantham, N. H., where he resided until 1821, then removed to the State of New York and lived on the farm known as the Holland purchase. In 1825 he removed and settled in Hartland, Vermont, where he lived on the same farm until his death. January 9, 1849, his wife

died, and July 1st of the same year, he married (2) Iantha Howard, daughter of Abiel and Kezia Howard, of Bridgewater, Massachusetts, where she was born February 25, 1799. Her parents removed to Grantham in 1805. Mr. Douglass died at his homestead January 5, 1873, aged 90 years.

Children by 1st wife all born in Grantham, N. H., except the youngest.

437 I. †Freelove E.,⁵ born February 13, 1808; married Nathan Mace.

438 II. †Sarah,⁵ born March 1st, 1813; married Calvin Raymond.

439 III. †John,⁵ born August 9, 1814; married Cynthia A. Douglass. [452.]

440 IV. †Mehitable C.,⁵ born December 22, 1817; married Elijah Douglass. [435.]

441 V. †Reuben,⁵ born April 9, 1820; married Catherine Thomas.

443 VI. †William,⁵ born in Hartland, Vt., January 23, 1827; married (1) Amanda Douglass, [458]; 2d, Hannah Stone.

123. Earl⁴ Douglas, (John,³ John,² John,¹) brother of the preceding, born in Middleborough, Mass., November 13, 1784; married Mary Reynolds, of Augusta, Me., born there, 1790. He was a farmer and settled first in Augusta. In 1813 he removed to Stafford, Genesee County, New York, and in the year 1819 removed to Gainsville, New York, where he and Jacob Reynolds (his wife's brother) had the homestead of his wife's father, willed to them in consideration of their supporting through life his wife's parents. In 1823 he sold his half of the farm to Rufus Jewett, and removed to Plymouth, Massachusetts. He committed suicide by hanging in 1851. His widow passed her last days at the residence of Nathan K. Douglass, in Plymouth, where she died 1852.

Their children:

443 I. †William,⁵ born in Augusta, August 14, 1820; married Mary Clark Vaughn.

444 II. Lewis,⁵ born in Plymouth, Massachusetts, March, 1824; unmarried; died May 9, 1847.

445 III. †Eliza,⁵ born in Augusta, March 1826; married Allen Raynolds.

124. Warren⁴ Douglass (John,³ John,² John,¹) brother of the preceding, born in Plymouth, Massachusetts, September 20, 1786; married June 5, 1808, Rhoda Thrasher, born June 10, 1792 His father, having a large family to support, at the early age of eight years, he was put out to live with a farmer, where he remained several years, and then went to sea, which business he followed most of the time until he was married. The day that he was married he and his wife united with the Presbyterian Church in Plymouth, Massachusetts. In 1815 he removed to the town of Lee, New York, where he lived a short time, and then bought a farm in Annsville, Oneida County, in the some State, where he built a log house, and lived in it two years; then he put up a framed house for himself; and in 1830 he built on the same farm a large, two-story, brick house, in which he resided until his death. In 1825 he and his wife withdrew from the Presbyterian Church, and united with the Freewill Baptist Church. They led a consistant and Christian life, and were much respected by those who knew them. He died June 8, 1842. His wife died June 17, 1843.

Their children were:—

446 I. Warren,⁵ born in Plymouth, Massachusetts, September 7, 1809; died September 11, 1809.

447 II. Luther,⁵ born in Plymouth, October 10, 1810.

448 III. †Betsey,⁵ born in Plymouth, September 13, 1812; married Caleb Evens.

449 IV. †Warren,⁵ born in Plymouth, July 9, 1814; married Sally Storms.

450 V. †Nancy Swift,⁵ born in Lee, N. Y., March 24, 1816; married Caleb Cushing.

451 VI. Lydia,⁵ born in Lee, June 12, 1818; died same day.

452 VII. †Cynthia Adaline,⁵ born in Annsvill, N. Y., May 28, 1819; married John Douglass. [489.]

453 VIII. †John Edward,⁵ born in Annsvill Oct. 4, 1821; married Mary Chapman.

454 IX. †Philanda,⁵ born in Annsvill July 8, 1823; two children.

455 X. Washington, born in Annsvill June 19, 1825; died June 28, 1825.

456 XI. Ira Gifforson,⁵ born in Lee, August 18, 1826; at the age of twenty-six he married Ruth Stockwell of Lancaster, Coos Co., N. H.; no children.

457 XII. Rhoda Harriet,⁵ born in Annsvill July 27, 1828; married Isaac Coffin.

458 XIII. †Amanda Maria,⁵ born in Annsvill April 25, 1830; married William Douglass. [442.]

125. Lucy⁴ Douglass, (John,³ John,² John,¹) sister of the preceding and daughter of John and Lydia (Southworth) Douglas; born in Plymouth, Mass., September 9, 1788; married, August, 1808, Joseph, son of Joseph and Rebecca (Harlow) Bates, born in Plymouth February 29, 1789. They settled and always resided in their native town. She died August 30, 1872 and her husband died 1816.

Their children, born in Plymouth, Mass. :

459 I. Benjamin (Bates), born November 2, 1809; married, March 9, 1831, Martha Pierce. They reside at Plymouth, Mass.

460 II. Lydia S. (Bates) born September 30, 1811; married John Sturtivant. She died May, 1866.

461 III. Lucy (Bates) born December 17, 1813; married, 1832, Lewis King of Plymouth. She died January 11, 1853.

462 IV. CYNTHIA (Bates) born September 17, 1815; married, 1835, George Phillips of Rochester, England.

463 V. JOSEPH (Bates) born October 7, 1816 or 17; married, 1839, Abigail Dunham of Carver, Mass.

126. GEORGE[4] DOUGLASS (John,[3] John,[2] John,[1]) brother of the preceding, was born in Plymouth, Mass., January 21, 1792; married, September, 1821, Eliza, daughter of Ellis and Abia Nightengale. He settled on the old homestead which was willed to him, in consideration of his taking care of his aged mother during the remainder of her life, which duty he cheerfully complied with. He was a man of steady habits and lived a consistant Christian life. He died January 14, 1858.

Their children, born in Plymouth, Mass.:

464 I. †ABIA,[5] born February 2, 1822; married, October 20, 1848, Branch Pierce.

465 II. GEORGE,[5] born September 1, 1823; unmarried; died April, 1859.

466 III. †ELIZA ANN,[5] born April 25, 1824; married Charles Henry Winship.

467 IV. JOHN,[5] born November 12, 1826; unmarried; residence unknown.

468 V. †MARTHA PIERCE,[5] born June 10, 1828; married, (1) Phineas Swift, (2) John P. Barrows.

469 VI. MARIA E.,[5] born July 26, 1834; married Abner Ellis.

470 VII. †ANDREW JACKSON, born December 13, 1835; married Priscilla H. Manter.

471 VIII. CYNTHIA P.,[5] born May, 1839; married, 1884, David Brown; resides in Plymouth, Mass.

472 IX. NOAH E.,[5] born April, 1841; died 1844.

127. JOSHUA[4] DOUGLASS, (John,[3] John,[2] John,[1]) brother of the preceding, was born at Half-way-Pond, Plymouth, Mass., January 25, 1794; married, October, 1813, Mary S. Pierce. He settled near the Agawam River in his native town. His beginning in life was small, for

those were truly hard times; labor was worth but little
and money was a rare article. Yet by hard work and
strict economy, aided by his noble wife, who was ever
ready to share with him in his toils and hardships, he
managed to acquire an ample competence. Though far
advanced in years he was hale and smart. He always
resided on the same farm that his father left him. All
his children are married and settled near the old homestead. He died at his home June 10, 1879, after a short
illness and was buried by the side of his wife in the family
graveyard.

Their children, born in Plymouth, Mass.:

473 I. †JESSE P.,⁵ born July 24, 1814; married Roxanna Manter.

474 II. †ELISHA,⁵ born August 12, 1816; married Susan P. King.

475 III. †WILLIAM MANTER,⁵ born March 15, 1819; married Sarepta Pierce.

476 IV. †MARY,⁵ born May 16, 1822; married Thomas Pierce.

477 V. †NATHAN King,⁵ born December 24, 1824; married, November 28, 1851, Angeline Thrasher.

478 VI. WARREN S.,⁵ born March 29, 1827; married Lydia W. Manter.

479 VII. †MARTIN VAN BUREN,⁵ born February 9, 1837; married Laura A. B. Swift.

480 VIII. †JOSHUA ALONZO,⁵ born December 4, 1840; married Lucy P. Raymond.

129. LYDIA⁴ DOUGLASS, (John,³ John,² John,¹) sister
of the preceding and daughter of John and Lydia (Southworth) Douglas, born in Plymouth, Mass., January 16,
1799; married, August 24, 1820, Prince Manter, son of
Belcher and Rebecca Manter, born in Plymouth, January
20, 1779. He was a widower at the time of their marriage and lived on a farm in Plymouth, where she went
to reside. She had eight children; three of them died

of canker rash within the brief space of six days. Her husband died November 7, 1854.

The compiler is much indebted to her for valuable assistance rendered in gathering the records and history of the descendants of her grandfather. She died at her daughter's, Mrs. Warren S. Douglass.

Their children, born in Plymouth, Mass.:

481 I. Capt. PRESTON (Manter) born May 21, 1821; married, (1) April 1, 1846, Ruth Pierce, (2) Sylvana E. Bates. He follows the sea; resides at Carver, Mass.

482 II. LYDIA (Manter) born February 25, 1823; died Oct. 15, 1833.

483 III. WILLIAM (Manter), born April 22, 1824; married, (1) January 1, 1846, Huldah Raymond; (2) Sarah Swift, May, 1854. He is a carpenter and resides in Plymouth, Mass.

484 IV. JOHN DOUGLASS (Manter), born November 6, 1827; married, November, 1850, Jennett Burgess. He was a cooper by trade and lived in Wareham, Mass. He enlisted August, 1862, in the Civil War in Company B., 3d Mass. Infantry, died in Newburn, North Carolina, Feb. 1863.

485 V. REBECCA (Manter), born Feb. 27, 1828; died October 10, 1833.

486 VI. THOMAS BELCHER (Manter), born March 9, 1830; married, October, 1849, Eliza Ann Finney. They reside at Ladoy, Indiana, where he works shoemaking.

487 VII. JAMES LUCAS (Manter), born March 5, 1832; died October 16, 1833.

488 VIII. LYDIA WARREN (Manter), born November 20, 1839; married Warren S. Douglas. [478.]

130. ELIJAH[1] DOUGLASS, (John,[3] John,[2] John,) brother of the preceding, born in Plymouth, Mass., May 24, 1801; married, March 24, 1835, Louisa, daughter of Ezra and Mary (Dudley) Freeman. At the age of eighteen he commenced going to sea, which business he followed for fifteen years. Being of an adventurous turn of mind, he went to the island of Jamaica, where he re-

mained some time prospecting. Becoming tired of a sailor's life he settled down in the town of Lewis, New York, where he married and lived several years on a farm. About the year 1838 he removed to Vermont. He enlisted in the Rebellion and was in the Mass. 12th Reg. of Infantry. He resides in his native town.

Their children:

489 I. †HARRIET GRAVES,[5] born in Lewis, N. Y., August 18, 1836; married, 1859, Ezra Freeman; farmer, resides at Read Oak, Iowa; one child, a daughter.

490 II. EZRA FREEMAN,[5] born in Lewis, N. Y., January 5, 1837; unmarried; lived some time in Missouri; has not been heard from for many years and is probably dead.

491 III. ELIZA ANN,[5] born in Hinsbury, Vt., May 31, 1840; married, 1856, Harry Stanton.

492 IV. RUTH A.,[5] born in Hinsburg, March 18, 1841; unmarried; resides in Elizabethtown, N. Y.

493 V. HENRY CLAY,[5] born in Hinsburg, February 16, 1845; died September 7, 1848.

156. ABSALOM[4] DOUGLASS, (Elisha,[3] John,[2] John,[1]) son of Elisha and Selah (Orkin) Douglas, born in Middleborough, Mass., November 27, 1795; married Realfy Caswell. He, with his father, removed to Troy, Maine. He was in the War of 1812. Soon after the close of the war he went south, probably to the State of New York, where he married. In 1827 he removed to Monroe, Me., where he lived three years; not being contented east he removed to the State of New York again and from there to Ohio and settled on a farm. He subsequently sold the farm and was removing to the State of Wisconsin and was taken sick and died on the way, September 2, 1862, in Spartar, Wisconsin.

Their children:

494 I. ELISHA,[5] born in New York, January 13, 1820; unmarried; died in Dickinson, Franklin County, New York, April, 1838.

495 II. †DAVID CASWELL,⁵ born in Shelba, New York, Nov. 15, 1821; married Maria Heath.

496 III. †JOHN BRALEY,⁵ born in N. Y., April 3, 1824; married Louisa Greenslit.

497 IV. JOSEPH BRALEY,⁵ born in New Hampshire, May 11, 1826; married, September 1, 1854, Lorana C. Kelley; one child.

498 RONNANZO M., born in Wisconsin August 23, 1855.

499 V. CHRISTOPHER RUSSELL,⁵ born in Monroe, Me., August 9, 1828; died August, 1851, in Geneva, Wisconsin.

500 VI. †LUCY ELIZABETH,⁵ born in Monroe July 17, 1830; married William Pathing.

501 VII. †EMILY,⁵ born in Bakerfield, Vt., July 26, 1832 ; married Andrew J. Patching.

502 VIII. †HIRAM,⁵ born in Dickinson, Franklin, New York, January 22, 1835; married Elizabeth Jordan. [522]

503 IX. †CHARLOTTE ADLEA,⁵ born in Dickinson, New York, October 10, 1837; married Rev. B. F. Kelley.

504 X. ABSALOM,⁵ born in Dickinson, New York, November 30, 1839; married June 14, 1862, Orra Johnson.

505 One child, John F., born September 5, 1863. Mr. D. died in Janesville, Minnesota, October 15, 1874.

506 XI. †SARAH ANN,⁵ born in Dickinson, New York, May 20, 1841; married Charles H. Jordan.

507 XII. †GEORGE WASHINGTON,⁵ born in Dickinson, New York, February 22, 1844; died August 2. 1848.

508 XIII. JAMES MADISON,⁵ born in Lawrence County, New York, March 4, 1846; died September, 1850.

158. CELIA DOUGLASS,⁴ (Elisha,³ John,² John,¹) sister of the preceding and daughter of Elisha and Selia (Orkin) Douglas, born in Middleborough, Massachusetts, January 13, 1799; married John Michols. They resided in several States at different times. Their last place of residence was in the State of Maine. No further record of them received.

Their children :

509 I. ELIAS (Michols) born

510 II. JOHN (Michols) born

511 III. REBECCA (Michols) born
512 IV. IRENE (Michols) born
513 V. OLIVER (Michols) born

HANNAH[4] DOUGLASS, (Elisha,[3] JOHN,[2] JOHN,[1]) daughter of Elisha and Hannah (Russell) Douglas, was born in Troy, Maine, December 20, 1882; married Isaac Jordan, reside in the west.

Their children:

514 I. MAHALA D., (Jordan) born in Monroe, Maine, October 21, 1820; married May 31, 1840, A. W. Twambly, reside in Monroe.

515 II. SALLEY (Jordan) born in Monroe, March 13, 1822; died August 14, 1825.

516 III. RUSSELL (Jordan) born in Monroe, February 19, 1824; died August 19, 1825.

517 IV. DANIEL R. (Jordan) born in Monroe, February 5, 1826; married July 9, 1845, Sarah Lewis; resides in Minnesota.

518 V. SARAH A. (Jordan) born in Monroe, December 23, 1827; married December 19, 1845, Simon Johnson, of M.; died in Minnesota, February 27, 1873.

519. VI. ISAAC (Jordan) born in Jackson, Maine, January 23, 1820; married May 16, 1854, Sarah Cunningham, of Monroe. He entered the army of the Civil War and never returned.

520. VII. HANNAH L., (Jordan) born February 9, 1832; married Winslow Webber, of Monroe; reside in Hamden.

521 VIII. JAMES (Jordan) born in Monroe, June 19, 1834; died October 27, 1854.

522 IX. ELIZABETH J(ordan) born in Exeter, November 23, 1836; married Hiram Douglas, [502] reside in Eagle Grove, Iowa.

523 X. THURSA M. (Jordan) born January 10, 1839; died February 24, 1861.

524 XI. PATIENCE P. (Jordan) born in Monroe, July 2, 1841; died August 5, 1865.

525 XII CHARLES H. (Jordan) born in Monroe, March 19, 1843, married Sarah A. Douglas, [506] resides in Okaman, Waseca County, Minnesota.

160. RUTH[4] DOUGLASS, (Elisha,[3] John,[2] John,[1]) sister of the preceding and daughter of Elisha and Hannah (Russell) Douglas, was born in Monroe, Maine, October 21, 1804; married February 18, 1827, Collins Pattee. He is a farmer and settled in Monroe, Maine, where he has always resided.

Their children born in Monroe, Maine.

526 I. HENRY (Pattee) born May 10, 1827; married Hannah Perry.
527 II. HIRAM (Pattee) born December 19, 1828; married Caroline Page; resides in Monroe.
528 III. COLLINS (Pattee) born October 26, 1830; died Feb 8, 1833.
529 IV. CAROLINE (Pattee) born December 14, 1832; died February 29, 1835.
530 V. EMILY (Pattee) born October 26, 1834; married Levi Bowen; resides in Monroe.
531 VI. COLLINS (Pattee) born December 11, 1836; married Lizzie Page; resides in Jackson.
532 VII. CAROLINE (Pattee) born February 26, 1838; married Thomas Batchelder.
533 VIII. MARY ANN (Pattee) born December 26, 1840; married Allen M. Batchelder; resides in Monroe.
534 IX. EZRA (Pattee) born January 4, 1843; married Estell Jeferde; resides in Monroe.
535 X. RUTH (Pattee) born September 27, 1845; married Pierce Randall; died December, 1865.

161. LUCY[4] DOUGLASS, (Elisha,[3] John,[2] John,[1]) sister of the preceding, born in Troy, Maine, June 3, 1808; married S. Emery Jewell, born in Monroe September 27, 1817. He is a farmer and resides in his native town.

Their children, born in Monroe:

536 I. LOUISA (Jewell) born December 15, 1839.
537 II. THOMAS E. (Jewell) born October 22, 1841; died in the War of the Rebellion April 19, 1863.

538 III. SARAH ANN (Jewell) born February 11, 1844.
539 IV. JULIA (Jewell) born March 13, 1848; died June 17, 1855.
540 V. REUBEN R. (Jewell) born April 14, 1851.

162. ELIZABETH[4] DOUGLASS, (Elisha,[3] John,[2] John,[1]) sister of the preceding, born in Monroe, May 21, 1810; married, May 30, 1830, Nathaniel Horton, born 1812; farmer, resides in Monroe.

Their children, born in Monroe:
541 I. LEMUEL C. (HORTON) born August 10, 1831.
542 II. CHRISTOPHER (Horton) born January 26, 1833.
543 III. ELIZA (Horton) born June 10, 1837.
544 IV. PHEBE (Horton) born October 26, 1839.
545 V. RUBE (Horton) born April 1, 1842.
546 VI. NATHANIEL (Horton) born June 16, 1844.
547 VII. BARBERY (Horton) born August 27, 1846.
548 VIII. HIRAM (Horton) born August 23, 1848.

163. HIRAM RUSSELL[4] DOUGLASS, (Elisha,[3] John,[2] John,[1]) brother of the preceding and son of Elisha and Hannah (Russell) Douglass, born in Monroe, April 27, 1812; married Fanny Twambly, daughter of Samuel Twambly, born March 23, 1815; settled in Lowell, Me., where he has since resided on a farm.

Their children, born in Lowell:
549 I. †HANNAH,[5] twin, born February 2, 1839; married Alonzo Curtis.
550 II. †BETSEY,[5] twin, born February 2, 1839; married Philemon Curtis.
551 III. †CALBERT DANIEL,[5] born August 3, 1843; married Lavinia McHenry.
552 IV. †MARY EMILY,[5] born July 4, 1847; married Orince Albert Hall.
553 V. HIRAM WILLIAM,[5] born October 3, 1849; died October 12, 1849.
554 VI. SARAH AMANDA,[5] born March 19, 1854; married Limon S. Sargent.
555 VII. HIRAM,[5] born November 3, 1856; died, 1858.

167. BARNABAS NYE[4] DOUGLASS, (George,[3] George,[2] John,[1]) son of George and Patience (Savery) Douglass, born in Middleborough (now Lakeville) Plymouth County Mass., November 11, 1791 ; married, September 19, 1828, Phebe N. Swift, born April 19, 1809. Soon after he was twenty-one years of age he commenced going to sea and for a number of years was employed on board a coasting vessel, running between New York and Savannah. He was mate on several voyages and was out in the great gale of 1815. In the year 1820, he, in company with a man by the name of Enoch Jenney, entered into the commission business in Savannah. They were in company several years, then he bought out his partner's interest and continued the business himself.

In 1840, he came back to his farm in Rochester, Mass., (which was his father's old homestead) where he remained until his death. He was a successful school teacher, having taught district schools in Middleborough, Wareham, Pierceville and in several districts in his own town. He was in feeble health several years. In attempting to rise from his chair when the family was out of the room, he fell, injuring himself so he lingered but three weeks and died March 9, 1873. His wife was a noble woman, a devoted wife, a loving mother and it can truly be said "her children rise up and call her blessed." She departed this life October 11, 1886.

Their children, born in Rochester, Mass.:

556   I.   †CAROLINE S.,[5] born August 8, 1830; married Emery Cushman.

557   II.   PHEBE NYE,[5] born May 18, 1832; married, May 28, 1853, Charles H., son of Charles B. and Abagail Damon, born Aug. 13, 1826. He is a painter by trade and resides in Wareham, Mass.

558   One child, Charles[6] B. (Damon) born November 24, 1857; died April 19, 1865.

559　III.　GEORGE,[5] born May 20, 1834; died July 24, 1836.

560　IV.　†MOSES SWIFT,[5] twin, born March 21, 1837; married, (1) Emiline F. Smith; (2) Celia H. Stevens.

561　V.　†GEORGE,[5] twin, born March 21, 1837; married Jane M. Mendall; she died in California February 25, 1873. He married (2) Alice Estelle Lindsay.

562　VI.　†PAMELIA C.,[5] born July 1, 1840; married Capt. Jas. R. Allen.

563　VII.　†JAMES OSCAR,[5] born August 12, 1843; married, February 12, 1870, Emma Elwood, daughter of Charles M. and Emily M. Blackman, of Rochester; (2) Sarah S. Clarke.

564　VIII.　†EDWIN DELAS,[5] born April 17, 1845; married, (1) Louisa C. Davis; (2) Rebecca Rhodes Ruedi.

565　IX.　†MARY A.,[5] born December 26, 1847; married Samuel Wing.

566　X.　LIZZIE FREEMAN,[5] born March 24, 1850; married, July 2, 1872, Capt. Geo. Fox, son of Sanford and Margaret Brightman, of Dartmouth, Mass., born there March 5, 1844. For several years he sailed as first mate of a whaling vessel. He subsequently became captain of the ship California, and has made many very successful whaling voyages to the South Pacific Ocean.

567　XI.　†CHARLES ALBERT,[5] born October 26, 1853.

168.　BETSEY[4] DOUGLASS, (George,[3] George,[2] John,[1]) sister of the preceding and daughter of George and Patience (Savery) Douglass, born in Middleborough, Mass., July 14, 1793; married, December 25, 1814, Nathaniel King, born January 1, 1791. He was a carpenter and resided in Rochester, where he died February 21, 1868. Mrs. King died February 7, 1868.

Their children, born in Rochester, were:

568　I.　CATHERINE C. (King) born August 27, 1815; married Joseph R. H. Braley.

569　II.　CHARLES F. (King) born March 4, 1818; married Julia Holmes.

570　III.　BETSEY M. (King) born February 9, 1820; married John Ryder, farmer; resides in Rochester.

571 IV. PATIENCE M. (King) born April 28, 1822; married Enos Hawes.

572 V. MARY ANN (King) born January 21, 1824; married Capt. Samuel T. Braley of Rochester; died at sea.

573 VI. NATHANIEL (King) born April 9, 1829; married Sabra Jane French.

574 VII. LUCY B. (King) born, —— married Simpson Jenney of Fairhaven, Mass., where they reside.

170. NOAH[4] DOUGLASS, (Noah,[3] George,[2] John,[1]) son of Noah and Mary (Sekel) Douglas, born in Middleborough, Mass. Married Rachel Maxfield of New Bedford, where they settled and resided a few years, then removed near Lake Erie. It is thought by his friends that he is dead.

Their children were:

575 I. NOAH,[5] born in New Bedford.
576 II. CAROLINE,[5] born.
577 III. HARRIET,[5] born in Ohio; married Giles Gilbert of Conneaut.
578 IV. JOSEPH,[5] born.

171. GEORGE[4] DOUGLASS (Noah,[3] George,[2] John,[1]) brother of the preceding and son of Noah and Mary (Seekel) Douglas, born in Middleborough, Mass., February 20, 1796; married (1) 1826, Hannah O. Churchill; (2) November 30, 1841, Alsada Pierce. He was a shoemaker and resided in Bridgwater, Mass., where he died April 30, 1859. His widow married David Ashley. Their place of residence is in Lakeville, Mass.

Their children, born in Bridgwater, Mass.:

579 I. SILAS S.,[5] born September 1, 1826; died June 15, 1827.
580 II. ELIZA ANN,[5] born November 28, 1828; married Edwin Howard.
581 III. HANNAH,[5] born October 25, 1832; died November 25, 1836.

582 IV. GEORGE ALLEN,[5] born July 12, 1845; married Villa L. Barrows.

173. MARY[4] DOUGLASS,(Noah,[3] George,[2] John,[1]) sister of the preceding and daughter of Noah and Mary (Seekel) Douglas, born in Middleborough, Mass.; married Job White, son of Abijah and Esther White of Dartmouth, Mass.

Their children;

583 I. AMY GIFFORD (White) born in Westport, Mass.; married William Albee Weeden of New Bedford; house joiner.

584 II. ALMIRA FRANCES (White) born in Dartmouth; married (1) Daniel Hartwell Reed, sea captain, who died in California; (2) Charles F. Brownell of New Bedford.

585 III. ALFRED (White) born in Dartmouth, Mass.; married Huldah Washburn of New Bedford. He died in California.

586 IV. MARY (White) born in New Bedford; unmarried; was a spinster in New Bedford where she died.

FIFTH GENERATION.

180. ABNER[5] DOUGLASS, (Cornelius,[4] Daniel,[3] Elijah,[2] John,[1]) son of Cornelius and Hannah (Whittemore) Douglass, was born in Freeport, August 28, 1802. At the age of ten years, he, with his father, removed to the town of Litchfield where he spent the remainder of his minority. He married (1) 1823, Abagail Allen. They resided in Litchfield, where she died. In 1850 he married (2) Elmira (Morrell) Douglass, his brother Levi's widow. In 1871 he and his two youngest children went to live with the Shakers at New Gloucester, where they still reside.

Children by first wife:

587 I. SARAH,[6] born in Litchfield, May 6, 1825; married Moses Turino.

588 II. WILLIAM,[6] born in Litchfield, January 22, 1827; married; went South where he died.

589 III. GEORGE,[6] born in Litchfield, March 14, 1829; married Mary Hilman.

Children by second wife:

590 IV. SIRENA,[6] born in Lewiston, March 1, 1853.

591 V. MARY,[6] born in Lewiston, June 27, 1855.

185. LEMUEL[5] DOUGLASS, (Cornelius,[4] Daniel,[3] Elijah[2] John,[1]) brother of the preceding; was born in Litchfield, April 12, 1812; married, December 11, 1834, Olive B. Berry of Rome. They have lived in several towns in the State of Maine and were residing in the city of Hallowell

at the time of their deaths. Mr. Douglass died October 25, 1876; his wife died May 12, 1885.

Their children, born in Hallowell, except two oldest:

592   I.   HANNAH M.,⁶ born in Rome, September 16, 1835; died August 8, 1852.

593   II.   CAROLINE LONGFELLOW,⁶ born in Rome March 7, 1837; died in Hallowell January 7, 1866.

594   III.   DANIEL BERRY,⁶ born August 9, 1839; died September 16, 1849.

595   IV.   BETSEY JANE,⁶ born December 17, 1843; died December 12, 1847.

596   V.   MARY E. W.,⁶ born September 12, 1845; died in Hallowell April 2, 1885.

597   VI.   CHARLES R.,⁶ born October 18, 1849; married, September 30, 1885, Louisa M. Lord; resides in Hallowell.

598   VII.   HANNAH JANE,⁶ born June 12, 1856; married Alden Sawyer. She died at Augusta May 24, 1878.

187.   MARY ANN⁵ DOUGLASS, (Cornelius,⁴ Daniel,³ Elijah,² John,¹) sister of the preceding and daughter of Cornelius and Hannah (Whittemore) Douglass, born in Litchfield February 25, 1821; married, February 25, 1848, Moses H. Arthor, son of Moses and Mary (Robinson) Arthor. They reside at Hallowell.

Their children, all born in Hallowell, except the two oldest:

599   I.   WILLIAM H. (Arthor) born in West Gardiner. August 16, 1849.

600   II.   MARY F. (Arthor) born in West Gardiner, December 8, 1850; married, August 11, 1872, William A. Morrill; reside in Hallowell.

601   III.   MARTHA H. (Arthor) born March 14, 1853; married, 1876, Benjamin Heath of Pittston; died May, 1877.

602.   IV.   GEORGE F. (Arthor) born September 5, 1855; died April 30, 1884.

603   V.   Augusta J. (Arthor) born January 30, 1860; died there February 28, 1861.

604   VI.   Sarah H. (Arthor) born March 10, 1862.

605   VII.   Charles E. (Arthor) born January 9, 1863.

218.   Dianna Dillingham Douglass (Daniel,[4] Daniel[3] Elijah,[2] John,[1]) daughter of Daniel and Sarah (Bailey) Douglass, was born in Freeport, May 28, 1822; married, September 20, 1850, Ezra Jordan Hoyt. He followed the sea for thirty years, then worked farming until his death, which occurred at his home in Freeport August 29, 1874. She died September 18, 1882.

Their children, born in Freeport:

606   I.   Charles Thomas (Hoyt) born September 10, 1851.

607   II.   Elbridge Jordan (Hoyt) born July 4, 1853; died May 4, 1879.

608   III.   Sarah Abbie (Hoyt) born February 22, 1857; married, April 23, 1881, Howard W. Chase.

609   IV.   George Amos (Hoyt) born April 4, 1861.

222.   Hannah[5] Douglas, (John,[4] Cornelius,[3] Elijah,[2] John,[1]) daughter of John and Judith (Collins) Douglas, born in Brunswick about 1794; married 1815, Abner Eaton, of Brunswick. They settled on his father's homestead, which was near Rocky Hill, in said town. They removed to the town of Lisbon, where they died.

Their children, all born in Brunswick:

610   I.   Paulene (Eaton) born September, 1817; married Israel W. Parker; died—she resides in Lewiston.

611   II.   Anstress (Eaton) born August 23, 1819; married Jeremiah Nowell; farmer; resides in Webster.

612   III.   Caroline (Eaton) born December, 1821; died in Fairfield, March 20, 1839.

613   IV.   Hannah (Eaton) born April 4, 1823; died in Lisbon, 1845.

614 V. DORCAS N. (Eaton) born April 9, 1826; married (1) November, 1847, William Hodges: (2) December 8, 1865, Rufus Nowell, house joiner; resides at Lewiston.

615 VI. ISRAEL (Eaton) born January, 1828; died same year.

616 VII. ALICE ISABELLA (Eaton) born January 24, 1831; married, 1855, Joseph A. Johnson; resides in South China.

617 VIII. MARIA S. (Eaton) born March 7, 1833; married, 1856, John Magonn of Litchfield; reside in California.

618 IX. ABNER HARRISON (Eaton) born May 28, 1836; married Elizabeth Carvill of Iowa, where they reside.

223. ABIJAH[5] DOUGLAS, (John,[4] Cornelius,[3] Elijah,[2] John,[1]) brother of the preceding and son of John and Judith (Collins) Douglas, born in Brunswick, June 25, 1796; married March 14, 1816, Phebe, daughter of James Estes, of Durham, born there November 11, 1798. Soon after they were married they went to Hebron where they resided two or three years; then removed to his father's homestead, where they lived one year, and in 1820 they removed to the town of Dixfield, where he bought a farm of a Mr. Goodall and paid for it in keeping sheep. In 1828 he and his family removed to Passadumkeage and lived three years where he worked at joinering. He and his wife experienced religion and joined the Free Will Baptist church in Dixfield. He was deacon of the church several years previous to his death. He built a saw-mill at the foot of Savery Hill, where he sawed lumber. He died very suddenly, having been absent from home on business, and was returning and fell dead in the road when within about a mile of his home, in Dixfield, February 17, 1838.

Their children:

619 I. †ELVIRA JANE,[6] born in Hebron, December 31, 1816; married Dudley Bean.

620 II. †WILLIAM ESTES,⁶ born in Brunswick, May 15, 1819; married Mahala Tucker.

621 III. †RHODA COOMBS,⁶ born in Dixfield, July 10, 1821; married (1) John Tarr, (2) Jonathan W. Forsaith. He is dead.

224. PHEBE⁵ DOUGLAS, (John,⁴ Cornelius,³ Elijah,² John¹) sister of the preceding; born in Brunswick, July 7, 1798; married June 10, 1827, Thomas Jones, of China, where they resided and where she died February 4, 1874.

Their children :

622 I. GEORGE (Jones) born in China, July 1, 1823; died in China, May 6, 1868.

623 II. AMOS (Jones) born in China, July 3, 1830; married October 27, 1852.

624 III. ANN (Jones) born in China, April 8, 1838; married May 12, 1853.

625 IV. JOHN (Jones) born in China, May 6, 1834; married July 26, 1853.

626 V. LEMUEL (Jones) born in Brooks, April 1, 1836; married June 7, 1862.

627 VI. ISRAEL (Jones) born in Brooks, March 3, 1841; married May 16, 1862. He was killed in the war of 1861, June 25, 1863.

225. RHODA⁵ DOUGLAS, (John,⁴ Cornelius,³ Elijah,² John,¹) sister of the preceding and daughter of John and Judith (Collins) Douglas; born in Brunswick, April 30, 1800; married December 6, 1821, Thomas Coombs, by Rev. Allen H. Cobb. They settled on her father's homestead, where they resided a number of years and then removed and settled on a farm near Storer's Corner, in Brunswick, where she died January 14, 1856. He died at South Durham, October 14, 1870.

Their children born in Brunswick :

628 I. JUDITH DOUGLAS (Coombs) born October 21, 1822; married John Williams, May 2, 1853, resides in Webster.

629 II. MARY OLIVE (Coombs) born October 9, 1824; died November 9, 1839.

630 III. HULDAH MARIA (Coombs) born July 5, 1827; died December 4, 1848.

631 IV. ELLEN (Coombs) born October 11, 1829; married January 1, 1860, William Jones. She died in the town of Wales.

632. V. BENJAMIN FRANKLIN (Coombs) born December 1, 1831; married July 22, 1855, Eliza A. Coombs; died in Temple, June 24, 1858.

633 VI. RHODA ELIZABETH (Coombs) born February 7, 1834; died March 19, 1853.

634 VII. HARRIET ABBIE (Coombs) born January 5, 1836; died April 14, 1854.

635 VIII. ELVIRA JANE (Coombs) born December 12, 1837; married September 16, 1861, Charles T. Coombs; reside in Kansas.

636 IX. MARY OLIVE (Coombs) born October 30, 1839; married January 1, 1859, James Henry Cox, farmer; resides on his father's homestead, formerly owned by David Douglas.

637 X. MARTHA WASHINGTON (Coombs) born March 12, 1842; married John L. Williams, farmer; resides in Webster.

638 XI. THOMAS ALBERT (Coombs) born October 11, 1844; married January 1, 1870, Fannie E. Lunt, daughter of Asa and Marcia Lunt, of Brunswick. He is a carriage maker and resides in Amesbury, Mass.

226. PAUL[5] DOUGLASS, (Edward,[4] Cornelius,[3] Elijah,[2] John,[1]) son of Edward and Esther (Collins) Douglas, born in Brunswick, March 18, 1798; married (1) September 21, 1823, Nancy, daughter of George Warren, of Durham, where she was born March 18, 1798. She died in Durham, March 5, 1837. October 11, 1837, he married for his second wife Emily Sawyer, of Durham. He lived one year on his father's homestead, after his first marriage, and in 1824 he sold his interest in the homestead to the heirs and bought a farm of Barnabas Strout, at the South West Bend, in Durham, where he resided until August 1, 1839, at which time he removed and settled on a farm in

the town of Dover, where he lived the remainder of his life. He was for many years engaged in the lumbering business both in Durham and in Dover; in 1830 he was elected Lieutenant of a Cavelry Company and in 1835 was elected its captain. He was elected one of the Selectmen of Dover for the years of 1844 and '45. He also held the commission of Justice of the Peace for many years and was an active business man. Religiously he was Universalist. In 1848 he was made a Free and Accepted Mason in Mosaic Lodge at Foxcroft. He departed this life at his home February 3, 1873. His wife died March 24, 1882.

Children by first wife, born in Durham:

639   I.   ALMIRA,[6] born May 5, 1825; died November 26, 1838.

640   II.   †IVORY WARREN,[6] born March 13, 1828; married Margaret Payne.

641   III.   †HARRIET JANE,[6] born October 3, 1831; married John C. Gerry.

Children by second wife:

642   IV.   †AMANDA,[6] born in Durham, May 14, 1839; married Frederick Hutchinson.

643   V.   ELVIRA NANCY,[6] born in Dover, December 8, 1841.

644.   VI.   GERALDINE,[6] born in Dover, July 15, 1844; married John Robinson; reside at La Cross, Wisconsin. No children.

645   VII.   GEORGE AUGUSTINE,[6] born in Dover, February 10, 1851; died in Dover, February 1, 1860.

227.   HULDAH[5] DOUGLASS (Edward,[4] Cornelius,[3] Elijah,[2] John,[1]) sister of the preceding, born in Brunswick February 4, 1800; married, November 24, 1831, Capt. Francis, son of Francis and Betsey (Dyer) Harmon, of Durham, born January 18, 1806. He was an industrious and enterprising farmer and carriage manufacturer. He had his father's homestead left him, in consideration of

his maintaining his parents during their lives. In 1830 he was elected captain of a military company, which office he held several years. On account of failing health he sold out his property in Durham and removed to Auburn. He and his wife were worthy members of the Congregational church and much esteemed by those who knew them. Mrs. Harmon died in Auburn February 4, 1869. Capt. Harmon died January 4, 1870. They were buried in Auburn.

Their children, born in Durham :

646 I. SARAH ELIZABETH (Harmon) born November 25, 1833; died in Durham, of consumption, May 29, 1853.

647 II. ESTHER COLLINS, (Harmon) born August 25, 1835; died at her father's home in Durham, May 24, 1855.

648 III. EDWARD FRANKLIN (Harmon) born June 5, 1837; married July 16, 1872, Jennie S. Rich, of Auburn. He resided in San Francisco, Cal., where he died October 4, 1875.

649 IV. GEORGE HARRISON, (Harmon) born May 18, 1839; married March 14, 1871, Orphia L. Vickery, of Auburn, where he resides.

650 V. FRANCES ELLEN (Harmon) born April 21, 1841; married February 11, 1869, Thomas Wheaton, of Brooklin, California. They reside at Oakland, California.

651 VI. HENRIETTA LOUISA (Harmon) born February 26, 1843, married September 24, 1867, Frank E. Young, of Auburn. She died at Auburn, June 10, 1876.

229. JOHN[5] DOUGLASS (Edward,[4] Cornelius,[3] Elijah,[2] John,[1]) brother of the preceding, born in Brunswick July 30, 1804; married, September 27, 1832, Charity P., daughter of John and Hannah (Morse) Coombs of Brunswick, born June 11, 1811. From 1825 to 1828 he followed the sea ; was on board the Brig Turner of Bath, Capt. William Thomas. May 15, 1828, they were shipwrecked on their passage from Bath to Cuba. Three out

of nine of the crew were washed overboard and lost. The surviving ones remained on the wreck seven days, having nothing but tallow candles to eat and no water to drink during that time. They were taken off the wreck by a passing schooner and safely landed in Boston. They resided at his father's homestead from the date of their marriage until March 5, 1835, when he removed to a farm in Dover that he bought of Nathan Toby for $350. There was only a porch on the farm and he built a house and made other improvements. He and his wife were members of the Free Will Baptist Church, in Dover. He died at his home, March 10, 1877. Mrs. Douglass died in Dover, June 10, 1886.

Their children, born in Dover, except Charles F., who was born in Brunswick:

652   I. †CHARLES FRANCIS,[6] born November 4, 1833; married Martha A. Cromwell.

653   II. †JOHN EDWARD,[6] born March 6, 1835; married Irene A. Phinney.

654   III. †RUFUS COLLINS,[6] born March 8, 1837; married Sarah E. Woodman.

655   IV. †ELBRIDGE THOMPSON,[6] born October 14, 1839; married Louisa Bigelow.

656   V. †ELLEN AUGUSTA,[6] born October 24, 1841; married Calvin Bigelow. She is dead.

657   VI. LORY HARMON,[6] born November 26, 1844; married February 17, 1874, Emma M. Morrill. They have no children.

658   VII. WINFIELD SCOTT,[6] twin, born May 21, 1847, and died October 8, 1847.

659   VIII. WHITEFIELD THOMPSON,[6] twin, born May 21, 1847; died October 15, 1847.

230. PHEBE[5] DOUGLASS (Edward,[4] Cornelius,[3] Elijah,[2] John,[1]) sister of the preceding and daughter of Edward and Esther (Collins) Douglas, born in Brunswick August

31, 1897; married, January 17, 1837. William P. Larrabee, son of William Larrabee of Brunswick He settled on his father's homestead where he resided a few years, then removed and settled on a farm in Dover, where he has since lived. Mrs. Larrabee died in Dover, June 24, 1851 and was buried in the grave-yard near Dover Village.

Their children, born in Dover, except the oldest ;

660　I.　GEORGE HENRY (Larrabee) born in Brunswick, November 16, 1837; died in Dover, October 21, 1850.

661　II.　LORY HARMON (Larrabee) born July 28, 1839; married April 10, 1864, Harriet M. Cole. Died October 5, 1865.

662　III.　WILLIAM FRANKLIN (Larrabee) born August 13, 1841; married May 1, 1866, Martha M. Beathall, of Fortress Monroe, Va., where they reside.

663　IV.　CHARLOTTE MARIA (Larrabee) born September 4, 1844; married June 7, 1871, John H. Warren; resided at Fortress Monroe, Va. Her husband is dead.

231.　RUFUS[5] DOUGLASS, (Edward,[4] Cornelius,[3] Elijah[2] John,[1]) brother of the preceding, born in Brunswick, August 21, 1809; married 1843, Marilla S. Nickerson, of Dover. When nineteen years of age he went to the South West Bend, Durham, where he served an apprenticeship of two years with his brother-in-law, Lory Harmon, at the carriage trade. In 1831 he went fishing one summer. He then worked at his trade in Bath, Durham, and other places, until 1829, at which date he visited Cincinnati, St. Louis and Chicago. In 1841, he and Lory Harmon formed a co-partnership and manufactured carriages at Dover Village, until the death of Mr. Harmon. In 1849 he went to California, where he remained six years. The remainder of his life was spent in the west at his trade and other kind of business.

In 1886 he was severely injured by the kick of a horse,

rendering him unconscious most of the time until his death, which occurred at Wenona, Ill., May 15, 1886. During his brief illness he was very kindly cared for by his Masonic friends, who took charge of his funeral.

One child:

664 I. HENRY CLAY, born in Dover, May 13, 1844. He was shot through the heart at the battle of Missionary Ridge, Chattanooga, Tenn., in the great rebellion, November, 1864.

232. EDWARD FRANKLIN^5 DOUGLASS (Edward,^{4} Cornelius,^{3} Elijah,^{2} John,^{1}) brother of the preceding and youngest son of Edward and Esther (Collins) Douglas, born in Brunswick August 19, 1812; married, February 7, 1840, Alvira Clark Starbird, born in Brunswick August 3, 1812. Being the youngest of the family it fell to his lot to have the care of his widowed mother, which duty he performed with pleasure. He sold the old homestead in Brunswick to James Merryman and March 19, 1841, he moved with his family to Dover, where he bought a farm, on which he has since resided. In 1843 he made great repairs on his house. He has always been a farmer. He has for many years had the agency for his county for Wood's Mowing Machine and other agricultural implements. He is also president of a cheese factory in his town, doing a large business.

665 NELLIE E.,^{6} born in Dover April 30, 1841; married, April 6, 1885, Frank A. Briggs of Dover, where they reside. He is a farmer.

248. JOSEPH DOUGLASS^5 (Joshua,^{4} Cornelius,^{3} Elijah,^{2} John,^{1}) eldest son of Joshua and Jane (Adams) Douglas, born in Brunswick March 24, 1819: married in Durham, January 16, 1842, Ann Gould Beal, daughter of Stephen and Charlotte (Gould) Beal, born in Lisbon September 9,

1819. In the spring of 1840, during a series of religious meetings held at the Booker Schoolhouse in Durham, he was converted to God and the following July he was baptized in the Androscoggin River and the same day joined the Free Will Baptist church of Durham. In the year 1841 he bought a farm of one hundred acres in Dover, where they settled soon after their marriage. There was no house on the farm and he built one in which he resided until 1847, when he exchanged his farm for a house in Orono, where he resided until his death. Previous to his marriage he served a few months apprenticeship at house joinering with a man in China, which trade he followed through life and by strict attention to it he became a good workman. He had charge of building the Methodist meetinghouses at Waterville and Skowhegan. March 1, 1862 he was chosen deacon of the Free Will Baptist church in Veazie and worthily filled the office to the close of life. He was a devoted christian, an active laborer in the cause of temperance, a kind husband and an affectionate father. His last sickness was congestion of the brain, which deprived him of his senses for the greater part of his illness. He died at his home in Orono, December 27, 1870. The funeral ceremonies were performed by the Methodist and Congregationalist clergymen of the village and Mechanic Lodge of Free and Accepted Masons of which he was a member. His body was interred in the cemetery two miles above the village in Orono.

Their children:

666 I. Lucy Jane,[6] born in Dover, February 19, 1843. She has taught district schools several terms; but owing to ill health was obliged to give up teaching. She resides with her mother at Orono.

667 II. Stephen Beal,[6] born in Dover April 14, 1845; died in Orono January 29, 1860.

668 III. Lewette Ann,⁶ born in Orono April 17, 1848; died there October 18, 1855.

669 IV. Clara Ella,⁶ born in Orono December 29, 1856; died there December 29, 1862.

670 V. †Lizzie Ann,⁶ born in Orono February 13, 1859 ; married J. Frank Beal of Durham, November 18, 1883.

249. Eliza Jane⁵ Douglas. (Joshua,⁴ Cornelius,³ Elijah,² John,¹) sister of the preceding and only daughter of Joshua and Jane (Adams) Douglas, born in Brunswick February 23, 1822 ; married at the Friends' meeting-house in Durham, June 20, 1848, James, son of Robert and Abagail (Winslow) Goddard, born in Brunswick November 12, 1822. They settled on a farm in Brunswick that he had of his father, where they resided a few years, then sold and bought a farm one mile from the Friends' meeting-house in the town of Durham. The house was, many years ago, Johnson's tavern, where many a traveler has slaked his thirst with the ardent. Here they passed the remainder of their days, with the exception of one or two years, when they lived with his father. They were both members of the Society of Friends. He died of typhoid fever January 4, 1866. She survived him a few years, taking a deep interest in the welfare of her children, the most of whom she lived to see grow up. She was ready at all times and at every one's call to go and watch by the sick and administer to their wants and comfort. Her sickness, like that of her husband's, was typhoid fever and was of short duration. She departed this life at her home on Sunday August 30, 1874. The funeral was held at the Friend's meeting-house. They were buried in the small grave-yard near his father's.

Their children :

671 I. Eli Franklin (Goddard), born in Brunswick July 13, 1849; died in Brunswick September 20, 1855.

672   II.   JAMES EMERY (Goddard), born in Brunswick December 9, 1851; married, December 27, 1874, Clara, daughter of Edward and Sarah T. Jones of Brunswick. He resides on his father's homestead in Durham.

673   III.   LUFKIN DOUGLAS (Goddard), twin, born in Durham September 19, 1854; married Annie A. Snow, January 13, 1879.

674   IV.   ABBY JANE (Goddard), twin, born in Durham September 19, 1854; married Oscar E. Douglass.

675   V.   CHARLES WINSLOW (Goddard) born in Brunswick, August 8, 1856; married September 7, 1876, Susie M. Swett, born in Bath, May 6, 1858. They reside at Amesbury, Mass. He is employed in a saw mill.

676   VI.   FRANKLIN ELI (Goddard) born in Durham, January 23, 1859; married September 24, 1881, Ida A. French, born in Seabrook, N. H., March 9, 1857. They reside at Amesbury, Mass. He works farming and jobbing.

677   VII.   ROBERT HENRY (Goddard) born in Durham, April 26, 1861; married March 18, 1882, Hattie A. Chambers.

250. GEORGE DOUGLAS, (Joshua,[4] Cornelius,[3] Elijah[2] John,[1]) brother of the preceding and son of Joshua and Jane (Adams) Douglas, born in Durham, May 11, 1824; married at the Friends' meeting-house in North Berwick, March 31, 1847, Elizabeth Ann, daughter of Josiah and Elizabeth Prescott, born in North Berwick July 30, 1823. His uprightness of character and strict integrity which he possessed strongly manifested itself even in his school-boy days. If innocent of a fault, of which he had been accused by his schoolmates, he did not rest until the matter was corrected. In the fall of 1843, becoming tired of farm work, he engaged with Lemuel Jones to learn the shoemaker's trade, serving one year. In 1849 he bought a small parcel of land of his father, in Durham, for which he paid one hundred dollars, on which he built a set of buildings. He continued to work at his trade and did some farming. In 1854 he sold his house and lot to G.

C. Crosman, and removed to North Berwick where he, in company with his brother-in-law, James Hussey, bought a shoe store; but finding the village too small to afford sufficient trade for the shop, they sold out the business. In 1856 he returned and settled once more in his native town where he built another set of buildings, more substantial and costly than the first. He and his wife were worthy members of the society of Friends and exemplified a christian life in their daily walks. In 1863 they were appointed elders in the society of Friends which society held them in high esteem and frequently chose them to important positions of trust. He was elected one of the selectmen of the town of Durham for the years 1868-9, which office he filled to the general satisfaction of his townsmen. In 1869, he removed to Portland, where he was employed in A. F. Cox's Boot and Shoe manufactory. In 1878 he removed back on his farm in Durham, where he spent his last days. He was elected collector of taxes for the years 1886-7 and 8. In 1886 he was taken sick of a disease which terminated his life April 20, 1888. No one had died in his town more lamented. The funeral was attended by a large gathering of his friends, some coming long distances to pay their last tribute ot respect to the deceased. The services were conducted by the society of Friends, assisted by ministers of other denominations. He was buried in the grave-yard near his late home.

Their children, born in Durham;

678 1. †STEPHEN ALBERT,[6] born September 16, 1848; married Olivia W. Powers.

679 II. †LEWIS MORRILL,[6] born February 1, 1852; married October 21, 1875, Emma A. Varney.

680 III. †ELLEN MARIA,[6] born February 25, 1854; married November 30, 1876, Clementine R. Hanson.

681 IV. GEORGIANNA,[6] born June 27, 1860; died in Durham, August 25, 1861, and was buried in the Friends' graveyard at South Durham.

682 V. †JOHN HENRY,[6] born April 19, 1862; married, 1881, Jennie L. Brown.

251. JOHN[5] DOUGLAS, (Joshua,[4] Cornelius,[3] Elijah,[2] John,[1]) brother of the preceding and son of Joshua and Jane (Adams) Douglas, born in Durham February 26, 1828; married, September 30, 1852, Ann Maria Hamblin, daughter of Allen and Lydia (Winslow) Hamblin of Windham, born there October 12, 1828. When about fourteen years of age his father employed a man to shave shingles. One day, while the men folks were at dinner, John undertook to learn the trade, which attempt came near costing him his life. Substituting his knee for the clamp, in holding the shingle, he cut a slight gash in it with the shave and taking cold in the wound a high fever set in and had it not been for the skill of the physician he would have lost his leg and probably his life. He received a fair education at the town school. Before he became of age he learned the shoemaker's trade of his brother George. He settled in his native town where he resided till 1853, when he removed to Little Falls, in Windham, and bought a cottage where he lived several years. After the death of his wife's father, he bought out the heirs and removed to the old homestead in Windham where he was engaged in farming during the summer and worked at his trade winters till his death. He and his wife were acceptable members of the society of Friends. In 1878 he was made an elder in that society which position he honored by a constant attendance on the means of grace and a devoted christian life. As he had a slender constitution the greater part of his life was attended by

ill health, having been a great sufferer for many years. In 1880 he was obliged to give up all labor. He was perfectly resigned and surrendered all earthly hopes and laid all upon God's altar. A few months previous to his death he awoke his wife in the night, praising God for the great joy which filled his soul. From that until his death, he enjoyed perfect peace, resting fully in the promises of his Savior. Death had no terrors for him. It was comforting to converse with him. A few moments before he died, raising his hand, he exclaimed, "Hallelujah, I see my home, O, how beautiful!" Then grasping the hand of his companion more firmly he uttered his last words, "Farewell Annie, farewell Annie," and the last cord that bound his spirit to earth was severed and his soul passed to its eternal rest on high, July 11, 1881. The funeral services were conducted by Charles Varney and were attended by a large circle of friends. He was buried in the Friends' grave-yard near their church in Windham. His widow and son now reside at Lisbon Falls.

One child:

683   I.   WALTER HENRY,[6] born in Windham, June 28, 1868.

252.   CHARLES[5] DOUGLASS, (Joshua,[4] Cornelius,[3] Elijah,[2] John,[1]) brother of the preceding, born in Durham, August 24, 1830; married, by Rev. Charles W. Morse, September 28, 1858, Annie Elizabeth Fisher, daughter of James Drummond and Lucinda (Pattie) Fisher of Bowdoinham, where she was born November 26, 1835. He received a good education at the town and high schools held in his native town. He also attended Litchfield Academy several terms. At the close of his studies he taught one term of winter school in Topsham and gave entire satisfaction both to parents and pupils. In the

CHARLES DOUGLASS.

autumn of 1854 he went to Bath and was engaged as a clerk in a shoe-store for Loran Fisher, one or more years. He also worked clerking for John Ballou and for Josiah Burleigh of Lewiston. The last two stores were for the sale of ready-made clothing. In 1855, under the labors of Rev. Howard B. Abbott, he experienced religion, was baptized and joined the Beacon Street Methodist Episcopal Church at Bath. In the church he was an active and zealous laborer and was soon called to serve as class-leader and steward. He was President of the Bath Young Men's Christian Association two years. In this capacity he was very active in establishing and sustaining prayer meetings and Sabbath schools in the neighboring towns. In 1857, he, in company with John L. Spofford, bought out John Ballou's clothing store in Bath. This co-partnership proved unfavorable and he sold out to his partner and opened a store next north of the old stand, where he remainded until Spofford closed out, then he returnded to his former place of business where he remained until 1866, when he sold out and was engaged as clerk in a wholesale clothing house in Boston several months.

He was in trade three years in Lewiston and was President of the Lewiston Young Men's Christian Association for nearly the entire period of time he spent in that city. During the War of the Rebellion he was very deeply interested in the work of the Christian Commission, going from town to town lecturing and collecting money and all articles of comfort for the soldiers which he forwarded to them. He spent several weeks with the wounded and dying soldiers, caring for their many wants and conversing with them in regard to the interests of their souls. In 1869 he removed to Toledo, Ohio, where he was in the ready-made clothing business. In 1877 he sold out his interest in the clothing business and the following year was elected Superintendent of Toledo House of Refuge, where he served until the spring of 1880, when he was elected Superintendent of the Boys' Industrial School of Ohio, where he remained till 1884, when, on account of change in the administration, he retired from the office and labored in the interest of the Society for the Prevention of Cruelty to Animals. In 1887 he was again elected Superintendent of the Boys' Industrial School. 1889 he resigned this position.

Their children, born in Boston:

684   I.   LUELLA CLARK,[6] born November 13, 1860; died at Toledo, Ohio, June 1, 1879.

685   II.   ANNIE JULIA,[6] born January 21, 1863; married December 31, 1887, Lewis I. Martin. They reside in Toledo, O.

685½.   One child, Douglass (Martin.)

686   III.   HENRY HOWARD,[6] born May 10, 1866.

253.   JOSHUA LUFKIN[5] DOUGLAS, (Joshua,[4] Cornelius,[3] Elijah,[2] John,[1]) brother of the preceding, born in Durham April 17, 1833; married in Lewiston by Rev. George Knox, November 25, 1856, Helen Lauraman Harvey, daughter of Daniel and Mehitable (Gott) Harvey of Dixfield, born in Leeds September 28, 1838. His education was obtained at the district school and at the age of fourteen, while attending to his studies, he spent his mornings and evenings in learning the shoemaker's trade of his brother John. In early manhood he took naturally to the art of writing and fitted himself for teaching penmanship which business he followed during the evening season for several years. In 1856 he bought twenty-two acres of land of his father (a portion of his homestead farm) for which he paid three hundred and fifty dollars. On this

lot he built a set of buildings where he resided, working at his trade, shoemaking, and farming until 1863, when he removed to Bath and was engaged as clerk for his brother Charles three years. January 1, 1866, he bought out his brother's stock of clothing and trade, which business he still continues to follow. In 1862, under the labors of his cousin, John Henry Douglas [260] he professed saving grace in Christ. He soon afterwards removed to Bath where he found a warm home among the Methodists and he and his wife were baptized and united with the Beacon Street Methodist Episcopal Church. In 1864 he was appointed class-leader, which position he continues to fill. He is also steward and has served as trustee of the church for several years.

Their children:

687 I. ELLA JANE,[6] born in Durham, February 27, 1860.

688 II. ROSA HARVEY,[6] born in Durham, November 9, 1862.

689 III. ALICE MAY,[6] born in Bath, June 28, 1865.

690 IV. IDA LAURA,[6] born in Bath, February 20, 1868; died in Bath, of canker rash, November 17, 1873.

691 V. CARRIE EMMA,[6] born in Bath, April 19, 1871; died in Bath of canker rash, November 8, 1873. They were both buried in Oak Grove cemetery in Bath.

> They have crossed the shining river,
> They have joined the angel band,
> And we know the Saviour called them,
> To that bright and happy land.

692 VI. MILTON HERBERT,[6] born in Bath, March 30, 1874.

254. WILLIAM HENRY[5] DOUGLAS,) Joshua,[4] Cornelius,[3] Elijah,[2] John,[1]) brother of the preceding and son of Joshua and Lucy (Beal) Douglas, born in Durham October 13, 1847; married in the town of Gray by the Rev. Charles Bean, May 15, 1869, Ella Herbert Rolfe, daughter of John and Melvina (Strout) Rolfe of Raymond, where

she was born March 21, 1847. He had his father's homestead given him in consideration of caring for his parents during their lifetime, where they resided several years. After the death of his wife, which occurred July 7, 1886. his daughter kept his house. January 12, 1889, he was married to Mrs. Eliza B. (Tibbetts) Clason, who owns a farm in Lisbon on which they, with his mother, now reside. He is a house joiner and contractor. His daughter occupies the homestead in Durham.

One child by first marriage:

693 I. MABEL MELVINA,[6] born in Durham February 16, 1870; married, May 11, 1889, Osburn J. Hoffman, son of Jacob and Elizabeth Hoffman, born in Canada June 13, 1865. He is a weaver in the Worumbo Mill at Lisbon Falls.

260. JOHN HENRY[5] DOUGLAS, (David,[4] Cornelius,[3] Elijah,[2] John,[1]) son of David and Chloe (Davis) Douglas, born in Fairfield November 27, 1832; married, April 23, 1856, Miriam Carter. daughter of Jesse and Malinda Carter, born August 31, 1831. She is a great grand-daughter of John Carter of North Carolina, who, in the early settlement of Ohio, removed to that State. He had the advantage of some education, such as was afforded in the district schools, the academy at Hartland and St. Albans, and three years at Friends' Boarding School, Providence, R. I. He was early converted and chose to remain in the Friends' church where he had a birthright. He felt himself called of God to devote his life to the ministry and entered heartily into the work which from the first was blessed by the conversion of souls, so that the path of the evangelist seemed clearly marked out before him. His first labors were in connection with elder ministers until 1858 he was officially ordained a minister of the gospel by the church. He has traveled and labored in the gos-

pel in most parts of the United States and Canada, also in England, Scotland and Ireland and in many parts of the continent of Europe, the result of which has been souls for the Master and many churches built up. He also spent much time in obtaining money and founding Wilmington College, Ohio, and for ten years was President of the Board of Managers. He spent two years as pastor of the Friends' church at Glen Falls, New York, to which souls were added every month. He labored as an evangelist in Ohio and Iowa until sickness compelled him for a short time to stop and seek a climate more adapted to his health. He finally removed with his family to Des Moines, Iowa, where they now reside. At the first yearly meeting of Friends, after his removal, he was appointed General Superintendent of pastoral and evangelistic work in its territory which includes Wisconsin, Iowa, Minnesota, Dakota Territory, Nebraska, Washington Territory, Oregon, California and Texas, which office he holds at the present time as chairman of the church extension board of the church in the Northwest. His wife has been a true help meet all the way through.

Their children are:

694 I. †CHLOE A., born at Bloomington, Ohio, February, 1857; married September 4, 1877, J. Frank Taylor.

695 II. JESSIE C., born at St. Albans, Maine, April 21, 1859; died at Glen Falls, N. Y., April 4, 1881.

696 III. MELLIE, born at Bloomington, Ohio, January 31, 1861.

697 IV. JOHN HENRY, JR., born at Bloomington, July 8, 1863; graduated at Oak Wood Seminary, N. Y., and Wilmington College, O., also spent some time in the University in Berlin and Geneva.

698 V. ROBERT, born at Oldtown, Ohio, March 11, 1866; lived only a short time.

699 VI. CHRISTINE, born at New Vienna, Ohio, January 2, 1869.

700 VII. MARY L., born at Wilmington, Ohio, April 14, 1872; died December 3, 1882.

261. ROBERT WALTER[5] DOUGLAS, (David,[4] Cornelius,[3] Elijah,[2] John,[1]) son of David and Chloe (Davis) Douglas, was born in the town of Fairfield, Maine, November 11, 1834; married, June 8, 1856, Margaret Ann Gifford. His parents moved to Palmyra when he was about six years old and in a few years from there to St. Albans. He lived at home on a farm at this place until he was twenty years of age, except the time spent away from home attending school. He attended district school in Palmyra, the High School at St. Albans Village, the Academy at Hartland Village and was two years at the Friends' Boarding School at Providence, R. I. When about twenty years of age he came to Ohio and engaged in teaching. He afterwards returned to Maine where he married, after which he again returned to Ohio and continued teaching and then, in company with his father, carried on a country store at Bloomington, in same State. About 1862 he moved to New Vienna, Ohio, where he resided several years; carried on a boot and shoe store and worked at the bench. It was at this place, in 1864, he was recorded a minister in the society of Friends by Clear Creek Monthly Meeting. Since then he has been actively engaged in preaching the gospel. For some years he traveled quite extensively in the northern States, made frequent visits to New York and New England, as well as laboring extensively in the western States. For some time he was city missionary in Cincinnati in connection with the Children's Home, which was then located on Park Street. In 1868 he moved to Wilmington, the

county seat of Clinton Co., where he was engaged in pastoral work, in connection with the meeting at that place. His labors were greatly blessed to the little church at that place, which grew from less than seventy-five to six hundred, the largest meeting of friends in Ohio. While living in Wilmington he was appointed the General Lecturing Agent of the Peace Association of Friends in America and in that capacity he visited all the Yearly Meetings in the United States, and also delivered lectures in important towns and cities throughout the western, eastern and southern States at a time when it required a great deal of moral courage to advocate the unpopular cause of Peace and Arbitration. In 1873 he went on a religious visit to Great Britain, Ireland and the Continent of Europe. He was absent from home about a year and a half and was warmly received by the Friends where he went. In 1873 and 4 he visited the principal cities in Europe. After his return he was engaged for a year as pastor of Friends' church at Kokomo, Indiana. In 1877 he was liberated by Indiana Yearly Meeting to go on a religious visit to Australia and was the first American Friend who ever went out to visit the Friends in that far off land, with a message of love from the churches in the United States. He also visited on this trip, the Sandwich Islands, New Zealand and Tasmania. Returning from thence he visited California, Oregon and Washington Territory. He resided at Wilmington about fourteen years. In 1886 he again visited the principal towns and cities in England, Ireland and Wales, being absent from home about eight months. For the past eight years, except the time just referred to, he has been engaged as the General Superintendent of the Evangelistic, Pastoral and Church extension work in Indiana Yearly Meeting of Friends. In

1882 he organized the West Milton Bank and since that time has been the President. His son, D. F. Douglas, is cashier and general manager, which relieves him from the details of business life so he can devote his entire time to religious work. In politics he is a republican, but never an active participant, yet always firm in his convictions. In business he is careful and conservative.

Their children :

701 I. †DAVID FRANKLIN,⁶ born in Bloomington, Ohio, June 15, 1857; married Emma R. Thornburg.

702 II. GEORGE GIFFORD,⁶ born in Wilmington, Ohio, July 29, 1859; died in Wilmington, January 13, 1870.

703 III. ANNIE BELLE,⁶ born in New Vienna, September 27, 1864.

704 IV. CHARLES BAILEY,⁶ born in Wilmington, May 10, 1872.

263. JOHN NICHOLS⁵ DOUGLAS, (Cornelius,⁴ Cornelius,³ Elijah,² John,¹) only son of Cornelius and Phebe (Nichols) Douglas, born in his grandfather's house in Durham November 15, 1820; married, September 3, 1846, Sarah Jones, daughter of Silas and Sophia Jones, of Albion, where she was born December 10, 1829. He settled on a farm that he bought in the town of Palmyra, where he resided three years. In the year 1849 he removed to Sligo, Clinton County, Ohio, and was employed as journeyman shoemaker for the first two years, then went into the boot and shoe manufactory for himself. In 1854 he removed to Bloomington, in the same county and State, where he has since resided and continued in the shoe business and worked farming a portion of the time. In the winter of 1875 he and his wife paid a visit to their friends and relatives in their native State, after being absent twenty-five years.

Their children :

705 I. MARIA,[6] born in Palmyra, November 24, 1847; married April 6, 1865, Iven H. Jackson.

706 CORA,[7] (Jackson) born in Ohio, 1871.

706½. GILBERT EUGENE,[7] (Jackson) born March 22, 1878.

707 II. LYDIA ELLEN,[6] born in Bloomington, Ohio, June 26, 1854; died there January 2, 1857.

708 III. PHEBE ANNA,[6] born in Bloomington, Ohio, October 17, 1857; died at her father's house, February 2, 1872.

709 IV. †MARY NARCISSA,[6] born in Bloomington, Ohio, August 30, 1860; married Charles L. Aldrige.

264. LYDIA[5] DOUGLAS, (Cornelius,[4] Cornelius,[3] Elijah,[2] John,[1]) sister of the preceding, born in Winslow February 26, 1824; married, May 22, 1845, Nathan C. Bailey, son of Ebenezer and Tabitha (Clough) Bailey, born in Litchfield July 2, 1817. He bought his father-in law's homestead in Winslow, where they now reside. They are both members of the society of Friends.

Their children, born in Winslow :

710 I. EBEN C. (Bailey) born March 17, 1850; married February 20, 1874, Mary H. Greenwood. He is a farmer and resides in China.

711 II. PHEBE ANNA, (Bailey) born December 13, 1852; married October 19, 1887, John A. Partridge, of Whitefield.

712 III. LYDIA JANE, (Bailey) born June 8, 1855, married Albert Estes. He is a farmer and shoemaker; resides in Freeport.

713 IV. JOHN HERBERT (Bailey) born November 30, 1857; married Annie May Lewis.

265. MARY DOUGLAS,[5] (Cornelius,[4] Cornelius,[3] Elijah,[2] John,[1]) sister of the preceding, and youngest daughter of Cornelius and Phebe (Nichols) Douglas, born in Winslow, August 26, 1835; married (1) September 29, 1856, Dr. E. F. Everest, of Ohio; (2) March 21, 1872, Philip P. Harner, house builder and contractor. She re-

sides at Morrow, Ohio. Mr. Harner died May 20, 1879.

Children by first husband, born in Ohio ;

714 I. CORELIUS JESSE, (Everest) born June 10, 1857; married Laura Johnson, 1879.

715 II. CHARLS FINELEY, (Everest) born February 26, 1859; died April 21, 1861.

716 III.' MARTHA PHEBE, (Everest) born May 12, 1862; died January 27, 1863.

374. MERCY[5] DOUGLAS, (David,[4] Joseph,[3] Elijah,[2] John,[1]) Eldest daughter of David and Weighty (Hawks) Douglas, born in Durham, January 26, 1808; married October 14, 1827, Mark Knight, son of Daniel and Sarah Knight, of Windham. He was a farmer and resided in his native town. They were both members of the society of Friends. She died in Windham, August 13, 1855. He married (2) Mary, a sister of his first wife.

Their children by first marriage, born in Windham:

717 I. MARY JANE (Knight) born August 2, 1828; died in Windham, May 5, 1845.

718 II. EUNICE DOUGLAS (Knight) born June 15, 1830; married March 25, 1859, John B. Cartland, a minister in the society of Friends. He is also a farmer. They reside at Parsonfield.

719 III. DAVID DOUGLAS (Knight) born October 14, 1831; died in Windham, April 20, 1845.

720 IV. DAVID DOUGLAS (Knight) born July 6, 1846; died in Windham, September, 1848.

276. NATHAN[5] DOUGLAS, (David,[4] Joseph,[3] Elijah,[2] John,[1]) brother of the preceding and son of David and Weighty (Hawks) Douglas, born in Durham, January 18, 1812; married October 2, 1834, Lucy Day, daughter of Isaiah and Deborah (Philbrook) Day, born January 6, 1812. His parents were members of the society of

Friends, and by their discipline their children inherit the privilege of being members of the Society.

At the age of twelve, he gave his heart to Christ, and for a time enjoyed much of the presence and love of the Saviour; but yielding to the temptations incident to the youth, he fell back into the world again, and mingled freely in the company of the gay and thoughtless. His mother's kind words and tears made deep and lasting impressions upon his young heart. It was during these years of waywardness, that the Lord appeared to him and called him to go forth and preach the gospel; but he told the Lord that he was but a child and could not speak in public. Thus he refused to obey the heavenly call, though his duty was plainly made known to him; and many of his fields of labor were clearly shown him and he frequently saw himself in distant parts of the country preaching the blessed gospel of the Lord Jesus Christ. He adds: "No pen can portray what I passed through until I yielded and obeyed the divine call, which was when I was twenty-two years of age."

He at once commenced the work of the ministry at the Friends' meetinghouse in his native town. His sermons were not studied, but delivered with zeal and great power, as the Holy Spirit gave utterance. Older ministers and elders in the society watched over him, fearing he was too forward, but he looked not to man, but to Him who had called him to the great work, and he pursued his labors with such earnestness and fervency that a general awakening was felt among the young people throughout the community and many were converted to God. Since that day he has been the principal minister among Friends at Durham. His labors have been very satisfactory and great good has resulted from them, which will tell in eternity. His sermons are plain and direct to the point, never shrinking to declare the whole council of God. He has many times been called upon by the good Master to visit different States and hold meetings among Friends and others, which duty he cheerfully performed and that too without any earthly compensation. On one visit he was absent from home nearly a year. He has visited nearly every yearly meeting of Friends on this continent and many meetings composing them. In all this labor he remarks: "I am nothing in myself, Christ is all my life, my light and my salvation. Glory be to God! Amen." He is respected and loved by all who know him. His wife died January 6, 1888.

Their children, born in Brunswick, were:

721 I. ISAIAH,⁶ born June 1, 1835. He was a promising young man and had acquired a good education. He was engaged in marriage to a young lady by the name of Abbie Cartland and while in the bloom of youth was stricken down by consumption and died at his father's residence February 23, 1858.

722 II. MARY,⁶ born June 3, 1838; died in Brunswick January 5, 1842.

277. EUNICE⁵ DOUGLAS (David,⁴ Joseph,³ Elijah,² John,¹) youngest daughter of David and Weighty (Hawks) Douglas, born in Durham October 15, 1813; married, April 12, 1834, George P. Day of Durham. He is a farmer and resides in Brunswick. She died——

Their children:

723 I. SUSAN MARIA (Day) born in Durham; died there in 1841.

724 II. DEBORAH (DAY) born in Brunswick; died in Durham, 1841.

725 III. EMELINE (Day) born in Durham May 5, 1841; married, October 22, 1864, Henry F., son of Eben Newell of Durham. He is a farmer and resides in Brunswick.

726 IV. GEORGE HENRY (Day) born in Windham August 11, 1847; married Mattie A. Page of Chicago. He resides in Idaho. He is a mining engineer.

278. JOSEPH[5], DOUGLASS (David,[4] Joseph,[3] Elijah,[2] John,[1]) brother of the preceding, born in Durham April 21, 1817; married, (1) September 23, 1841, Phebe Jones of Falmouth, daughter of Robert and Lydia Jones of China. He married (2) October 4, 1848, Mary Jane, daughter of Daniel and Jane Cook of Casco. He settled in his native town on a part of his father's homestead, where he worked at his trade shoemaking. His first wife died there January 1844, aged 26 years. After her death he sold his house and lot in Durham and removed to Windham, where he worked at his trade and did some farming until 1868, when he removed and settled on the Joseph Bailey homestead in Freeport which he bought of Silas Goddard, where he resided. He and wife were worthy members of the society of Friends and much respected by all who knew them. He died April 29, 1886.

Child by first wife, born in Durham:

727 I. †DAVID J.,[6] born October 15, 1843; married Lydia Myers.

Children by second wife, born in Windham:

728 II. NATHAN,[6] born March 26, 1850; married, November, 1872, Emma S. Cartland. He is a farmer and resides in Brunswick.

729 III. SARAH M.,[6] born February 14, 1851; died in Windham November 3, 1862.

730 IV. SARAH M.,[6] born May 20, 1852.

731 V. CHARLES,[6] born June 22, 1854; died in Windham, Nov. 8, 1862.

732 VI. †ISAIAH,[6] born August 24, 1856; married Affie A. Lunt.

733 VII. PHEBE J.,[6] born December 1, 1858.

734 VIII. JOSEPH H.,[6] born October 21, 1861.

279. JAMES[5] DOUGLASS, (Joseph,[4] Job,[3] Elijah,[2] John,[1]) son of Joseph and Elizabeth (Sawyer) Douglas, born in Durham September 1, 1801; married Elmira Burgess of Phipsburg, where they settled. In 1825 they removed to Bath, where they resided until the year 1834, when they removed to the town of Litchfield, where he passed the remainder of his days. His death was caused by fits, A. D. 1848. His widow married Ephriam Plummer of North Vassalboro, where she resides.

Their children:

735 I. †JOHN W.,[6] born in Phipsburg November 8, 1825; married (1) Mary E. Chase; (2) Abby A. Hall.

736 II. ELIZABETH,[6] born in Bath; married Samuel Cowles of Springfield, Mass.; died 1854.

737 III. †RACHEL R.,[6] born in Bath June 15, 1830; married Zina Spinney.

738 IV. MARY L.,[6] born in Bath; married Albert Plummer of Vassalboro.

284. JOSEPH[5] DOUGLAS (Joseph,[4] Job,[3] Elijah,[2] John[1]) brother of the preceding, born in Litchfield January 11, 1809; married, December 18, 1828, Mercy, daughter of Dr. Samuel and Sarah (Preble) Douglas. He resided in Bath, where he died March 7, 1844.

Their children, born in Bath:

739 I. GILMAN S.,[6] born November 8, 1829; married Rosanna Shaw. After his death in 1866, his widow married V. B. Killey of Boston.

740 II. REBECCA HELEN,[6] born September 9, 1834; married John Henry, a resident of one of the Southern States.

741 III. GEORGE HENRY,[6] born October 3, 1837; died in Bath in the year 1847.

289. BETSEY[5] DOUGLAS (Samuel,[4] Job,[3] Elijah,[2] John[1]) eldest daughter of Dr. Samuel and Sarah (Preble) Douglas, born in Litchfield December 27, 1802; married, Jan-

uary 17, 1824, Abraham, son of Abraham and Dorcas (Booker) Preble of Bowdoinham. They settled in Brunswick and afterwards removed to Bowdoinham, where they settled on a farm one mile north of the village in said town. He was a Justice of the Peace and a smart active man. She died May 4, 1848. He died later.

Their children, born in Bowdoinham:

742   I.   SARAH ELIZABETH (Preble) born July 20, 1824; married, September 4, 1845, Soren Holm of Copenhagan, Denmark.

743   II.   ABRAHAM FRANCIS (Preble) born October 20, 1826; married, April 5, 1849, Almira R. Grant. He died March 1, 1864.

744   III.   JOSEPH (Preble) born July 29, 1828; died October 2, 1863.

745   IV.   MARY OCTAVIA (Preble) born June 23, 1830; married, January 6, 1856, William P. Bibber of Harpswell, where they reside.

746   V.   LEONARD GARDINER (Preble) born February 27, 1832; died August 25, 1833.

747   VI.   ZELIA (Preble) born March 26, 1834; unmarried.

748   VII.   BETSEY (Preble) born April 8, 1836; unmarried.

749   VIII.   REBECCA (Preble) born October 8, 1837; married James G. Potter September 17, 1855; reside in Harpswell.

750   IX.   OLEVIA (Preble) born August 31, 1839; married, April 13, 1864, Wm. King of Parkman.

751   X.   MARTHA ANN (Preble) born October 25, 1841; married, May 15, 1862, William S. Bibber of Harpswell.

291.   SAMUEL[5] DOUGLASS (Samuel,[4] Job,[3] Elijah,[2] John,[1]) brother of the preceding, born in Litchfield, March 17, 1806; married, December 2, 1830, Theodates, daughter of Joseph and Elizabeth (Sawyer) Douglas, born February 11, 1807. They resided at Bowdoinham Village, where he was Station Agent for the Portland & Kennebec Railroad Co. many years and resigned the position on account of ill health. He died about the year 1863 and was buried in the cemetery at Bowdoinham Village.

Their children, born in Bowdoinham ;

752　I.　†HARRIET ANN[6] born October 7, 1833; married Joseph Sedgley.

753　II.　†HANNAH ELIZABETH[6] born November 23, 1835; married, first, Albion B. Jack; second, Edward S. Sparks.

754　III.　†MARY STINSON[6] born February 11, 1838; married George L. Card.

755　IV.　SUSAN FISHER[6] born December 1, 1839; unmarried.

756　V.　†MELVINE WILCHIER[6] born November 19, 1841; married Clara J. Hill.

757　VI.　ISAAC FISHER[6] born June 2, 1843; unmarried.

758　VII.　JANE MARIA[6] born June 29, 1845; died April 8, 1860.

293.　CAPT. ABRAHAM[5] DOUGLASS (Samuel,[4] Job,[3] Elijah,[2] John,[1] (brother of the preceding, born in Litchfield May 10 1811; married, November, 1833, Hannah E., daughter of Joseph and Elizabeth (Sawyer) Douglas [287] born April 5, 1814. He is a ship master and has followed the sea most of the time since he was sixteen years of age, mostly in the West India trade. He lives in Bowdoinham Village where he has resided since 1835.

Their children, born in Bowdoinham, except Asa A.:

759　I.　†ASA ALBION[6] born in Bath November 29, 1834; married Josephine Knight.

760　II.　SARAH ANN[6] born September 7, 1836; died January 26, 1858.

761　III.　SUSAN OFELIA[6] born May 19, 1838; died August 19, 1854.

762　IV.　ARABINE FRANCES[6] born December 9, 1839; married September 7, 1867, Ira Dingley. He died and she married, second, Fred Patten of Bowdoinham, where they reside.

763　V.　†AMANDA JANE[6] born April 5, 1842; married, first, George G. Williams; second, Joseph G. Washburn.

764　VI.　ELLEN ELIZABETH[6] born December 30, 1845; married Jefferson M. Clark, farmer. They reside in Augusta.

765. VII. MARGARET EMMA[6] born March 8, 1847. She married Standish Reed; he resides on a farm in Durham.

766 VIII. WILLIAM HARRIS[6] born January 19, 1850; died October 19, 1854.

767 IX. WILLIAM HARRIS[6] born November 15, 1854. He died in Bowdoinham April 1, 1882.

768 X. LEONA MAY[6] born May 6, 1858; died March 8, 1864.

294. REV. GARDINER[5] DOUGLASS (Samuel,[4] Job,[3] Elijah,[2] John,[1]) brother of the preceding, born in Litchfield October 11, 1812; married, 1835, Asenath S., daughter of John Orr, of Bowdoin. At the age of three years he went to live with Isaiah Gardiner of East Bowdoinham, where he remained until he was sixteen years old; then went to sea, which business he followed seven years; was second mate on several voyages and first mate on one voyage. After he married he settled on the homestead of Isaiah Gardiner. In 1840 he was ordained a minister of the gospel, under the auspices of the Free Will Baptist church. His ministerial labors have been in Bowdoinham, Richmond, Dresden, Phipsburg, Edgecomb, the island of Monhegan and in various other towns lying near the mouth of the Kennebec river. During the years of his ministry he lived in Woolwich, Gardiner, Topsham, Bath, Lewiston and Harpswell. As a minister, he was favored with a good degree of success, having had many revivals and was instrumental in the conversion of many precious souls. He resides with his son in Lewiston.

Their children, born in Bowdoinham;

769 I. †OSCAR GARDINER[6] born June 24. 1836; married Phebe W. Cook.

770 II. SUSAN T.,[6] born January 16, 1840; married, 1857, Samuel T. Rogers of Topsham.

771 III. ARVILLA[6] born November 24, 1844; died in Westbrook, 1851.

297. JOANNA[5] DOUGLASS (Samuel,[4] Job,[3] Elijah,[2] John,[1]) daughter of Samuel and Sarah (Stevens) Douglas, born in Litchfield December 30, 1817; married John Roff of Rumford, where he settled.

Their children, born in Rumford:
772 I. HENRIETTA (Roff). About 1840.
773 II. MARIA (Roff) 1842.
774 III. HENRY (Roff) born about 1845.

298. MARIAM[5] DOUGLASS (Samuel,[4] Job,[3] Elijah,[2] John,[1]) sister of the preceding, born in the town of Mexico July 10, 1819; married, in Lowell, Mass., January 1, 1844, Stephen Davis Ward of Bradford, N. H. They settled in Dracut, Mass., removed to West Moreland, N. H., and to Putney, Vermont. In 1855 they removed to Warrenville, Illinois, where they have since resided. Mr. Ward was in the Rebellion and was taken prisoner in the State of Georgia and shot by the rebels August 21, 1864.

Their children:
775 I. CHARLES HENRY (Ward) born in Dracut, Mass., Nov. 2, 1844. He was in the Rebellion and received a wound and died in the hospital at Washington July 24, 1864.
776 II. JAMES ALFRED (Ward) born in West Moreland, N. H., February 21, 1847; he was in the Rebellion; was taken prisoner, but escaped and took refuge in the mountains. He is married and resides at Cedar Rapids, Iowa.
777 III. SARAH ELIZABETH (Ward) born in Putney, Vermont, March 24, 1849; married, November 16, 1867, Benjamin Purier. They reside at Lincoln Park, N. J.
778 IV. EMMA JANE (Ward) born in West Moreland June 11, 1854. She is lame and lives with her mother.

311. JOHN BANKS[5] DOUGLASS (James,[4] Job,[3] Elijah,[2] John,[1]) son of James and Eliza M. (Banks) Douglas born in Litchfield April 1, 1803. At the age of sixteen he left the parental roof to obtain a living for himself. From

1819 to 1823 he hired with farmers during summer seasons and attended school winters. In 1824 he engaged with Capt. John O'Brine of Brunswick, to clerk in his store. In the fall of the same year he visited Quebec on business for his employer. The following winter he went to the Lakes at the head waters of the Androscoggin River, logging for G. F. Richardson. In the year 1827, he bought a tract of wild land in the township of letter B, now Upton, Oxford County. He cleared a portion of the land for cultivation and built a set of buildings. In his house was built the first brick chimney in the township. He kept bachelor's hall a short time, making butter and cheese as best he could. Becoming tired of his lonely life and feeling the full force of that true saying "It is not good for man to be alone," he married, March 8, 1829, Nancy, daughter of John and Sarah (Booker) Douglas of Durham. Soon after their marriage he took his widowed mother home to live with him. In 1831 he sold his farm and removed to Canton Mills where he learned the blacksmith's trade of his wife's brother Hugh, which business he followed six years. In 1835 he was elected Lieutenant of Company H. He was subsequently elected Capt. of said company, which office he held until 1837, at which time he sold his shop and other property in Canton and removed to Little River Village, Lisbon, where he bought a farm of David Metcalf.

In 1855 he was elected one of the selectmen of his town. He was a very active business man. He took great pride in keeping his farm in good order. He died October 25, 1877. His wife died February 8, 1881. They were buried in the cemetery at Lisbon Falls.

Their children:

779   I.   †JOHN ALBION⁶ born in Letter B Plantation (now Upton) January 1, 1830; married Margaret Springer.

780   II.   EDWIN⁶ born in Letter B Plantation January 15, 1832. He learned the house joiner's trade, which business he followed several years. His health failing him he thought a change in business might be for the better; so he learned the tailor's trade which he followed but a short time when he was obliged to stop work almost entirely. He died at his father's residence February 24, 1875 and was buried in the graveyard at Lisbon Falls.

781   III.   ELIZA⁶ born in Canton December 27, 1833; married, July 24, 1875, Oringe F. Small.

782   IV.   †NOAH H.⁶ born in Canton March 29, 1836.

783   V.   EMILY⁶ born in Canton February 5, 1838; married Emery Douglass [801].

784   VI.   NANCY A.⁶ born in Lisbon June 16, 1840; married, July 5, 1873, Alfonzo W. Horn. She died of consumption, 1876.

785   VII.   OTIS H.⁶ born in Lisbon November 23, 1842; died June 6, 1862, at New Orleans while in the War of the Rebellion.

786   VIII.   †WILLIAM W.⁶ born in Lisbon July 11, 1845; married Ellen R. Jordan.

787   IX.   CHARLES H.⁶ born in Lisbon June 16, 1847; died December 9, 1871.

788   X.   †OSCAR EATON⁶ born in Lisbon August 14, 1849; married, July 2, 1876, Abbie J. Goddard, daughter of James and Eliza J. (Douglas) Goddard.

789   XI.   ISAAC WESLEY⁶ born in Lisbon March 4, 1852; died January 2, 1874.

312.   JAMES S.⁵ DOUGLASS (James,⁴ Job,³ Elijah,² John,¹) brother of the preceding, born in Litchfield, March 24, 1807; married Azubah, daughter of James and Apphia (Segar) Godwin, born February 9, 1816. When quite young he removed with his father to Freeport. At the age of fourteen he left his home and lived with Samuel Starbird, Jr., in Bowdoin, seven years. In 1828 he worked farming one year for Nathaniel Osgood of Durham. In the year 1829 he went to the township of Letter B (now Upton) which at that time was almost a dense

wilderness and contained only eight families. In 1842, he felled the first tree on the place where he has since resided and cultivated it into a thrifty farm. Since the organization of the town he has held some town office. He was a man much respected in the community for his upright and moral character. He died at his home in Upton, September 3, 1882.

Their children, born in Upton:

790 I. JOHN HENRY[6] born January 11, 1837; married, Sept. 1, 1868, Susan E. Locke. He has always resided in his native town and followed the business of farming. He has been one of the selectmen and held other important town offices. In 1852 he was appointed Justice of the Peace. He died October 22, 1882.

791 One child, Ellen E.[7] born July 28, 1869.

792 II. †CHARLES LYMAN[6] born June 4, 1839; married Hester A. Ballard.

793 III. MARIA GODWIN[6] born January 23, 1841; married, first, Joseph H. West; second, Henry W. Chapman.

794 IV. SOPHIA BRAGG[6] born November 20, 1843; married James Locke; resides in Kansas.

795 V. EDWIN WESTON[6] born March 6, 1845; married Abbie S. Penley. They reside in Colorado.

796 VI. WARREN OSGOOD[6] born January 7, 1847; married, 1873, Hortense French of Plainview, Minn.

797 VII. LUCINDA FRENCH[6] born July 29, 1850; died September 14, 1861.

798 VIII. CALVIN HOWE[6] born September 20, 1852; died September 17, 1861.

799 IX. IDA AFFIE[6] born August 1, 1858; married Asa K. Frost and resides in Upton.

313. REV. WILLIAM BOOKER[5] DOUGLASS (James,[4] Job[3] Elijah,[2] John,[1]) brother of the preceding, born in Freeport April 7, 1809; married Mary, daughter of Deacon Samuel Duren, born January 20, 1811. He was a shoemaker by trade. When a young man he gave his heart to Christ and joined the Methodist church. Feeling it

enjoined upon him to labor in the Master's cause as a minister, he was ordained to the work and labored earnestly in his own and the adjoining towns; but his usefulness was destined to be of short duration, for that fatal disease, consumption, marked him for its prey. He lingered a few years and died in great faith and hope of a bright immortality, April 22, 1843. His widow married, second, Elisha Gatchell of Durham; removed to Raymond where she died November 9, 1860.

Their children, born in Lisbon:

800 I. †William Sidney[6] born October 12, 1832;. married Mary E. Nash.

801 II. †Louisa[6] born September 1, 1835; married Henry C. Johnson.

802 III. Wilber F.[6] born July 2, 1837. While living with his step-father in Durham, he, with other boys, on Sunday May 29, 1853, visited the mouth of Pinkham's Brook, which had risen very high by recent rains and while at play on a log fell off and was drowned.

803 IV. Emery[6] born April 22, 1839. His father died when he was four years old and by the advice of friends his mother consented to have him go and live with Deacon John Whitmore, a farmer living on Bowdoinham Ridge. Here he had but few opportunities for attending school, which, however, he improved to the best advantage. At the age of fourteen he went to live with his mother, who had again married and resided in Durham, where he remained a few years and learned the joiner's trade of his step-father, which he worked at summers and attended school during the winter months. In the winter of 1859 he taught a district school in the town of Raymond. In 1860 he commenced the study of law with N. M. Whitmore of Gardiner, which he continued with good progress and at the August term of court, held at Augusta, was admitted a member of the bar. He opened an office at Little River, now Lisbon Falls, but finding the place too small for his ambitious desires he soon closed it. About this time the teacher at the Village having some trouble left the school and he was engaged to finish out the term. March 23, 1862 he married Emily, daughter of John B. and Nancy B. Douglass of Lisbon Falls. June, 1862, he opened a law office in Brunswick with very flattering pros-

pects of a brilliant career in his chosen profession. Here he commenced keeping house and pleasantly passed the few more years allotted him on earth. He died very suddenly, July 3, 1865, and was interred in the grave-yard at Lisbon Falls.

804   V.   MARY JANE born November 7, 1841; died in Raymond February 11, 1860.

316.   NEHEMIAH OWEN[5] DOUGLASS (James,[4] Job,[3] Elijah,[2] John,[1]) brother of the preceding, born in Durham, September 3, 1814 ; married, first, 1838, Jane Hall.

Owing to a protracted sickness of his father he left home at the age of seven years to live with one Lemuel Jenkins, a farmer of Bowdoin. He worked on the farm summers and received only a few weeks schooling each year. In those days nearly every farmer had his "little brown jug" well filled with intoxicating drink, and it fell to his lot to replenish this jug frequently—as often as three times a week—from a store some three miles away. So disgusted was he with his adopted home and the life he was forced to live, that at the age of fourteen he left Mr. Jenkins and soon afterwards went and lived with his eldest brother, where he remained until he was about twenty years of age, at which time he went with Elisha Moulton of Canton and learned the cabinet maker's trade, remaining with him three years and then went into the business for himself in Canton. Soon after his marriage he settled in Lisbon but owing to poor health he was obliged to give up his trade. He removed to Canton Village and opened a stove and hardware store. In 1842 he sold out his store and removed to Buckfield. In 1856 he married, second, Mrs. Lydia E. (Willis) daughter of William Cole of Buckfield and removed to Little River, Lisbon, and opened a dry goods and grocery store. In 1858 he removed to Cape Elizabeth where he went into trade.

Seeing so much of the evils of intemperance in his boyhood led him to take a decided stand in favor of total abstinence. He signed the pledge when a young man and has never broken it. He has ever been foremost in the noble cause and has delivered many lectures on the subject.

He was for a short time in the dry goods business in Portland; has retired from active business and resides in Deering.

One child:

805 I. CEPHAS HENRY[6] born in Lisbon April 14, 1840; married, January 1, 1866, Nellie J. Willis. He succeeded his father in trade at Lisbon Falls and removed to Westbrook and opened a variety store at Morrill's Corner. Here his stock was burned and he removed to Portland and opened a dry goods store. He died at his home in Portland, very suddenly, November 15, 1376.

317. PHILIP BANKS[5] DOUGLASS (James,[4] Job,[3] Elijah,[2] John,[1]) brother of the preceding, born May 20, 1816; married, February 14, 1842, Mary Ann, daughter of John and Hannah (Beal) Knight, born November 30, 1813. Settled in Lisbon. In 1854 removed to Durham and bought the farm on which the old Strout tavern sits. In 1886 he bought a farm in Wales, where he remained till his death, which occurred June 13, 1887.

Their children were:

806 I. CHARLES HENRY[6] born in Lisbon June 25, 1843; died in Durham February 16, 1844.

807 II. EDWARD BERRY[6] born in Lisbon November 10, 1845; died in Durham September 14, 1866.

808 III. JAMES HENRY[6] born in Lisbon August 9, 1848; died in Lisbon July 29, 1850.

809 IV. STILMAN NEWELL[6] born in Lisbon September 18, 1850; died December 10, 1862.

810 V. WILLARD METCALF[6] born in Bowdoin November 22, 1852; died in Durham October 10, 1854.

324. Charles[5] Douglass (Job,[4] Job,[3] Elijah,[2] John,[1]) son of Job and Margaret (Brown) Douglass, born in Litchfield in 1812; married by Rev. Silas Stearns, May 11, 1834. Emeline Poor, born January 8, 1817 He was a blacksmith by trade and resided in Bath, where he died March 17, 1855. His widow died January 10, 1861.

Their children, born in Bath:

811 I. Mary Ellen[6] born September 10, 1835; died April 14, 1854.

812 II. Charles William[6] born January 26, 1838; died June 20, 1839.

813 III. Lydia Margaret[6] born February 24, 1840; married Boyington Beal; resided in Bowdoinham where she died February 24, 1871. Children:

814 Nellie (Beal), Fred (Beal), Mary (Beal).

815 IV. Isaac Martin[6] born November 16, 1843; went to sea; probably dead.

816 V. Esther Ann[6] born February 17, 1845; she died in Bath from severe burning, caused by her clothing taking fire, October 22, 1862.

817 VI. Thomas Jackson[6] born February 18, 1849; died at Gardiner April 9, 1881.

818 VII. Maria[6] born about 1850; died February 10, 1853.

819 VIII. Alfred Eugene[6] born January 21, 1852; unmarried: died in Bath May 23, 1882.

325. Esther Douglas[5] (Job,[4] Job,[3] Elijah,[2] John,[1]) sister of the preceding, born in Litchfield; married by John Neal, Esq., March 4, 1831, Alexander Bubier, born April 12, 1804. He is a farmer and resides on a small farm in South Gardiner. She is dead but no date given of her death.

Their children, born in Gardiner, are:

820 I. Maria M. (Bubier) born March 12, 1823.

821 II. George B. (Bubier) born August 1, 1830; died August, 1867.

822 III. ALONZO W. (Bubier) born May 1, 1833.
823 IV. CHARLES H. (Bubier) born November 22, 1837.

326. MARY ANN⁵ DOUGLASS (Job,⁴ Job,³ Elijah,² John,¹) sister of the preceding, born in Litchfield December 1, 1815; married, January 8, 1834, William S. Gordon, born in Mount Vernon September 2, 1807. She died at Manchester January 26, 1855.

Their children, born in Litchfield:

824 I. BETSEY T. (Gordan) born 1835; married, first, ——— Stone, second, Jacob Libby; reside at Augusta.
825 II. WILLIAM THURSTON (Gordan) born 1844.
826 III. MARY ELLEN (Gordan) born March 31, 1846.
827 IV. SETH (Gordan) born in 1848; died in California.
828 V. JOHN EDWARD (Gordan) born November 26, 1850.
829 VI. DANIEL EMERY (Gordan) born in 1851.
830 VII. LAURA C. (Gordan) born May 7, 1852; married August 27, 1870.

329. ALFRED⁵ DOUGLASS (Job,⁴ Job,³ Elijah,² John,¹) brother of the preceding, born in Litchfield September 15, 1822; married, February 15, 1844, Frances E. Nash, born November 16, 1822. He died 1870.

Their children:

831 I. CHARLES ALFRED⁶ born in Hallowell May 17, 1845; married Lizzie L. Howland, daughter of Jesse and Sophia Stewart, born November 24, 1853.
832 II. †HENRIETTA⁶ born in West Gardiner October 20, 1848; married, first, Jesse Stover; second, James Jones.
833 III. ANNA LUCRETIA⁶ born in Gardiner April 2, 1852; married James Bartlet of New Brunswick.
834 IV. THOMAS NASH⁶ born in Gardiner July 6, 1855.

330. SETH⁵ DOUGLASS (Job,⁴ Job,³ Elijah,² John,¹) brother of the preceding, born in Litchfield April 14, 18—; married, September 11, 1844, Mary Jane Smith of Brunswick where they settled and resided until his death, which

occurred December 25, 1870. His widow still resides in Brunswick Village.

Their children, born in Brunswick:

835 I. MARGARET JANE[6] born April 14, 1848; married, 1870, Harley Bacan. He is a jeweller and resides in Boston. She died June 28, 1887.

836 II. †BENJAMIN FRANKLIN[6] born September 17, 1855; married Lizzie B. Southard.

837 III. ALICE G.[6] born February 17, 1860; married Edward D. Beaman, October 29, 1882; reside in Yarmouthville.

331. REV. GEORGE[5] DOUGLASS (Benjamin,[4] Job,[3] Elijah,[2] John,[1]) son of Benjamin and Betsey (Potter) Douglas, born in Bowdoin August 7, 1816; married Rebecca, daughter of Barnabas and Lydia Cook. The year he was eighteen there was a powerful revival of religion in his father's neighborhood, under the labors of Rev. Samuel Hathorn and other ministers of the gospel. At these meetings he became interested in religion and gave his heart to the Savior and was baptized and joined the Free Will Baptist church. Soon after his conversion he felt it his duty to labor in his Master's vineyard as a preacher; and at the age of twenty-two he was ordained for the work of the ministry, which calling he pursued until his death. His last place of residence was at Fairfield, where he died of typhoid fever August 12, 1846.

Their children:

838 I. GEORGE HENRY[6] born in Bowdoin January 5, 1840; married, May 2, 1860, Adelaide Helen, daughter of Lonis Asa and Caroline Gowell. He served in the War of the Rebellion as Sergeant in the 15th Maine Regiment, Company B, four years. He now resides in Gardiner and is a wholesale dealer in confectionery. One child.

839. LEONORA ARDELL born July 27, 1873.

840 II. ALBION C.[6] born in Litchfield, March, 1842. He was a tailor. He went to California, where he remained three years; then

came home sick. He was engaged in marriage to Sarah Smith, who took care of him until his death, which occurred Nov. 19, 1866.

841 III. MARY ELIZABETH[6] born in Fairfield; died there May 1846.

332. CHARLES[5] DOUGLASS (Benjamin,[4] Job,[3] Elijah,[2] John,[1]) brother of the preceding, born in Bowdoin August 7, 1816; married Eunice, daughter of Rev. Benajah Pratt of Belfast. He settled on a farm in his native town. He was deeply interested in the cause of religion and respected by all who knew him for his genial disposition and integrity of character. He died June 14, 1859.

Their children, born in Bowdoin:

842 I. †EDWIN CHARLES[6] born March 6, 1841; married Hattie R. Smith.

843. II. SARAH JANE[6] born October, 1843; married Charles Hall; resided in Bangor, where she died. One child, Charles M. (Hall) born November 18, 1865.

844 III. †WARREN P.[6] born October 5, 1845; married, first, Lois J. Fisher; second, Ida F. Field.

845 IV. MARY AUGUSTA[6] born, 1847; died, 1864.

846 V. †ELLA A.[6] born July 27, 1859; married, first, Isaiah Merrifield; second, J. Eben Butler.

334. WILLIAM[5] DOUGLASS (Benjamin,[4] Job,[3] Elijah[2] John,[1]) brother of the preceding, born in Bowdoin March 31, 1821; married, August 20, 1843, Roxcilla, daughter of Capt. James and Patience (Douglas) Rodick, born in Freeport August 15, 1825. They settled in Bowdoin where he died October 10, 1863. His widow died July 9, 1865. They were buried in the graveyard on Litchfield Plains.

Their children, born in Bowdoin:

847 I. BENJAMIN F.[6] born August 15, 1845; died May 18, 1846.

848 II. †DANIEL A.[6] born April 22, 1847; married Mary Eliza Douglas. [850.]

849   III. WILLIAM WILLIS[6] born June 16, 1859.

336. BENJAMIN BOOKER[5] DOUGLASS (Benjamin,[4] Job,[3] Elijah,[2] John,[1]) brother of the preceding, born in Bowdoin December 10, 1825; married Rachel J. Bates. He settled near his father's residence in Bowdoin; removed to Richmond Village and finally removed back to Bowdoin, where he passed the remainder of his days. He was a farmer and shoemaker. He died July 6, 1862.

Their children, born in Bowdoin:

850   I. MARY ELIZABETH[6] born August 7, 1847; married Daniel A. Douglass, [848]; second, Abizah Small.

851   II. †JAMES ALEXANDER[6] born April 24, 1849; married, first, Sarah Davis; second, Georgia Lawrence.

852   III. †FREDERICK BATES[6] born April 16, 1851; married Hester Robinson.

853   IV. RACHEL JANE[6] born November 24, 1853; married first, Peter Nelson; second, —————— Batchelder.

854   V. †BENJAMIN BOOKER[6] born October 2, 1858; married Minnie S. Buker.

364. CLARISSA[5] DOUGLASS (David,[4] Israel,[3] Elijah,[2] John,[1]) eldest daughter of Capt. David and Sally (Merryman) Douglas, born in Harpswell December 29, 1803; married, February 28, 1828, Robert Merriman of Harpswell. They settled in Bowdoin, removed to Richmond and to Bowdoinham, where they both died.

Their children:

855   I. ISABELLA (Merriman) born in Harpswell November 14, 1830.

856   II. DAVID DOUGLAS (Merriman) born in Harpswell November 27, 1832; married, November 26, 1859, Emeline Perkins of N. H. He is a tailor, also a trader at Readfield, where he resides.

857   III. ELI (Merriman) born in Bowdoin June 14, 1837; married Almeda Gilman of Litchfield. He is Postmaster and trader at North Litchfield, where he resides.

858 IV. SARAH J. (Merriman) born in Bowdoin March 27, 1836 She is engaged in a cloak and dress manufactory at Richmond.

859 V. FRANCES (Merriman) born in Bowdoin February 9, 1838; married, 1867, Charles Dunn of Portland.

860 VI. SUSAN A. (Merriman) born in Bowdoin July 14, 1841; married, 1864, Henry M. Gardiner of Richmond, where they reside. He is a harness maker.

366. JANE[5] DOUGLASS (David,[4] Israel,[3] Elijah,[2] John[1]) sister of the preceding and daughter of Capt. David and Sally (Merriman) Douglas, born in Harpswell June 15, 1809; married, August 26, Nehemiah, son of Nehemiah and Jane (Alexander) Curtis of Harpswell, born there August 18, 1807. Settled in his native town, removed to Bowdoin previous to 1835, where he still resides. His wife died October 1, 1852.

Their children:

861 I. SAMUEL E. (Curtis) born in Harpswell November 20, 1833; married Elizabeth L. Goud. He is a carpenter; resides in Topsham.

862 II. ROBERT M. (Curtis) born in Bowdoin June 13, 1835; married Sarah J. Bibber; carpenter; resides in Harpswell.

863 III. NEHEMIAH (Curtis) born in Bowdoin July 5, 1838; married Rachel H. Bubier; resides in Bowdoin.

864 IV. DAVID F. (Curtis) born in Bowdoin July 3, 1841; married Eliza F. Danforth; resides in Lisbon.

865 V. JOSEPH P. (Curtis) born in Bowdoin January 8, 1843; married Rosilla Dunham; farmer; resides in Litchfield.

866 VI. GEORGE S. (Curtis) born in Bowdoin November 23, 1844; married Alice Smith. He works in the Worumbo Mills at Lisbon Falls, where he resides.

368. DELIGHT[5] DOUGLASS (David,[4] Israel,[3] Elijah,[2] John,[1]) sister of the preceding, born in Harpswell June 30, 1813, married, December 10, 1832. Samuel, son of Thomas and Esther Longley, born August 30, 1813; farmer; settled in Green, then removed to Leeds; now resides in Green.

Their children, born in Green :

867 I. THOMAS HENRY (Longley) born May 28, 1834; married Eleanor Skinner. He is a harness manufacturer in Lewiston, where he resides.

868 II. SARAH JANE (Longley) born August 20, 1837; married John H. Hodgkins; was a farmer and resided in Green, where he died.

869 III. WILLIAM EDWARD (Longley) born July 25, 1839; married Augusta Thompson. He follows farming for a business in his native town.

870 IV. GEORGE EARL (Longley) born July 21, 1841; married Susan Thompson. He is a farmer and resides in Green; died April, 1875.

871 V. ESTHER ANN (Longley) born April 20, 1847; she married Wilber F. Mower of Green, where they reside on a farm.

386. JULIA ANN DOUGLASS[5] (William,[4] Elijah,[3] Elijah,[2] John,[1]) daughter of William and Mary (Sinnott) Douglas, born in Harpswell October 14, 1823, married, December 15, 1847, Jotham R. Chipman. They reside at Bucksport Centre.

Their children, born in Bucksport :

872 I. ISAIAH LEWIS (Chipman) born September 15, 1848.

873 II. WILLIAM RICH (Chipman) born October 14, 1850; died November 2, 1852.

874 III. GEORGE WILLIAM (Chipman) born November 2, 1854; married, May 28, 1879, Lida E. Hopkins.

875 IV. MARY SINNETT (Chipman) born February 11, 1857; died November 11, 1861.

876 V. STEPHEN FRANKLIN (Chipman) born January 16, 1860.

877 VI. JULIA RICH (Chipman) born September 16, 1864.

878 VII. ANN HOWARD (Chipman) born September 1, 1867.

387. CAPT. WILLIAM[5] DOUGLASS (William,[4] Elijah,[3] Elijah,[2] John,[1]) brother of the preceding and son of William and Mary (Sinnott) Douglas, born in Bucksport April 12, 1825; married, April 12, 1846, Thankful W. Hinks,

born February 26, 1827. He followed the sea for a living. He died in Philadelphia November 1, 1885.

Children, born in Bucksport:

879 I. STOWERS ABEY[6] born December 11, 1847; married, May, 1869, Sophia A. Hurst of New York city. She died March 12, 1886.
880 II. WILLIAM WARREN[6] born July 30, 1854; married, Oct. 26, 1874, Lizzie Maria, daughter of David and Dorothy Atwood.
881. III. FRANK PIERCE[6] born November 23, 1859.
882 IV. GEORGE HINKLEY[6] born June 13, 1868.

392. MARY JANE[5] DOUGLASS (William,[4] Elijah,[3] Elijah,[2] John,[1]) sister of the preceding and daughter of William and Mary (Sinnott) Douglass, born in Bucksport February 23, 1840; married, October 18, 1857, William Williams. He is a farmer and resides in Bucksport.

Their children, born in Bucksport, are:

883 I. MARY ELLA (Williams) born August 30, 1858; died May 13, 1867.
884 II. WILLIAM ALBERT (Williams) born December 4, 1860.
885 III. MARY ABBY (Williams) born August 9, 1862.
886 IV. HARRIET ELIZABETH (Williams) born February 6, 1864.

407. JOHN WILLIAM[5] DOUGLASS (Isaac,[4] Elijah,[3] Elijah,[2] John,[1]) son of Isaac and Mary (Pinkham) Douglas, born in Harpswell August 3, 1829; married, December 22, 1850, Martha C. Randall, daughter of William and Hannah Randall, born December 11, 1831. He resides near his father's homestead in Harpswell. He followed fishing for a business. He died January 29, 1889.

Their children, born in Harpswell:

887 I. ALBERT HENRY[6] born June 28, 1851; died November 15, 1852.
888. II. HARRIET RANDALL[6] born September 29, 1853.

889. III. WILLIAM RANDALL[6] born August 15, 1855; died August 28, 1865.
890. IV. CHARLES BISHOP[6] born May 22, 1858.
891. V. ALONZO CAMPBELL[6] born November 30, 1860.
892. VI. MARY PINKHAM[6] born March 24, 1862.
893. VII. HANNAH RANDALL[6] born November 19, 1864.
894. VIII. JENNIE BLAKE[6] born June 12, 1869.

408. DANIEL K.[5] DOUGLASS (Isaac,[4] Elijah,[3] Elijah[2] John,[1]) brother of the preceding and son of Isaac and Mary (Pinkham) Douglas, born in Harpswell December 16, 1830; married, December 26, 1856, Deborah A. Randall, born September 22, 1833. He, like his brother, follows the fishing business and resides in the same house with his brother, John W., on Harpswell Neck. Their house commands the view of Casco Bay and is a delightful residence.

Their children, born in Harpswell, are:
895. I. ALBERT H.[6] born August 5, 1859.
896. II. FRANK R.[6] born October 1, 1861.
897. III. ISAAC[6] born July 28, 1863. He died in Harpswell September 13, 1886.

420. ISAAC HUGH[5] DOUGLASS (Isaac,[4] John,[3] Elijah,[2] John,[1]) son of Isaac and Abigail (Webber) Douglas, born in Harpswell April 26, 1851; married, April 26, 1879, Etta Martha Taylor of Vassalboro, daughter of Amos and Harriet P. Taylor. They reside at Lisbon Falls. He is pressman in the Worumbo Mills.

Their children:
898. I. MABEL ALBERTINA born January 17, 1880; died July 5, 1882.
899. II. CORA EDITH born December 9, 1882; died January 22, 1884.

421. DEANNA[5] DOUGLASS (Waitstill Webber,[4] John,[3] Elijah,[2] John,) daughter of Waitstill W. and Jane (Day)

Douglass; was born in Durham January 17, 1842; married, March 1872, Alden Moulton of Green; farmer; resides on her father's homestead in Wales.

One child:

900 WAITSTILL DOUGLASS MOULTON, born in Wales March 17, 1873.

423. ORLANDO KELLOG[5] DOUGLASS (Waitstill Webber[4] John,[3] Elijah,[2] John,[1]) brother of the preceding; was born in Durham August 30, 1846; married, January 1, 1872, Cynthia R., daughter of Capt. George T. and Charlotte J. Howe of Green. He is a house carpenter; they reside in Lewiston.

Their children:

901 I. HARRY ELMER born at Walpole, Mass., December 14, 1873; died in Lewiston April 11, 1881.
902 II. MYRA C. born in Lewiston August 7, 1876.
903 III. FRED EVANS born in Lewiston June 2, 1882.

424. GEORGE EMERY[5] DOUGLASS (Waitstill W.,[4] John,[3] Elijah,[2] John[1]) brother of the preceding and son of Waitstill W. and Jane (Day) Douglass; was born April 28, 1850; married, May 9, 1876, Ella B., daughter of Furber and Betsey Libby of Wales. Mr. Douglass is a carpenter and resides in Waterville.

Their children:

904 I. DANA C. born in Wales February 2, 1877.
905 II. BERTIE F. born in Winslow September 2, 1878; died September 5, 1880.
906 III. FRANK L. born in Waterville December 19, 1881.

433. LYDIA[5] DOUGLASS (Ephriam,[4] John,[3] John,[2] John,[1]) daughter of Ephriam and Deborah (Haskins) Douglas, born in Grafton April 30, 1817; married at Sandwich, Mass., July 25, 1845, George W. Marsh, glass blow-

er. They resided at Sandwich New Bedford and several other places in Massachusetts, where he worked at his trade. Mrs. Marsh died in Somerville, Mass., May 15, 1861.

Their children, born in Sandwich, Mass.:

907 I. NETTIE G. (Marsh) born May 6, 1846; married in Boston, September 12, 1875, George Emery. They reside in Boston.

908 II. GEORGE W. (Marsh Jr.) born February 14, 1849; died in Philadelphia February 14, 1862.

909 III. ISADORA F. (Marsh) born June 6, 1851; died in Sandwich November 25, 1857.

429. DEBORAH[5] DOUGLASS (Ephriam,[4] John,[3] John,[2] John,[1]) son of Ephriam and Deborah (Haskins) Douglass; born in Grafton, N. H., February 7, 1810; married Robert Clark. They settled in Middleborough, Mass.

Their children:

909½ I. MARY R. (Clark) born in Plymouth December 30, 1832; married John K. Robinson.

910 II. SARAH R. (Clark) born in Plymouth August 6, 1837; married Elijah N. Osborn. They reside in Brockton, Mass.

911 III. DEBORAH F. (Clark) born in Middleboro, Mass., Nov. 27, 1838; married Henry A. Eaton.

912 IV. HATTIE C. (Clark) born in Middleboro April 12, 1841; died February 25, 1870.

913 V. ALICE H. (Clark) born in Middleboro December 14, 1842; married George B. Whitmarsh.

914 VI. HELEN M. (Clark) born in Middleboro September 1, 1845; died August 4, 1870.

915 VII. ROBERT R. (Clark) born in Middleboro December 14, 1847; married Sarah Thayer.

434. HANNAH[5] DOUGLASS (Ephriam,[4] John,[3] John,[2] John,[1]) daughter of Ephriam and Deborah (Haskins) Douglas, born in Plymouth, Mass.: married in Killingly, Conn., August 21, 1842, John K. Robinson, they resided in Pawtucket, R. I., until November 1842, when they

sailed for Europe, where they arrived and resided with his parents two years, then returned to America and resided several years in Charlestown, Boston and East Boston, where he worked at his trade, house and sign painting. He subsequently removed to Franklin, Mass., where they resided twenty years. Mrs. Robinson died in Franklin, April, 1859. Mr. R. married, second, Mary R. Clark of Middleborough, Mass.; 1870 removed to Medway, Mass.

Children born in Franklin, except oldest, who was born in Boston:

916 I. JANE K. (Robinson) born December 27, 1846; married Charles Grant; reside in Medway, Mass.

917 II. JOHN QUINCY (Robinson) born August 11, 1848.

918 III. WILLIAM GEORGE (Robinson) born in 1850.

919 IV. CHARLES FURGUS (Robinson) born in 1852.

920 V. COLIN CAMPBELL (Robinson) born in 1854.

921 VI. MARY H. (Robinson) born in 1856.

922 VII. ROBERT DAVIS (Robinson) born July 27, 1857.

435. ELIJAH W.^{5} DOUGLASS (Ephriam,^{4} John,^{3} John,^{2} John,^{1}) son of Ephriam and Deborah (Haskins) Douglas, born in Plymouth, Mass., October 5, 1822; married, October 22, 1846, Mehitable C., daughter of John and Mehitable (Elliot) Douglass [440] born in Grantham, N. H., December 22, 1817. He settled in Middleborough, Mass.; his wife died in Carver, Mass.

Their children, born in Middleborough, Mass:

923 I. ELIJAH ELLIOT^6 born July 18, 1847; married October 25, 1868, Mary Sherman.

924 One child, Elliot S., born November 30, 1874.

925 II. ALBERT FREEMAN^6 born August 19, 1850; married, January 5, 1870, Nellie W. Sherman.

926 One child, Freeman W., born December 12, 1872.

927 III. †ELIZA ELLEN, born August 5, 1852; married Frederick Pratt.

928 IV. HENRY HOWARD^6 born July 3, 1855.

929   V. MERCY JANE[6] born September 8, 1858.

436. LUTHER[5] DOUGLASS (Ephriam,[4] John,[3] John,[2] John,[1]) brother of the preceding, born in Plymouth, Mass., July 18, 1826; married, first, Lucy S. Gibbs, born in Sandwich, Mass., September 25, 1824. He followed the sea twenty-four years of the early part of his life. He then bought a farm in the town of Carver, where he resided and worked farming. His wife died in West Sandwich, June 26, 1869. He married, second, November, 1870, Mrs. Abba J. (Hamblin) Dunham. He resided on a farm at Monument Pond; removed and now lives at Sagamore, Mass.; married for his third wife, October 17, 1889, Mrs. Jane E. (Marsh) Allister, daughter of Rev. Joseph Marsh of Sandwich, Mass.

Children by first wife, born in Sandwich:

930   I.   †LUTHER ANDERSON[6] born July 25, 1847; married, June 1, 1878, Ella Brewer.

931   II. ANSEL GIBBS[6] born June 18, 1849; married in Plymouth, 1871, Anna Vaughn; married, second, Mary Blaisdell of Lincoln, Mass., where they reside on a farm.

932   One child, Rosella,[6] born August 2, 1877.

933   III. †FRANK MILLARD[6] born July 25, 1851; married Josephine N. Foley.

934   IV. †CHARLES EVERETT[6] born September 27, 1853; married Ella Gibbs.

935   V.   ELLA JANE[6] born July 27, 1855; married William H. Brett. She died in Deerfield, N. H., November 5, 1882.

936   VI. †MARY MARTHA[6] born October 18, 1858; married Charles Sherman.

437. FREELOVE E.[5] DOUGLAS (John,[4] John,[3] John,[2] John,[1]) eldest daughter of John and Mehitable (Elliot) Douglas, born in Grantham, N. H., February 13, 1808; married, December 4, 1828, Nathan Mace, born in Tukesbury, Mass., May 24, 1801. He was a farmer and settled in Hartland, Vermont, where he resided until his death,

which occurred May 8, 1869; his widow lives with her brother William at Maidstone, Vt.

Their children, born in Hartland, Vt.:

937 I. ELIZABETH (Mace) born September 11, 1829; married William Clark, a farmer; he resided in Woodstock until his death.

938 II. NATHAN (Mace) born January 5, 1833; married Frances Perkins; he resides at Lancaster, N. H.; she died November 18, 1871.

939 III. CLARISSA (Mace) born June 20, 1846; married Norman A. Jenks; they reside in Orange, Michigan.

940 IV. DANIEL (Mace) born November 14, 1847; died October 14, 1852.

438. SARAH[5] DOUGLASS (John,[4] John,[3] John,[2] John,[1]) sister of the preceding, born in Grantham, N. H., March 1, 1813; married, May, 1843, Calvin, son of Caleb and Deborah (Harlow) Raymond, born February, 1793; they settled in Plymouth, Mass., where they resided until after the year 1854. They removed to Hyde Park and to Walpole, Mass. He died September 8, 1867; she died at Walpole about 1886.

Their children, born in Plymouth, Mass.:

941 I. SARAH VIOLA (Raymond) born April 5, 1849; married George A. Pierce; she died of consumption September 10, 1872, at Hyde Park.

942 II. DORA AMANDA (Raymond) born September 22, 1851; married Martin S. Smith.

943 III. SAMUEL TURNER (Raymond) born March 3, 1854.

439. JOHN[5] DOUGLASS (John,[4] John,[3] John,[2] John,[1]) brother of the preceding, born in Grantham, N. H., August 9, 1814; married, September 19, 1842, Cynthia, A., daughter of Warren and Rhoda Douglas [1001]. He settled in Hartland. Vt., where he resided nine years, and in March, 1852, removed to Northumberland, N. H., where he remained one year; then he bought a farm of one

hundred and thirty acres in the town of Lancaster, N. H. In 1859 he removed back to Hartland. In 1870 he removed and settled on a farm in Reading, Windsor County, Vermont, where he resided until his death. He and his wife died in 1887. There were only fifteen days between their deaths.

Their children:

944   I.   SETH[6] born in Hartland, Vt., January 7, 1844; died there January 14, 1844.

945   II.   †ALONZO[6] born in Hartland November 29, 1844; married Emma Evens.

946   III.   †NANCY AMANDA[6] born in Hartland August 7, 1846; married Levi Bishop.

947   IV.   JOHN WARREN[6] born in Hartland December 27, 1847; died December 20, 1867, of heart disease.

948   V.   †RHODA MEHITABLE[6] born in Hartland September 25, 1850; married Lyman B. Stoddard.

949   VI.   †ADDIE BESTEY[6] born in Northumberland, N. H., July 1, 1852; married Franklin Stoddard.

950   VII.   REUBEN SETH[6] born in Lancaster, N. H., November 16, 1853.

951   VIII.   †ANSEL MORRIS[6] born in LancasterMarch 19, 1856; married, February 9, 1876, Arvilla Davis, of Hartland, Vt.

952   IX.   MELVIN PHILANDER[6] born in Lancaster April 13, 1858.

953   X.   CYNTHIA ADELIA[6] born in Hartland January 20, 1860; married, George W. Mathews of Grandville, Vt; he is a blacksmith.

954   One child, ——— (Mathew) born October 19, 1878.

955   XI.   MARY ETTA[6] born in Hartland January 31, 1862.

956   XII.   CHARLES LINCOLN[6] born in Hartland November 5, 1863.

441.   REUBEN[5] DOUGLASS (John,[4] John,[3] John,[2] John,[1]) brother of the preceding, born in Grantham, N. H., April 9, 1820; married, August 18, 1844, Catherine A. Thomas, born March 25, 1821. They settled in school district No. 14, in the town of Woodstock, Vt.; he was a prosperous

farmer; he resided in Woodstock, Vt., where he died February 13, 1882.

Their children, born in Woodstock, Vt.:

957 I. Mary Diantha[6] born August 18, 1846; married, December 11, 1872, Austen Kingsley Leach; he is a farmer and resides in Woodstock, Vt.

958 II. †Julia Maria[6] born September 29, 1849; married Augustus P. Whitney.

959 III. Kate Meroa[6] born June 4, 1852; married Walter P. Darling.

960 One child, Walter E. (Darling) born February 12, 1882.

961 IV. Frank Leslie[6] born September 19, 1856; married, August 26, 1883, Nellie Moore. They reside at Cleveland, Ohio; they have two children, births and names not received.

442. William[5] Douglass (John,[4] John[3] John,[2] John,[1]) brother of the preceding, born in Hartland, Vt., January 23, 1827; married, first, February 22, 1851, Amanda Maria Douglas [458]. She died of consumption in Northumberland, N. H., June 11, 1853. He married, second, August 17, 1853, Hannah Stone, born in Lancester, N. H. Mr. Douglass is a prosperous farmer and resides at West Concord, Vt.

Their children :

962 I. †Maria A., born in Northumberland, N. H., May 17, 1852; married Henry D. Underwood.

Children of second wife :

963 II. Albert L., born September 29, 1854; married, December 3, 1881, Hattie Sanderson.

964 III. Charles Henry, born July 24, 1856; married, November 20, 1883, Carrie J. Taylor.

964½ One child, Pearl (Taylor) born February, 1887.

965 IV. Frank L., born April 18, 1858; married, June 24, 1882, Maggie M. Mitchell.

965½ One child, Abbie, born May 6, 1883;

966 V. William Edward, born April 27, 1860; married, December, 1885, Bessie E. Buchanan ; resides at West Concord, Vt.

966½ One child, Hattie E., born April 20, 1887.
  967 VI. FLORA D., born May 22, 1863; married, May 5, 1881, Frank F. Reed, farmer; she died June 16, 1884.
  968 VII. MARY L., born February 17, 1865; married William E. Ball; resides at West Concord, Vt.
  969 VIII. WALTER, born February 1, 1867.
  970 IX. HUBERT, twin, born in 1871.
  971 X. HERBERT, twin, born in 1871.
  972 XI. BLANCH, born June 6, 1875.
  973 XII. BERTHA A., born in Concord, Vt., May 20, 1878.

443. WILLIAM[5] DOUGLAS (Earl,[4] John,[3] John,[2] John,[1]) son of Earl and Mary (Raynols) Douglas, born in Augusta, Maine, August 14, 1820; married, May 20, 1845, Mary Clark Vaughn. He followed the sea for a living; on his way home from the Grand Banks, August, 1850, was drowned.

Their children, born in Plymouth, Mass:
  974 I. †WILLIAM L.,[6] born August 22, 1845; married, September 6, 1868, Naomi Augusta Terry.
  975 II. †MARY ANNIE,[6] born March 26, 1847; married Frank L. Moor.
  967 III. MAGGIE P.,[6] born August 5, 1848.
  977 IV. HATTIE P.,[6] born February 5, 1850; married, July 18, 1874, Sidney L. Morse; they reside at Brockton.

445. ELIZA[5] DOUGLASS (Earl,[4] John,[3] John,[2] John,[1]) sister of the preceding and daughter of Earl and Mary (Reynolds) Douglass, born in Augusta, Maine, March, 1824; married, January, 1847, Allen, son of Calvin and Polly Raymond, born December. 1823. They settled and always resided in Plymouth, Mass., where she died 1851.

  978 I. ALLEN LEWIS (Raymond) born in 1847.
  979 II. ELIZA FRANCES (Raymond) born in Plymouth, Mass., October 1851; died there 1872.

447. LUTHER[5] DOUGLASS (Warren,[4] John,[3] John,[2] John,[1]) son of Warren and Rhoda (Thrasher) Douglas,

born in Plymouth, Mass., October 13, 1810; married, April 16, 1834, Eliza Storms, born June 19, 1814. At the age of four years he, with his father's family, removed to the State of New York, where he resided until he was twenty-four years old. In 1853 he removed to Almond, Portage County, Wisconsin, where he has since lived; he has always followed farming.

Their children, all born in Taberg, Oneida County, N. Y., except the youngest:

 980 I. Maria S.,⁶ born March 6, 1835.
 981 II. Theodore," born April 28, 1836; died June 20, 1836.
 982 III. †Theodore Warren,⁶ born September 3, 1838; married Mary Ann Wannastrand.
 983 IV. Lodiac,⁶ born December 29, 1839.
 984 V. Charles Albert,⁶ born August 27, 1843. He enlisted in the 21st Regiment of Voluuteers, Company C. Wisconsin, in the rebellion and died while in the army, April 12, 1863.
 985 VI. Franklin Jay, born November 11, 1846; died March 13, 1847.
 986 VII. Emma Jane,⁶ born October 16, 1849.
 987 VIII. Polly Adaline,⁶ born March 8, 1850.
 988 IX. Franklin Jay,⁶ born February 28, 1854.
 989 X. Lilla Ann,⁶ born in Almond, Wisconsin, January 24, 1857.

448. Betsey⁵ Douglass (Warren,⁴ John³ John,² John.¹) daughter of Warren and Rhoda (Thrasher) Douglas, born in Plymouth, Mass., September 13, 1812; married, December 25, 1833, Caleb, son of Hugh and Jerusha Evans, born in Paris, Oneida County, New York; he was a farmer and settled in Amesville, N. Y. He died January 9, 1853, on board the steamer Tennessee on her passage to California. He was a worthy member of the Methodist church and much respected by those who knew him. His widow still resides at their old homestead.

Their children, born in Amesville, N. Y.:

THE DOUGLAS GENEALOGY. 161

990 I. LUTHER (Evans) born January 19, 1835; died September 29, 1851.

991 II. WARREN HUGH (Evans) born March 12, 1836.

992 III. RHODA JERUSHA (Evans) born March 26, 1838; married, June 24, 1854, Thomas B. Magood.

993 IV. GEORGE WASHINGTON (Evans) born August 6, 1843; died, September 8, 1862, from the effect of a wound received at the battle of Bull Run.

994 V. EMMA JANE (Evans) born in Lee, N. Y., May 30, 1848; married, October 11, 1865, Alonzo Douglass.

449. WARREN[5] DOUGLASS (Warren,[4] John,[3] John,[2] John,[1]) brother of the preceding and son of Warren and Rhoda (Thrasher) Douglas, born in Plymouth, Mass., July 9, 1814; married, February 11, 1836, Sally Storms, born March 22, 1818. He is a farmer.

Their children:

995 I. HARRIET[6] born April 21, 1839; died April 22, 1839.

996 II. MAYNARD H.[6] born October 11, 1840; died September 11, 1841.

997 III. †HARRIET AMANDA[6] born December 2, 1843; married, July 1, 1861, Charles Wilson.

998 IV. †ALBERT M.[6] born February 5, 1847; married Clara C. Hule.

999 V. SARAH A.[6] born November 12, 1848; married, January 1, 1868, Almon Perkins.

1000 VI. JENNIE M.[6] born January 5, 1860.

450. NANCY SWIFT[5] DOUGLASS (Warren,[4] John,[3] John[2] John,[1]) sister of the preceding, born in Lee, N. Y., March 24, 1816; married, April 24, 1834, Charles Evans, a brother to her sister Betsey's husband, born March 11, 1810. They settled and have since resided on a farm in Lee, Oneida County, New York; they are members of the Methodist Episcopal Church and enjoy the esteem of their many friends where they reside.

Their children, born in Lee, N. Y.:

1001 I. DANIEL FRANKLIN (Evans) born November 15, 1837; married, August 15, 1862, Adelaide Tupper.

1002 II. NATHAN (Evans) born January, 1840; died November 5, 1862.

1003 III. MARIAN (Evans) born August 22, 1843; died same day.

1004 IV. ELI HUGH (Evans) born December 1, 1847; died December 21, 1847.

1005 V. ALBERT MELVIN (Evans) born October 25, 1848; died December 2, 1849.

1006 VI. CHARLES WELLINGTON (Evans) born January 11, 1852; married, May 25, 1870, Adelia Lour.

453. JOHN EDWIN^5 DOUGLASS (Warren,^{4} John,^{3} John,^{2} John,^{1}) brother of the preceding and son of Warren and Rhoda (Thrasher) Douglas, born in Amesville, Oneida County, N. Y., October 4, 1821; married, January 8, 1842, Mary Chapman; he enlisted in the War of the Rebellion, was wounded in the battle at Fair Oaks and died June 1, 1862.

Their children:

1007 I. GEORGE HENRY^6 born in Woodstock, Vt., September 1847.

1008 II. NANCY^6 born about 1855.

1009 III. MARTHA^6 born about 1857.

1010 IV. AMY CYNTHIA^6 born about 1859.

454. PHILANDER^5 DOUGLASS (Warren,^{4} John,^{3} John,^{2} John,^{1}) brother of the preceding and son of Warren and Rhoda (Thrasher) Douglas, born in Amesville, Oneida Co., N. Y., July 8, 1823; married, July 6, 1843, Roxcinda Cornish, daughter of George and Mary (Setton) Cornish, born September 30, 1822. He is a farmer; he settled in Amesville, Oneida County, N. Y. By the birthplaces of his children it appears that he resided in four different towns in Oneida County. His wife died December 23, 1872.

Their children:

1011   I.   MARY JANE[6] born in Amesville, Onedia County, N. Y., September 14, 1844.

1012   II.   GEORGE WARREN[6] born in Lee, Oneida County, N. Y., October 15, 1848; died January 12, 1853.

1013   III.   WILLIAM MARCILOUS[6] born in Camden, Oneida Co., N. Y., September 12, 1852; died May 8, ——.

1014   IV.   FRANKLIN PORTER[6] born in Floyd, Oneida County, N. Y., February 3, 1857.

464.   ABIA[5] DOUGLASS (George,[4] John,[3] John,[2] John,[1]) eldest daughter of George and Eliza (Nightengale) Douglas, born in Plymouth, Mass., February 2, 1822; married, February 18, 1839, Branch, son of Branch and Rebecca Pierce. born April 16, 1815. They settled in Plymouth, where they resided for several years and then removed to Rochester, Mass., where she died October 20, 1848.

Their children:

1015   I.   BRANCH HENRY (Pierce) born in Plymouth, Mass., June 4, 1840; died in Plymouth June 2, 1844.

1016   II.   MARY THOMAS (Pierce) born in Plymouth January 8, 1842; married January 8, 1859; died February 11, 1865.

1017   III.   CAROLINE ELIZABETH (Pierce) born in Rochester, Mass., February 10, 1845; died there October 7, 1850.

1018   IV.   BRANCH HENRY (Pierce) born in Rochester, February 4, 1848; married November 27, 1870.

466.   ELIZA ANN[5] DOUGLASS (George,[4] John,[3] John,[2] John,[1]) sister of the preceding and daughter of George and Eliza Douglas, born at Half-way Pond, Plymouth, Mass., April 25, 1824; married, August 15, 1850, Charles Henry Winship, born January 1, 1821; they settled in Monument, Mass. In 1855 they moved to Grafton, N. H., and finally removed back to Monument, where he died, May 9, 1862. She married for her second husband, May 4, 1864, Moses Gibbs Bumpus, son of Edward and

Lucy (Hill) Bumpus, born in South Carver, Mass., July 15, 1822; they reside in Monument, Mass.

One child by first marriage:

1019 I. JULIA ANN (Winship) born in Monument April 5, 1851.

468. MARTHA PIERCE[5] DOUGLASS (George,[4] John,[3] John,[2] John,[1]) sister of the preceding, born in Plymouth, Mass., June 10, 1828; married, first, February 11, 1846, Phineas Swift, born in Plymouth, Mass., April 14, 1823. He was a seaman and resided during the greater part of his life in his native town, where he died October 4, 1855. Mrs. Swift married, second, October 31, 1858, John P. Barrows. He is a farmer and they reside at East Wareham, Mass.

Children, all by first husband, born in Plymouth, except eldest:

1020 I. SARAH FRANCES (Swift) born in Sandwich, Mass., Dec. 14, 1846; married, 1864, William Manter, son of Prince and Lydia (Douglas) Manter of Plymouth.

1021 II. NEHEMIAH GIPSON (Swift) born July 21, 1848; he is a moulder by trade.

1022 III. ELLEN MARIA (Swift) born October 14, 1851; married, 1869, Daniel Nickerson of Nova Scotia; she died November 29, 1873 and was buried in Plymouth.

1023 IV. RUTH BRIANT (Swift) born November 8, 1852.

1024 V. PHINEAS (Swift) born November 20, 1854.

469. MARIA E.[5] DOUGLASS, (George,[4] John,[3] John,[2] John,[1]) sister of the preceding born in Plymouth, Mass., July 26, 1834; married, February 16, 1854, Abner Ellis, son of Bartlett and Maria Ellis of West Sandwich, Mass., where he was born March 12, 1829. He is a farmer and settled in his native town; then moved to Monument, Mass. He subsequently returned to West Sandwich, where they have since resided. Mr. Ellis died May 12, 1885.

Their children, all born in West Sandwich, except the third:

1025 I. EMILY FRANCES (Ellis) born January 23, 1858.
1026 II. LIZZIE JENNETTE (Ellis) born August 26, 1859.
1027 III. WINFIELD EVERETT (Ellis) born in Monument, Mass., May 25, 1866.
1028 IV. REBECCA HOWLAND (Ellis) born May 22, 1869.
1029 V. FRANKLIN BARTLETT (Ellis) born March 9, 1872.

470. ANDREW JACKSON[5] DOUGLASS (George,[4] John,[3] John,[2] John,[1]) brother of the preceding and son of George and Eliza (Nightengail) Douglas, born in Plymouth, Mass., December 13, 1835; married, December 11, 1865, Priscilla H. Manter, daughter of William and Huldah R. (Raymond) Manter, born January 4, 1847; he is a farmer and resides on the same farm that his grandfather and father owned and occupied in Plymouth.

Their children, born in Plymouth, Mass.:

1030 I. CLARABEL MAY[6] born September 13, 1866.
1031 II. LILLIAN ELIZA[6] born November 10, 1865.
1032 III. GEORGE ALFRED[6] born March 26, 1872.

473. JESSE P.[5] DOUGLASS (Joshua,[4] John,[3] John,[2] John,[1]) eldest son of Joshua and Mary S. (Pierce) Douglas, born in Plymouth, Mass., July 24, 1814; married, January 24, 1839, Roxanna Manter. In his younger days he followed fishing at the Banks for several years; later he was engaged in the oyster business. He died at his home in East Wareham, October 15, 1889.

Their children:

1033 I. ROXANNA F.[6] born November 11, 1840; married, 1864, J. H. Burgess; she died in 1882.
1034 II. †JESSE P.[6] born December 5, 1845; married Maria Benson.
1035 III. SUSAN F.[6] born January 5, 1852; married Elliot Blackwell of Bourne, Mass., where they reside.
1036 IV. NANCY M.[6] born October 16, 1857; married, first,

—— White; second, Wm. Ackerman; they reside at Stoughton Center, Mass.

474. ELISHA[5] DOUGLAS (Joshua,[4] John,[3] John,[2] John[1]) brother of the preceding, born in Plymouth, Mass., August 12, 1816; married, December 31, 1840, Susan P. King, daughter of William and Huldah (Battles) King, born July 23, 1821. At the age of seventeen he went cod-fishing, which business he followed twenty-seven summers; he was engaged during the winter months in chopping cord wood, having chopped two thousand cords; he has killed seventy-five deer in the Plymouth woods; he had a pleasant residence near the Half-way Pond in Plymouth, where he lived until November, 1873, when he and his family removed and settled in Plymouth Village; he died at his home March 26, 1889. The following card was published and forwarded to friends and relatives:

In loving memory of
Elisha Douglas.
Died March 26, 1889,
Aged 72 years, 7 mos., 14 days.

A precious one from us has gone,
A voice we loved is stilled;
A place is vacant in our home
Which never can be filled.
God in his wisdom has recalled
The boon his love has given,
And though the body slumber here
The soul is safe in Heaven.

Their children, born in Plymouth, Mass:

1037 I. SUSAN M.[6] born October 14, 1841; died in Plymouth August 13, 1844.

1038 II. †EMILY S.[6] born November 14, 1843; married Pelham Sampson.

1039 III. ELLEN D.[6] born December 25, 1846; married, Nov. 2, 1885, Jahaziel J. Howard of Fair Haven, Mass. Mr. Howard has spent twenty-four years of his life in China where he was engaged in the commission business, with which he is still connected. They reside with Mrs. Howard's mother at Plymouth, Mass.

1040 IV. †ELISHA T. P.[6] born October 22, 1851; married, April 14, 1873, Evvie A. Barrett; married, second, Annie Reamy.

475. WILLIAM MANTER DOUGLAS (Joshua,[4] John,[3] John,[2] John,[1]) brother of the preceding, born in Plymouth, Mass., March 15, 1819; married, March 28, 1847, Sarepta Pierce, daughter of Dennis and Melintha Pierce of Rochester, Mass., born there June 18, 1828. In 1847 he bought a farm in Rochester, for which he paid the sum of three hundred and fifty dollars. The house was so dilapidated that it had to be taken down and another built in its place; he works on his farm and a portion of the time in a stave mill; he is an honest, upright man and is much esteemed in the community where he lives.

Children born in Rochester, Mass.:

1041 I. †CLARA F.[6] born April 23, 1851; married, July 24, 1869, Thomas W. Gault.

1042 II. JOSHUA E.[6] born June 18, 1855; married, December 25, 1878, Ida M. Pierce; he works in a nail factory in Rochester, Mass.

1042½ One child, Mabel F., born February 15, 1881.

1043 III. †MARIA L.[6] born January 31, 1857; married, first, Frank W. Ryan; second, Albert W. West.

1044 IV. JULIA E.[6] born January 13, 1863; married, November 23, 1881, Edward F. Handy, Jr.

1045 One child, Sarah E. (Handy) born June 4, 1882.

476. MARY[5] DOUGLASS (Joshua,[4] John,[3] John,[2] John,[1]) sister of the preceding and only daughter of Joshua and Mary S. Pierce Douglas, born in Plymouth, Mass., May 16, 1822; married, December 31, 1839, the Hon. Thomas Pierce, son of Thomas and Nancy (Freeman) Pierce, born in West Wareham, Mass., May 25, 1820. When a lad he learned the trade of making nails. In 1837 he went to Half-way Pond, so called, in the town of Plymouth,

where he learned to make nail casks and subsequently set up in the business for himself, which he continued to follow until within a few years, acquiring a handsome fortune and giving employment to a large number of men in that vicinity. In 1851 he received the appointment of Justice of the Peace, which commission has been renewed as often as it run out, up to the present time. In 1863 he was elected to represent his town in the State Legislature which office he filled so satisfactorily that he was re-elected the following year. He is a professor of religion and an exhorter of much worth and ability; he now resides at Plymouth Village.

Their children, born in Plymouth, Mass.:

1046 I. JERARD (Pierce) born February 20, 1845; died February 20, 1845.

1047 II. MARY S. (Pierce) born October 6, 1846; married, January 24, 1866, Coleman B. Chandler.

1048 III. PHILIP R. W. (Pierce) born April 18, 1848; married, November 16, 1871, Laura L. Washburn; they resided in East Wareham, where he died October 20, 1877.

1049 IV. LAURA A. (Pierce) born November 12, 1850; married, January 2, 1871, Thomas G. Savery; they reside in their native town.

1050 V. SARAH T. (Pierce) born March 8, 1853.

1051 VI. CHARLES M. (Pierce) born July 3, 1856.

1052 VII. THOMAS J. (Pierce) born January 4, 1860; died July 17, 1862.

1053 VIII. NELLIE A. C. (Pierce) born December 1, 1867.

477.　NATHAN KING[5] DOUGLASS (Joshua,[4] John,[3] John[2] John,[1]) brother of the preceding, born in Plymouth, Mass., December 24, 1824; married, November 28, 1851, Angeline, daughter of Jonathan and Cynthia Thrasher, born April 10, 1832. Soon after their marriage he bought a farm in Plymouth, on which he lived a few years, but not liking farming for a business, he sold his farm and removed to Half-way Pond, where he resided in the house with his brother Warren and resumed his former occupation of sawing staves. In 1874 he built himself a house in Plymouth Village, where he resided until his death, which occurred February 21, 1885.

Children, born in Plymouth, Mass.:

1054 I. NATHAN WINSLOW[6] born January 22, 1852; married, September 7, 1881, Nellie Manter; resides at Plymouth.

1055 II. CHARLES EVERETT,[6] born January 28, 1855; married, November 7, 1878, Mercy Holbrook. They reside at Plymouth.

1056 III. HENRY LEWIS,[6] born May 28, 1868.

1057 IV. ELMER EDWARD,[6] born February 9, 1871.

478. WARREN SOUTHWORTH[5] DOUGLASS (Joshua,[4] John,[3] John,[2] John,[1]) brother of the preceding, born in Plymouth, Mass., March 29, 1827; married, December 14, 1854, Lydia W. Manter, daughter of Prince and Lydia (Douglas) Manter, born in Plymouth, Mass., November 21, 1839. At the age of twenty-one he went to sea, which business he followed summers and during the winter months he stopped at home and worked in the stave mill. His leisure hours were devoted to hunting, trapping and fishing, which pursuit afforded him much enjoyment as well as some remuneration. His wife died at Half-way Pond, Plymouth, July 31, 1885.

Their children, born in Plymouth:

1058 I. JAMES WARREN,[6] born February 8, 1855; married, November 26, 1878, L. Ella Holmes, of Wareham, Mass. He died January 14, 1880.

1059 II. ALBERT,[6] born June 1, 1857; died June 22, 1857.

1060 III. WILLIAM,[6] born September 18, 1859; died——

1061 IV. LUCY ELIZABETH,[6] born October 22, 1862; married, March, 1880, Martin Powers, of Sandwich, Mass.

1062 V. GEORGE F.,[6] born August 2, 1865; died August 14, 1865.

1063   VI. GEORGE WATSON,[6] born December 22, 1868. Resides on the homestead.

479. MARTIN VAN BUREN[5] DOUGLASS (Joshua,[4] John,[3] John,[2] John,[1]) brother of the preceding, born in Plymouth, Mass., February 9, 1837; married, April 14, 1858, Laura A. B. Swift, daughter of Isaac B. and Abigail N. (Raymond) Swift, born November 29, 1838; he settled on the old homestead in Plymouth, residing in the family with his father since his marriage; he is engaged in farming and teaming; he is a man of very steady and industrious habits and has laid by a few hundred dollars for old age; he is kind and charitable to the needy and of a cheerful temperament; his wife is justly entitled to be classed with the smart women of New England, as she picked with her hands, in one day, a barrel of cranberries.

They have one child, born in Plymouth:

1064   MARTIN ALONZO, born January 31, 1866.

480. JOSHUA ALONZO[5] DOUGLASS (Joshua,[4] John,[3] John,[2] John,[1]) brother of the preceding and youngest son of Joshua and Mary S. (Pierce) Douglas, born in Plymouth, Mass., December 4, 1840; married, February 23, 1868, Lucy P. Raymond; they reside in Plymouth Village, where he is janitor at the Court House.

Their children, born in Plymouth Mass.:

1065   I. ALFRED N., twin, born January 31, 1871.
1066   II. EDWARD A., twin, born January 31, 1871.
1066½ III. HOWARD MARTIN, born August 3, 1876.

489. HARRIET GROVES[5] DOUGLASS (Elisha,[4] John,[3] John,[2] John,[1]) eldest daughter of Elijah and Louisa (Freeman) Douglass; married, 1859, Ezra Freeman, farmer, born August 18, 1836. They reside at Red Oak, Iowa.

Their children:

1067 I. WILLIAM (Freeman) born in Clintonville, N. Y., August 18, 1862; died September 7, 1862.

1068 II. CARRIE MAY (Freeman) born in Black River, N. Y., May 4, 1865.

1069 III. ARTHUR H. (Freeman) born in Black Eagle Point, Ill., November 20, 1868; died there July 24, 1869.

1070 IV. ALBERT E. (Freeman) born at Red Oak, Iowa, January 7, 1874; died August 14, 1874.

491. ELIZA ANN[5] DOUGLASS (Elijah,[4] John,[3] John,[2] John,[1]) sister of the preceding and daughter of Elijah and Louisa Douglass, born at Steens, N. Y., May 31, 1840; married, 1856, Harvey Stanton.

Children:

1071 I. JOHN WILBUR (Stanton) born in Lewis, N. Y., 1857.

1072 II. WILLIAM WESLEY (Stanton) born in Franklin, N. Y., 1860.

1073 III. FREDERICK (Stanton) born in Franklin, 1867.

1074 IV. MERRITT (Stanton) born in Franklin, 1869.

495. DAVID CASWELL[5] DOUGLASS (Absalom,[4] Elisha,[3] John,[2] John,[1]) son of Absalom and Realfy (Caswell) Douglass, born in Shelba, Genesee Co., New York, November 15, 1821; married, April 8, 1849, Maria Heath; he is a farmer and resides in Janesville, Minnesota.

Their children, born in Wisconsin:

1075 I. MARY O.,[6] born in Walworth County, Wisconsin, February 6, 1850.

1076 II. GEORGE E.,[6] born in Waushara County, September 6, 1859.

1077 III. CARRIE MAY,[6] born in Waushara County, August 14, 1863.

496. JOHN BRAILEY[5] DOUGLASS (Absalom,[4] Elisha,[3] John,[2] John,[1]) brother of the preceding and son of Absalom and Realfy (Caswell) Douglas, born in Shelba, Genesee County, New York, April 3, 1824; married, November 25, 1846, Louisa Greenslick.

Their children:

1078 I. BETSEY L.,⁶ born in Waushara County, Wisconsin, October 26, 1849.
1079 II. ABSALOM G.,⁶ born in Elysian, Minn., January 29, 1851.
1080 III. JOHN E.,⁶ born in Elysian, January 20, 1860.
1081 IV. CHARLES,⁶ born May 2, 1862; died April 28, 18—

500. LUCY ELIZABETH⁵ DOUGLASS (Absalom,⁴ Elisha,³ John,² John,¹) sister of the preceding, born in Monroe, State of Maine, July 17, 1830; married, December 29, 1849, William Patching.

Their children:

1082 I. REALFY (Patching) born in Rossie, St. Lawrence Co., N. Y., December 20, 1848.
1083 II. ALMIRA (Patching) born in Plainfield, Wis., December 20, 1859.
1084 III. EMILY (Patching) born in Plainfield, Wis., August 23, 1860.
1085 IV. WILLIAM A. (Patching) born in Plainfield, Wis., August 29, 1862.
1086 V. THOMAS P. (Patching) born in Janesville, Minn., November 23, 1865.

501. EMILY⁵ DOUGLASS (Absalom,⁴ Elisha,³ John,² John,¹) sister of the preceding and daughter of Absalom and Realfy (Caswell) Douglas, born in Bakerfield, Vt., July 26, 1832; married, October 16, 1852, Andrew J. Patching.

Their children:

1087 I. SARAH E. (Patching) born in Waushara County, Wis., February 16, 1863.
1088 II. HIRAM P. (Patching) born in Waushara County, January 22, 1866.

502. HIRAM⁵ DOUGLASS (Absalom,⁴ Elisha,³ John,² John,¹) brother of the preceding and son of Absalom and Realfy (Caswell) Douglas, born in Dickinson, Franklin

County, New York, January 22, 1835; married, December 25, 1851, Elizabeth Jordan.

Their children:

1089 I. ALBION,[6] born in Plainfield, Waushara County, Wis., March 9, 1858.

1090 II. DAVID,[6] twin, born in Plainfield, March 16, 1861.

1091 III. HENRY,[6] twin, born in Plainfield, March 16, 1861.

1092 IV. MERRILLA,[6] born in Waseca County, Minn., September 21, 1863.

1093 V. ROSELLA,[6] born in Hambolt, Iowa, December 20, 1870.

1094 VI. WALTER,[6] born in Hambolt, January 14, 1874.

503. CHARLOTTE ADLEA[5] DOUGLASS (Absalom,[4] Elisha,[3] John,[2] John,[1]) sister of the preceding, born in Dickinson, Franklin County, New York, October 10, 1837; married, January 30, 1856, Rev. B. F. Kelley; they reside at Waushara County, Wisconsin.

Their children, all born in Waushara County, Wisconsin, except the youngest:

1095 I. LAURA A. (Kelley) born November 29, 1857.

1096 II. L. R. (Kelley) born September 22, 1858.

1097 III. LUCY A. (Kelley) born October 8, 1860.

1098 IV. MARY E. (Kelley) born January 14, 1861.

1099 V. AMANDA A. (Kelley) born November 22, 1862.

1100 VI. VIOLA A. (Kelley) born March 6, 1864.

1101 VII. BENJAMIN F. (Kelley) born in Lewiston, Minnesota, July 22, 1867.

506. SARAH ANN[5] DOUGLASS (Absalom,[4] Elisha,[3] John,[2] John,[1]) sister of the preceding and daughter of Absalom and Realfy (Caswell) Douglas, born in Dickinson, Franklin County, New York, May 20, 1841; married, February 18, 1862, Charles H. Jordan; they settled in Okeaman, Waseca County, Minn.: removed to Janesville in same State.

Their children:

1102 I. CHARLES E. (Jordan) born in Waseca County, Minn., December 13, 1863.

1103 II. ALICE (Jordan) born in Waseca County, Minn., June 19, 1865.

1104 III. THERSA L. (Jordan) born in Janesville, Minn., February 24, 1871.

1105 IV. LILLIAN L. (Jordan) born in Janesville, January 18, 1874.

549. HANNAH[5] DOUGLASS (Hiram Russell,[4] Elisha,[3] John,[2] John,[1]) daughter of Hiram Russell and Fanny (Twambly) Douglas, born in Lowell, Maine, February 21, 1839; married, first, 1859, Alonzo Curtis; he was a farmer and resided in Lowell, where he died August 9, 1864; she married, second, April 28, 1866, Thomas R. McKinney who is also a farmer and resides in Lowell.

Their children, all born in Lowell, Maine, by first husband:

1106 I. HIRAM (Curtis) born July 4, 1860; died August 9, 1862.

1107 II. DAVID (Curtis) born November 3, 1861; died Nov. 15, 1863.

1108 III. ALONZO (Curtis) born December 25, 1863; died March, 1864.

Children by second marriage:

1109 IV. LEFORIST (McKenney) born January 27, 1867.

1110 V. HIRAM W. (McKenney) born October 3, 1868.

1111 VI. FANNY (McKenney) born August 3, 1869.

1112 VII. THOMAS E. (McKenny) born June 27, 1872.

550. BETSEY[5] DOUGLASS (Hiram Russell,[4] Elisha,[3] John,[2] John,[1]) sister of the preceding, born in Lowell, February 2, 1839; married, November 25, 1858, Philemon Curtis, a brother to Alonzo, her sister Hannah's first husband. He is a farmer and resides in Lowell.

Their children, born in Lowell :

1113   I.   MARY JANE (Curtis) born March 25, 1860.
1114   II. CHARLES NELSON (Curtis) born May 13, 1862.
1115   III. HORACE (Curtis) born September 23, 1864.
1116   IV. HIRAM HERBERT (Curtis) born June 3, 1867.

551. CALBERT DANIEL[5] DOUGLASS (Hiram,[4] Elisha,[3] John,[2] John,[1]) brother of the preceding and son of Hiram R. and Fanny (Twambly) Douglas, born in Lowell, Maine, August 3, 1843; married, September, 1866, Lovina McHenry, born in Lincoln, 1845 ; he is a farmer and resides in the town of Lincoln, Maine.

Their children, born in Lincoln:

1117   I. HERBERT CHANDLER[6] born June 8, 1868.
1118   II. GEORGE CHRISTOPHER[6] born September 4, 1870.

552. MARY EMILY[5] DOUGLASS (Hiram,[4] Elisha[3] John[2] John,[1]) sister of the preceding and daughter of Hiram and Fanny (Twambly) Douglas, born in Lowell, Maine, July 4, 1847; married, July 27, 1868, Prince Albert Hall ; he is a farmer and resides in the town of Lincoln.

Their children, born in Lincoln:

1119   I. HIRAM GRANT (Hall) born March 27, 1870.
1120   II. EUGENE (Hall) born October 4, 1872.

556. CAROLINE S.[5] DOUGLASS (Barnabas N.,[4] George,[3] George,[2] John,[1]) daughter of Barnabas N. and Phebe N. (Swift) Douglas, born in Rochester, Mass , August 8, 1830; married, January 2, 1853, Emery Cushman ; he was a box manufacturer at Acushnet, Mass., where they resided ; Mr. Cushman died April, 1884.

Their children :

1121   I. JULIA L. (Cushman) born in Providence, R. I. September 25, 1853 ; married Mr. Gardiner ; she died January 6, 1887, leaving one child.

1122 II. Carrie D. (Cushman) born in Providence, R. I., Oct. 25, 1856 ; married, June, 1886, Silas Pope.

1123 III. Henry (Cushman) born in Acushnet, Mass., February 20, 1859; married, October 29, 1885, Frances Russell Eldridge of Acushnet, Mass.

1124 IV. Emery (Cushman) born in Acushnet, October 13, 1866.

560. Moses Swift[4] Douglass (Barnabas N.,[4] George[3] George,[2] John,[1]) brother of the preceding, born in Rochester, Mass., March 21, 1837; married, first, December 18, 1864, Emeline F., daughter of Consider Smith of Acushnet, Mass.; she died in her native town December 10, 1871. He married, second, September 14, 1873, Sylvia H. Stevens of Fairhaven, Mass. She died at Acushnet, January 14, 1885.

Children by first wife, born in Acushnet, Mass.:
1125 I. Edgar Emerson[6] born June 4, 1867.
1126 II. Walter Franklin[6] born August 1869.

Child by second marriage :
1127 III. Myron Erle[6] born August 15, 1874.

561. Capt. George H.[5] Douglass, (Barnabas N.,[4] George,[3] George,[2] John,[1]) brother of the preceding; born in Rochester, Mass., March 1, 1837 ; married, January 27, 1865, Jane M. Mendell. She died February 17, 1873. He married for his second wife, August 25, 1879, Alice Estelle Lindsay.

His boyhood was spent at home on the farm till the year 1854 : when seventeen years of age he sailed from New Bedford in the whale ship Roman, before the mast, in which he remained six years, returning home after the second voyage as second mate.

In 1860 he went mate of the schooner Cyclone from New York to Portugal, Spain and South America and thence to Scotland and England, bringing a cargo of coal to Providence, R. I.

The next few years he made several voyages as second mate until 1869, when he went as first mate on a vessel sailing from Yokohama to Shanghai, remaining one year. He then went to San Francisco and for three years served on the Panama Line. He was master of the steamer Pacific, which was lost after he took command of the Mohongo, which ran on the coast of California as far south as San Diego. The Pacific Mail, in whose employ he had served eleven years, sold out their line of steamers that ran south, and for two years he was in the employment of the California State Navigation Company as master of the Montana, which ran between San Francisco and Mexican ports and the Colorado River. They sailed on the night of December 17, 1876, and as Capt. Douglass was going to his room discovered fire coming from the after ventilation. Alarm was sounded and immediately they turned the vessel and headed for land. They threw over seventy packages of powder. In ten minutes the ship was one mass of flames. The crew, together with forty soldiers and officers, fought the fire bravely, but of no avail. They ran the ship ashore and at one o'clock in the morning the fore and mainmasts burned and fell over. A crew was sent up to the harbor of Guaymas, where the American Consul sent them relief.

Capt. D. then went overland to San Francisco and in twenty-four hours after his arrival the company put him in command of the steamer Idaho. He left the service of this Company to go east and on his return built, in March 1878, the schooner Rosario, which carried 260 tons cargo and sailed the first voyage in June for Mexico. After making several voyages he sold the schooner to John D.

Spreckles & Bros., of San Francisco, and accepted the position of superintendent of their vessels and steamers, which he now faithfully fills. The Speckles have lately purchased a brig which they placed under the Hawaiian flag and in honor of their faithful employee named her the "George H. Douglass."

Child by first marriage:

1128 I. GEORGE[6] born at Acushnet, Mass., December 20, 1866.

562. PAMELIA C.[5] DOUGLAS (Barnabas N.[4] George,[3] George,[2] John,[1]) sister of the preceding, born in Rochester, Mass., July 1, 1840; married, October 23, 1859. Capt. James R. Allen, born July 30, 1818. He commenced going to sea when only thirteen years of age and continued to follow the business for a livelihood for many years; he made many whaling voyages, in which he was very successful, enabling him to lay by a handsome competence. They reside at Acushnet, Mass.

Their children:

1129. I. JOSEPHINE CHATMAN (Allen) born September 24, 1860; married, December 20, 1886, James L. Humphrey, Jr.

1130 II. SARAH JANE (Allen) born November 27, 1862; married, May 2, 1882, Joseph T. Leonard.

1131 III. JAMES EDWIN (Allen) born October 11, 1865.

1132 IV. MELLIE DOUGLASS (Allen) born February 26, 1872.

1133 IV. LESLIE CHAPMAN (Allen) born August 22, 1874.

563. JAMES OSCAR[5] DOUGLASS (Barnabas Nye,[4] George[3] George,[2] John[1]) brother of the preceding and son of Barnabas N. and Phebe N. (Swift) Douglas, born in Rochester, Mass., August 12, 1843; married, February 12, 1870, Emma Elwood, daughter of Charles M. and Emma M. Blackman; born in Rochester September 4, 1850; she died March 1, 1880; he married for his second wife, August 24, 1882, Sarah Clark, daughter of Peleg W. and

Sarah S. Clark, born March 23, 1851; he resided on his father's homestead and cared for his parents during their lifetime. He now resides at New Bedford.

One child by first marriage:

1134   I.   MABEL B., born August 20, 1877.

564.   EDWIN DELAS[5] DOUGLASS (Barnabas N.,[4] George,[3] George,[2] John,[1]) brother of the preceding and son of Barnabas and Phebe N. (Swift) Douglass, born in Rochester, Mass., April 17, 1845; married, October 11, 1870, Louisa Davis, daughter of John R. and Abbie Leavitt Davis of Acushnet; he resides in Philadelphia and carries on the business of manufacturing packing boxes of all kinds; his wife died November 8, 1885; January 26, 1887, he married for his second wife Rebecca Rhodes Ruedi, daughter of George W. and Susan Ruedi, born in Reading, Pa., March 16, 1864.

Children by first marriage:

1135   I.   EDWIN ALLEN, born in Acushnet, Mass., December 20, 1874.

1136   II.   LOUISA ESTELLE, born in Philadelphia, March 25, 1881; died July 25, 1882.

565.   MARY ANN[5] DOUGLASS (Barnabas N.,[4] George,[3] George,[2] John,[1]) sister of the preceding, born in Rochester, Mass., December 26, 1847; married, May 26, 1866, Samuel Wing, son of Levi and Rachel Wing of Acushnet, where he was born October 2, 1842.

Their children, born in Acushnet, Mass.;

1137   I.   HAROLD CLIFTON (Wing) born May 11, 1869.

1138   II.   CHESTER BRAINARD (Wing) born September 29, 1870. He was thrown from a carriage and so severely injured that he died September 4, 1888.

1139   III. ALFRED BOARDMAN (Wing) born March 27, 1875.

567. CHARLES ALBERT[5] DOUGLASS (Barnabas N.,[4] George,[3] George,[2] John,[1]) youngest son of Barnabas N. and Phebe N. (Swift) Douglass, born in Rochester, Mass., October 26, 1853; married, December 31, 1878, Ella C. Hoagland, daughter of Elijah H. and Emeline S. Hoagland; he lived at home on the farm with his parents, where he received his education at the district school. Previous to his marriage he spent a few years in Philadelphia, working with his brother Edwin manufacturing packing boxes; he now resides in his native town, where he is engaged in the milling business.

They have one child:
1140 I. EDITH MAY[6] born at Philadelphia, September 18, 1880.

SIXTH GENERATION.

619. ELVIRA JANE[6] DOUGLAS (Abijah,[5] John,[4] Cornelius,[3] Elijah,[2] John,[1]) daughter of Abijah and Phebe (Estes) Douglas, born in Hebron, December 31, 1816; married, May 31, 1840, Dudley Bean, born June 6, 1816, son of Israel and Betsey (Payn) Bean of Jay; he was a farmer in his lifetime; resided in his native town; she died September, 1885.

Children born in Jay:

1141 I. MARCIA ANNA (Bean) born August 4, 1841; married, March 8, 1878, Samuel H. Leighton of Philips.

1142 II. ABIJAH LAFAYETTE (Bean) born November 16, 1842; he resides in California.

1143 III. MARY AUGUSTA (Bean) born September 15, 1844; married, August 3, 1866, George H. Bean; resides at Canton.

1144 IV. RHODA ALICE (Bean) born August 2, 1846; married, December 11, 1882, Frank H. Russell; resides in Everett, Mass.

1145 V. PHEBE FRANCES (Bean) born April 7, 1849; married Ferdinand Jordan of Lewiston.

1146 VI. HARRISON DUDLEY (Bean) born May 20, 1850; married, October 16, 1871, Emma L. Richardson of Jay.

1147 VII. LYDIA EMMA (Bean) born April 10, 1852; married, March 15, 1887, William M. Halley; reside in Farmington.

1148 VIII. ELLA JANE (Bean) born February 23, 1855; married, February 23, 1886, Alvah O. Moulton; he is a farmer and resides in Parsonfield.

1149 IX. CLARA MELISSA (Bean) born January 2, 1857; married George E. Lowell; they reside on a farm in Farmington.

1150 X. ELIZA SMALL (Bean) born December 2, 1858; married Greenleaf M. Walton; they reside on a farm in Wilton.

620. WILLIAM ESTES[6] DOUGLAS (Abijah,[5] John,[4] Cornelius,[3] Elijah,[2] John,[1]) brother of the preceding and only son of Abijah and Phebe (Estes) Douglas, born in Dixfield, May 15, 1819; married, February 3, 1848, Mahala Tucker, born October 31, 1824; he has always followed farming for a livelihood; he is honest and upright in all his dealings and much respected in the community where he resides; his wife died September 11, 1879.

Their children, born in Dixfield:

1151 I. ALBION L. born October 11, 1848.
1152 II. MARION, born September 29, 1849.
1153 III. HERBERT, born March 29, 1851; died February 23, 1866.
1154 IV. RUFUS, born August 30, 1855.
1155 V. ISABEL, born July 15, 1859.
1156 VI. EFFIE S., born November 18, 1862.
1157 VII. DAISY H., born February 26, 1864.

621. RHODA COOMBS[6] DOUGLAS (Abijah,[5] John,[4] Cornelius,[3] Elijah,[2] John,[1]) sister of the preceding, born in Dixfield July 10, 1821; married John Tarr, born October 1818; he died in the Army of the Rebellion November 3, 1863; she married, second, Jonathan W. Forsaith, December 20, 1874; Mr. Forsaith died December 25, 1884; she resides at her home in Brunswick.

Children born in Brunswick;

1158 I. ABBIE JANE (Tarr) born November 16, 1845; married M. Grant, who died during the Rebellion.
1159 II. GEORGE (Tarr) born October 5, 1847; married Flora E. Hallowell; they reside at Livermore Falls.
1160 III. WILLIAM A. (Tarr) born September 21, 1849; married, Hattie B. Locke; she died June 8, 1880; he married, second, Lucy A. Locke, his first wife's sister; they reside in Lewiston; he is Road Master on Maine Central Railroad.
1161 IV. JOHN F. (Tarr) born July 6, 1853, married Lizzie F. Hutchinson; he died November 11, 1881.

1162 V. MARSHAL M. (Tarr) born January 16, 1855; married Belle Pickens; he is conductor on the Maine Central Railroad.
1163 VI. LEONARD M. (Tarr) born November 19, 1858; married M. Gertrude Davis; he is a graduate of Bates College; is now in the U. S. Signal Service.
1164 VII. HENRY C. (Tarr) born April 21, 1861; he was a school teacher; he died November 28, 1887.

Child by second marriage :
1165 VIII. ANNIE L. FORSAITH, born March, 1885.

640. IVORY WARREN[6] DOUGLAS (Paul,[5] Edward,[4] Cornelius,[3] Elijah,[2] John,[1]) son of Paul and Nancy Warren Douglass, born in Durham, March 13, 1828; married, March 13, 1851, Margaret Guilford, he is a house joiner; he is in trade in Dover, where they reside.

Children born in Dover:
1166 I. MELISSA A., born December 19, 1851; died ———
1167 II. IDA MAY, born October 13, 1855; married in Dover, July 21, 1877, Arthur J. Lansin of Bangor; she died August 25, 1877.
1168 III. HATTIE M., born September 17, 1857.
1169 IV. ANNIE M., born May 28, 1859.

641. HARRIET JANE[6] DOUGLAS (Paul,[5] Edward,[4] Cornelius,[3] Elijah,[2] John,[1]) sister of the preceding, was born in Durham October 3, 1831; married, January 5, 1852, John C. Gerry; farmer, resides in Dover.

Children born in Dover:
1170 I. WILLIAM W. (Gerry) born October 22, 1852.
1171 II. SUSAN E. (Gerry) born February 10, 1854.
1172 III. GERALD A. (Gerry) born October 22, 1860.

642. AMANDA[6] DOUGLAS (Paul,[5] Edward,[4] Cornelius,[3] Elijah,[2] John,[1]) sister of the preceding; was born in Durham May 14, 1834; married, March 21, 1863, Frederick Hutchinson of Dover. He settled on a farm in the town of Eastern, Aroostook County; he was a kind husband and an affectionate father; he became deranged and fearing

that he would come to want, November 3, 1882, he killed his wife and then took his own life. It is presumed that he intended to have taken the lives of the whole family but the two children escaped.

Children born in Dover:

1173   I.   LILLIAN A. (Hutchinson) born November 16, 1867; married, March 21, 1883, Wallace Lafayett Bowe.

1174   II.   ERNEST EUGENE (Hutchinson) born September 15, 1869.

652.   CHARLES FRANCIS[6] DOUGLAS (John,[5] Edward,[4] Cornelius,[3] Elijah,[2] John,[1]) son of John and Charity Page (Coombs) Douglass; was born in Brunswick November 4, 1833; married, September 18, 1860, Martha Ann, daughter of Augustine W. and Charlotte (Varney) Cromwell of Norridgwock, born there April 23, 1837. At the age of two years he removed with his parents to Dover and settled on a farm (then a vast wilderness) where he spent the greater part of his boyhood in assisting his father on the farm and attending the town school and Foxcroft Academy. At the age of eighteen he commenced and served three years apprenticeship in the house-building business. Having a natural taste for architecture, he devoted much time to the study of that profession and in after years established himself as architect and builder, carrying on both branches of the business for several years in his native state, erecting many private and public buildings. He now resides in Philadelphia.

Children:

1175   I.   ALICE FRANCES[7] born in Norridgewock December 22, 1861.

1176   II.   CARRIE AGNES[7] born December 15, 1863.

653.   JOHN EDWARD DOUGLASS[6] (John,[5] Edward,[4] Cornelius,[3] Elijah,[2] John,[1] (brother of the preceding, was born

in Dover March 6, 1835; married, November 14, 1865, Irene A., daughter of John G. and Ann W. Phinney. Soon after the breaking out of the Rebellion of 1861, he enlisted in the Sixth Regiment of Maine Volunteers for 18 months, at the end of which time he re-enlisted in the 30th Regiment of Maine Veteran Volunteers, in which he served until the close of the war, passing through many hard-fought battles, but fortunately received no wound. He was a farmer and resided in his native town not far from his father's homestead. August 17, 1874, he took his gun, which he had carried through the war, and went out back of his barn to shoot a hawk and by some mishap the gun was discharged and its contents took effect in his head, it is presumed, killing him instantly.

Children born in Dover:

1177 I. JOHN FRANK PHINNEY[7] born September 10, 1867.
1178 II. MARIANNE SOUTHWORTH[7] born December 14, 1868.
1179 III. CHARLES EDWARD[7] born August 9, 1872.

654. RUFUS COLLINS[6] DOUGLASS (John,[5] Edward[4] Cornelius,[3] Elijah,[2] John,[1]) brother of the preceding and son of John and Charity P. (Coombs) Douglass, born in Dover March 8, 1837; married, December 24, 1865, Sarah E., daughter of Hon. Reuel and Eliza (Woodman) Weston, of Skowhegan, born April 14, 1844. He received a liberal education at the town school and Foxcroft Academy; he was an assistant teacher in the latter institution two years; he also taught several district schools; his health failed him and he spent several months at Newfoundland Banks; he was then engaged for three years as a commercial traveler.

Soon after his marriage he was connected with the insurance business in Burlington, Iowa. In 1867 he removed and settled at La Crosse, Wis., where he was engaged in the drug business in company with his brother-in-law, J. W. Western. In 1871 he sold his interest in the drug business to his partner, and set up a jewelry and music store in the same village, having for his partners A. T. Clinton and A. D. Loomis.

In 1880 he purchased a farm of 250 acres in La Crosse County, on which he resided until the spring of 1886, when he rented the farm and is now traveling agent for D. H. Houghtaling, of New York, selling teas in Wisconsin, Minnesota and Iowa.

At the age of nineteen he was converted and joined the Free Baptist church at Dover, and remained a member until his removal to his present residence, when, with his wife, he united with the First Congregational church of La Crosse, of which they have since been active and worthy members, and of which all their children, except the youngest, have become members.

Their children:

1180 I. ELLA AUGUSTA[7] born in Burlington, Iowa, October 20, 1866; died there June 18, 1867.

1181 II. ELSIE WESTON[7] born in La Crosse, Wisconsin, May 17, 1869.

1182 III. ALICE CAREY[7] born in La Crosse, Wisconsin, June 13, 1871.

1183 IV. REUEL ELMER[7] born in La Crosse, Wisconsin, Sept. 15, 1874; died there August 25, 1876.

1184 V. JOHN WESTON[7] born in La Crosse, Wisconsin, August 7, 1876.

1185 VI. RUFUS HARMON[7] born in La Crosse, Wisconsin, Apr. 26, 1880; died December 9, 1881.

1186 VII. SADIE GERALDINE,[7] born in Hamilton, Wisconsin, July 29, 1885.

655. ELBRIDGE THOMPSON[6] DOUGLAS (John,[5] Edward,[4] Cornelius,[3] Elijah,[2] John,[1]) brother of the preceding, born at Dover, October 14, 1839; married, September 27, 1866,

Louisa, daughter of James and Louisa Bigelow, born June 29, 1841. He attended district school and assisted his father on the farm. April 27, 1861, he enlisted in Co. A. 6th Regiment Maine Volunteers, for the suppression of the great rebellion of 1861; was in the army of the Potomac. In the fall of 1862 he was discharged on account of sickness, but on recovering his health he enlisted September 1, 1864, in the Navy. He was in the South Atlantic Blocking Squadron, where he served until the close of the war. He has been elected Captain of a State Military Company, of his native town. He occupies the old homestead farm; a portion of his time is spent in moving buildings.

Their children born in Dover:

1187 I. NELLIE MAY[7] born May 2, 1869.
1188 II. HERBERT EUGENE[7] born July 16, 1872.
1189 III. MYRTIE EDNA[7] born April 2, 1877.

656. ELLEN AUGUSTA[7] DOUGLASS, (John,[5] Edward,[4] Cornelius,[3] Elijah,[2] John,[1]) sister of the preceding, born in Dover, October 24, 1841; married October 21, 1866, Calvin, son of James and Louisa Bigelow, born March 29, 1839; she was an accomplished lady and of fine culture. Previous to her marriage she was a teacher, in which capacity she was successful. They resided in St. Albans. She died October 1, 1881. In 1884 he went to California.

One child:

1190 I. HARMON ELMER (Bigelow) born in St. Albans May 12, 1870. He resides in California.

670. LIZZIE ANN[6] DOUGLASS (Joseph,[5] Joshua,[4] Cornelius,[3] Elijah,[2] John,[1]) daughter of Joseph and Ann G. (Beal) Douglass, born in Orono, February 13, 1859; married, November 18, 1883, J. Frank Beal; he is a house joiner and millwright. They reside at Orono.

Children:

1191 I. MARY ANN (Beal) born in Durham May 16, 1885.
1192 II. LIZZIE ELLA (Beal) born in Orono April 20, 1886.

678. STEPHEN ALBERT[6] DOUGLAS (George,[5] Joshua,[4] Cornelius,[3] Elijah,[2] John,[1]) son of George and Elizabeth Ann (Prescott) Douglas, was born in Durham, September 16, 1848; married August 7, 1870, Olivia W., daughter of Michael and Mary (Johnson) Powers, of Bath, born in Robinston, July 7, 1846. He received his education at the town school and one term each at Oak Grove Seminary and Litchfield Academy. In 1867, he went to Lewiston and clerked two years in dry goods business for Goddard & Paul. In 1869 he clerked for a firm in Bath; He then went to Portland, where he passed several years clerking and in business, a part of the time in company with N. O. Douglass. In 1877 he went to Boston and entered the dry goods store of Jordan & Marsh as salesman, for two years; then with R. H. White & Co., as salesman for a short time, when he was promoted to superintendent of the dress goods department; in 1888 he entered the employment of Houghton & Dutton, of Boston, as buyer of dry goods for their establishment, where he can be found at the present time.

Children born in Portland:

1193 I.   HARRY A.,[7] born May 27, 1871.
1194 II. ELANORA BAILEY,[7] born June 29, 1873.
1195 III. LIZZIE MARIA[7] born November 24, 1877.

679. LEWIS MORRELL[6] DOUGLAS (George,[5] Joshua,[4] Cornelius,[3] Elijah,[2] John,[1]) brother of the preceding and son of George and Elizabeth Ann (Prescott) Douglas, born in Durham February 1, 1852; married, October 21, 1875, Emma A., daughter of John C. and Eunice H. (Jones) Varney, born at China, January 15, 1851. During his

minority he lived at home, attended town school and learned the shoemakers' trade of his father. August 25, 1869, he entered the employ of Tyler, Lamb & Co., afterwards A. F. Cox & Son, as salesman in their shoe manufactory, in Portland, where he continued until 1878, and then opened a shoe store at Rochester, N. H., where he remained a few years, but finding the place too small for him to succeed as well as he wished, he closed out the stock and soon afterwards entered into co-partnership with a Mr. Elder, at Portland, who was already in the shoe trade. In 1888, he bought his partner's interest in the store and now continues the business alone.

He and his wife are active and acceptable members of the Society of Friends.

680. ELLEN MARIA[6] DOUGLAS, (George,[5] Joshua,[4] Cornelius,[3] Elijah,[2] John,[1]) only daughter of George and Elizabeth Ann (Prescott) Douglas, born in Durham, February 25, 1854; married at Portland, November 30, 1876, Clementine R. Hanson, son of Timothy and Almira Hanson, born in Thorndike. He is a minister in the Society of Friends; he carries on a large milk farm at Salem, Mass.

Children:

1196 I. LUEMMA DOUGLAS (Hanson) born in Deering September 28, 1880; died in Salem, Mass.
1197 II. ALMIRA LIZZIE (Hanson) born in Salem May 27, 1883.

682. JOHN HENRY[6] DOUGLAS, (George,[5] Joshua,[4] Cornelius,[3] Elijah,[2] John,[1]) son of George and Elizabeth Ann (Prescott) Douglas, born in Durham, April 19, 1862; married Jenney L. Brown. He resides on his father's homestead farm in Durham.

Children born in Durham:

1198 I. GEORGE WARREN[7] born March 14, 1882.

1199 II. EDITH JANE[7] born August 12, 1885.
1200 III. SADIE BROWN, born February 8, 1887.

694. CHLOE ANNA[6] DOUGLAS, (John Henry,[5] David,[4] Cornelius,[3] Elijah,[2] John,[1]) daughter of John Henry and Miriam (Carter) Douglas, born in Bloomington, Ohio, February, 1857; married, September 4, 1877, J. Frank Taylor; they reside at Iowa Falls, Iowa.

Children born in Spiceland, Ind.
1201 I. DOUGLAS (Taylor) born May 27, 1880.
1202 II. ETHEL (Taylor) born February 17, 1882.

701 DAVID FRANKLIN[6] DOUGLAS, (Robert W.,[5] David,[4] Cornelius,[3] Elijah,[2] John,[1]) son of Robert Walter and Margaret Ann Douglas, born at Bloomington, Clinton County, Ohio, June 15, 1857; married July 8, 1880, Emma R. Thornburg, born August 6, 1859, daughter of Edward and Rachel Thornburg. Mr. Douglas graduated at Earlham College in 1879. Taught school among the Indians in a Government school in the Indian Territory Since 1882 he has been cashier of the West Milton Bank, Ohio.

Children born in West Milton, Ohio:
1203 I. ROBERT EDWARD[7] born February 27, 1882.
1204 II. GIFFORD[7] born October 17, 1884.
1205 III. VERA[7] born December 25, 1887.

709. MARY NARCISSA[6] DOUGLAS, (John N.[5] Cornelius,[4] Cornelius,[3] Elijah,[2] John,[1]) daughter of John N. and Sarah (Jones) Douglas, born in Bloomington, Ohio, August 30, 1860; married October 10, 1878, Charles L. Aldrige; they reside on a farm in Wilson Township, Clinton Co., Ohio.

Children born in Wilson Township, Clinton Co., O.
1206 I. VESTA ANN (Aldrige) born October 28, 1879.
1207 II. HENRY ALTON (Aldrige) born September 7, 1881.

1208 III. John Ernest (Aldrige) born September 17, 1884.
1209 I. Fred Lawernce (Aldrige) born February 19, 1888.

727. David J.[6] Douglas, (Joseph,[5] David,[4] Joseph,[3] Elijah,[2] John,[1]) son of Joseph and Phebe Douglas, was born in Durham, October 15, 1843 ; married, August 28, 1867, Lydia E., daughter of James and Emeline C. Myers, of Manchester.

In May, 1861, he was converted and immediately felt called upon to devote his life to the work of the ministry and at once began preaching among Friends, of which society he was already a member. He assisted in the first revival meeting ever held in New England among Friends. In 1760, he sought and found the experience of sanctification. In 1871, he accepted a call to become pastor of Friends' Church at Martinsville. In 1880, he succeeded J. H. Douglas as pastor at Glen Falls, N. Y. During this pastorate of three years the church was blessed with several revivals. At one of these seven hundred knelt at the altar for pardon and holiness.

After a little rest he engaged as an evangelist in Ohio Yearly Meeting. In 1885 he again settled as pastor in Kokomo, Ind. In 1887 by failing health he was compelled to retire. He then settled in Maine where he resides in the town of Manchester, doing what work his health will admit.

One child :
1210 I. Robert Walter[7] born February 12, 1879.

732. Isaiah[6] Douglass, (Joseph,[5] David,[4] Joseph,[3] Elijah,[2] John.[1]) son of Joseph and Mary Jane (Cook) Douglas ; married Effie Lunt, of Brunswick, where they reside on a farm. They are worthy members of the Society of Friends.

Children born in Brunswick :

1211 I. CHARLES LEONARD[7] born August 17, 1880.
1212 II. AFFIE MAY[7] born November 29, 1881.
1213 III. FRANK ELLWOOD[7] born August 17, 1883.
1214 IV. ISAIAH WILLIS[7] born April 28, 1886.
1215 V. JOSEPH NATHA[7] born February 28, 1888.

735. JOHN W.[6] DOUGLASS, (James,[5] Joseph,[4] Job,[3] Elijah,[2] John,[1]) son of James and Elmira (Burgess) Douglass, was born in Phipsburg, November 8, 1825 ; married (1) 1847, Mary E. Chase, of Hallowell, who died August 2, 1852 ; he married (2) Abby A. Hall, of Chelsea, 1854 ; she died October 2, 1863.

When a small boy he lived four months with Dr. Israel Putnam, of Bath ; he then went to Litchfield, where he remained for a time and finally settled in Hallowell, where he lived till 1847 ; he is a book binder and now resides in Gardiner.

Children by first marriage :

1216 I. IDA M.[7] born in Hallowell December 15, 1848; died May 22, 1870.
1217 II. ALICE E.[7] born in Gardiner March 22, 1852; died October 4, 1852.
1218 III. CHARLES F.[7] born in Chelsea, November 4, 1855.
1219 IV. ARTHUR B.[7] born in Gardiner November 12, 1857.
1220 V. ALVIN W.[7] born in Chelsea November 16, 1859.
1221 VI. JOHN C.[7] born in Gardiner February 22, 1860; died August 22, 1863.

737. RACHEL R. DOUGLASS[6] (James,[5] Joseph,[4] Job,[3] Elijah,[2] John,[1]) sister of the preceding, was born in Bath, June 15, 1830 ; married Zina H. Spinney, 2d, of Georgetown ; Mr. Spinney is a farmer and fisherman : resides at Long Island, Georgetown.

Their children, born in Georgetown ;

1222 I. ELIJAH M. (Spinney) born October 11, 1852.

1223   II.   WILLIAM P. (Spinney) born September 11, 1854.
1224   III. ZINA H. (Spinney) born September 23, 1861.
1225   IV.   FREDERICK H. (Spinney) born August 30, 1867.

752. HARRIET ANN[6] DOUGLASS (Samuel,[5] Samuel,[4] Job,[3] Elijah,[2] John,[1]) daughter of Samuel and Theodates Douglas of Bowdoinham, born there October 7, 1833; married (1) Joseph Sedgley of Bowdoinham, where he lived and died; (2) Charles Melcher of Boston, a painter. They reside in Boston.

Children by first marriage, born in Bowdoinham:

1226   I.   INEZ ROSILLA (Sedgley) born February 12, 1854; died February, 1858.
1227   II. IONA ESTELLA (Sedgley) born ———
1228   III. MARSHAL INGERSON (Sedgley) born July 4, 1859.
1229   IV. WILLIAM CLAPP (Sedgley) born 1860.

753. HANNAH ELIZABETH[6] DOUGLASS (Samuel,[5] Samuel,[4] Job,[3] Elijah,[2] John,[1]) sister of the preceding, born in Bowdoinham, November 23, 1835; married, (1) February 9, 1855, Albion B. Jack, of her native town; he was accidentally shot dead by a man named Brown. She married, (2) May 30, 1865, Edward S. Sparks: they reside in Bowdoinham.

Children:

1230   I.   IDA ELENOR (Jack) born in Bowdoinham October 5, 1857.
1231   II. CORA ALBERTIA (Jack) born in Bowdoinham April 6, 1859.
1232   III. JANE MARION (Jack) born in Bowdoinham, July 23, 1861.
1233   IV. CLARA ALBINA (Jack) born in Bowdoinham July 13, 1863.

Children by second husband:

1234   V.   MINNETTA ESTELLORE (Sparks) born in Bath May 30, 1867.

1235 VI. JOSEPH SEWELL (Sparks) born in Richmond October 12, 1870.

1236 VII. FREDERICK BERRY (Sparks) born in Bowdoinham May 1, 1873.

1237 VIII. EARL (Sparks) born in Bowdoinham October 5, 1874.

754. MARY STINSON[6] DOUGLASS (Samuel,[5] Samuel[4] Job,[3] Elijah,[2] John,[1]) sister of the preceding: was born in Bowdoinham February 11, 1838; married George L. Card. stevedore and carpenter; resides in Bowdoin.

Children, seventh generation:

1238 I. GEORGE FRANKLIN (Card) born in Bowdoinham May 10, 1858.

1239 II. MELVIN WILCHIER (Card) born in Bowdoinham February 24, 1861.

1240 III. INEZ ESTELLA (Card) born in Bowdoin May 1, 1862.

1241 IV. MAY ELIZABETH (Card) born in Bowdoinham, 1863.

1242 V. SUSAN ELLEN (Card) born in Bowdoin December 30, 1865.

1243 VI. LYDIA ANN (Card) born in Bowdoin April 15, 1867.

756. MELVIN WILCHIER[6] DOUGLASS (Samuel,[5] Samuel,[4] Job,[3] Elijah,[2] John,[1]) brother of the preceding and son of Samuel and Theodates Douglas; was born in Bowdoinham November 19, 1841; married, June 8, 1864, Clara J. Hill, of St. John, New Brunswick. He is a ship carpenter and resides at Bowdoinham Village.

Children, born in Bowdoinham:

1244 I. MARY ABBY[7] born in Saco August 5, 1865.

1245 II. ANNIE VESTY[7] born in Bowdoinham March 27, 1869.

1246 III MARY ELENIA[7] born in Bowdoinham.

759. ASA ALBION[6] DOUGLASS (Abraham[5] Samuel[4] Job[3] Elijah,[2] John,[1]) son of Capt. Abraham and Hannah Douglass, born in Bath November 29, 1834, married Josephine Knight; they reside in Pilot Town, La., where he has been

employed as pilot and at the present time is Superintendent of Schools.

Children:

1247   I. WILLIAM R.[7] born in New Orleans August 15, 1861; died September 20, 1863.
1248   II. WILLIAM B.[7] born in New Orleans August 13, 1863, died August 13, 1865.
1249   III. ALBION F.[7] born in New Orleans November 16, 1865.
1250   IV. WARREN D.[7] born in New Orleans March 11, 1868.
1251   V. VIOLA E.[7] born in New Orleans July 27, 1871.

763. AMANDA JANE[6] DOUGLASS (Abraham,[5] Samuel,[4] Job,[3] Elijah,[2] John,[1]) sister of the preceding and daughter of Capt. Abraham and Hannah E. Douglass, born in Bowdoinham April 5, 1842; married, October 30, 1864, George G., son of Gardiner and Elizabeth (Adams) Williams, born in Bowdoin March 14, 1842. Mr. Williams lived for a time in Bath, working at his trade, shoemaking. He afterwards removed to Bowdoinham, where he died October 24, 1878. His widow married, (2) Joseph G. Washburn, August 13, 1881. He is a dealer in pianos and organs. They now reside in Bath.

Children by first marriage:

1252   I. LEONA M. (Williams) born in Bath September 13, 1865.
1253   II. SELDEN F. (Williams) born November 6, 1867.
1254   III. EVELYN F. (Williams) born in Bowdoinham February 8, 1877.

769. OSCAR GARDINER[6] DOUGLASS (Gardiner,[5] Samuel,[4] Job,[3] Elijah,[2] John,[1]) only son of Rev. Gardiner and Aseneth S. (Orr) Douglass, born in Bowdoinham June 24, 1836; married, September 6, 1860, Phebe W. Cook, daughter of Hanson and Nancy Cook of Lewiston, born in Madrid, 1835. Previous to his marriage he taught several terms of district school, giving good satisfaction; he settled in Lewiston and in 1870, 1871 and 1875 was

elected City Marshal of that city, which office he filled with much credit to himself and terror to the offenders of the law. He is a man of public spirit, of generous impulses and takes a deep interest in all public affairs. In personal appearance he resembles the robust Douglases of the olden times, tall and portly and of fine proportions. He, in company with his brother-in-law, Mr. Cook, are engaged in the book and stationery business in Lewiston.

One child :
1255   I.   MAUD M.[7] born in Lewiston November 2, 1866.

779.   JOHN ALBION[6] DOUGLASS (John B.,[5] James,[4] Job[3] Elijah,[2] John,[1]) oldest son of John Banks and Nancy Douglass, born in the plantation of Letter B, now Upton, January 14, 1830 ; married, October 18, 1855, Margaret Springer. Soon after his marriage he went to Bath, where he worked in the shipyard several years. He subsequently entered into partnership with his uncle Nehemiah O., in a variety store at Lisbon Falls. He shortly sold his interest in the store to his partner and went in company with Rev. George Plummer in the grist mill in the same village. After running the mill a few years he sold out and removed and settled at Richmond and worked in the shipyard the remainder of his life. He died December 28, 1874.

One child :
1256   I.   DELIA J. born April 18, 1856.

782.   NOAH H.[6] DOUGLASS (John Banks,[5] James,[4] Job[3] Elijah,[2] John,[1]) brother of the preceding and son of John B. and Nancy B. Douglass, born in Canton March 29, 1836 ; married, November 24, 1860, Harriet Mountford, of Lisbon. They settled in Lewiston, where he worked in a tannery ; removed on a farm in Bowdoin, known as the Berry farm. He died of consumption January 23, 1871. She died November 20, 1870.

Children:

1257　I.　WALTER SCOTT[7] born in Auburn July 13, 1861; married Clara Campbell.

1258　II.　WILLIS P.[7] born December 29, 1863; died April 29, 1864.

1259　III.　HATTIE E.[7] born in Bowdoin November 5, 1864; married Herbert Crosman.

1260　IV.　WILLIAM HENRY[7] born in Bowdoin April 29, 1867.

1261　V.　CHARLES[7] born about 1869.

1262　VI.　LIZZIE[7] born November 4, 1870; she has been adopted by George F. Williams of Bath and now bears his name.

786.　WILLIAM W.[6] DOUGLASS (John Banks,[5] James,[4] Job,[3] Elijah,[2] John,[1]) brother of the preceding and son of John B. and Nancy B. Douglass, was born in Lisbon, July 11, 1845; married, May, 1866, Ellen R. Jordan, born August 16, 1846; he was a farmer and resided in his native town. July, 1886, for some unknown cause, took poison, which terminated his life.

Children:

1263　I.　NETTIE L.[7] born in Lisbon July 19, 1868.

1264　II.　FRANK EMERY[7] born in Lisbon July 26, 1870.

788.　OSCAR EATON[6] DOUGLASS, (John,[5] James,[4] Job,[3] Elijah,[2] John,[1]) son of John B. and Nancy B. Douglass, born in Lisbon August 14, 1849; married, July 2, 1876, Abbie Jane, daughter of James and Eliza Jane (Douglas) Goddard. They settled on his father's homestead, which he subsequently sold and bought a small farm in the same town; he died at his residence in Lisbon, January 2, 1888. His widow lives at Amesbury, Mass.

Their children, born in Lisbon:

1265　I.　OTIS NEHEMIAH[7] born May 13, 1877.

1266　II.　FRED WESLEY[7] born February 16, 1879; died May 12, 1879.

1267　III.　CARRIE MAY[7] born August 16, 1881.

1268   IV.   BERTHA JANE[7] born August 5, 1883; died January 22, 1885.
1269   V.   JOHN ELMER[7] born September 28, 1884; died April 1, 1885.
1270   VI.   ESTELLA ALICE[7] born April 5, 1886.
1271   VII.   OSCAR EVERETT[7] born May 5, 1888.

792.   CHARLES LYMAN[6] DOUGLAS (James S.[5] James,[4] Job,[3] Elijah,[2] John,[1]) son of James S. and Azabah (Godwin) Douglass, born in Letter B plantation, now Upton, Oxford County, June 4, 1839; married, October 13, 1864, Hester A. Ballan. In 1861 he enlisted in the 14th Maine Regiment in the War of the Rebellion; he was in the engagement at New Orleans, under Gen. B. F. Butler; he has served his town as one of the selectmen and has held the office of Town Clerk of Upton several years; he now resides at South Paris.

Children born in Upton:

1272   I.   HERBERT C.[7] born October 26, 1865.
1273   II.   ISABEL J.[7] born August 3, 1867.
1274   III.   ALICE M.[7] born July 6, 1869.

800.   WILLIAM SIDNEY[6] DOUGLASS (William Booker,[5] James,[4] Job,[3] Elijah,[2] John,[1]) son of Rev. William B. and Mary (Duren) Douglass; was born in Lisbon October 12, 1832; married, November 21, 1861, Mary E. Nash. He has always been an industrious man and is much respected by his large circle of friends. He now resides at Gray Corner.

Children born in Raymond:

1275   I.   FRANK N.[7] born November 3, 1862.
1276   II.   FLORA[7] born August 10, 1864; married, October 22, 1887, Edson O. Nay.
1277   III.   CORA REBECCA[7] born July 4, 1866.
1278   IV.   GEORGE W.[7] born ———
1279   V.   MABEL F.[7] born December 8, 1870.
1280   VI.   HERBERT L.[7] born December 17, 1872.

1281 VII. LEANDER M,[7] born May 8, 1875.
1282 VIII. HARRY R.[7] born January 27, 1878.

801. LOUISA[6] DOUGLASS (William Booker,[5] James,[4] Job,[3] Elijah,[2] John,[1]) sister of the preceding and daughter of Rev. William B. and Mary Douglass, was born in Lisbon September 1, 1835; married Henry C., son of Aaron and Martha (Lamb) Johnson, born in Durham January 15, 1834. He is a house joiner and resides at Auburn.

Children, seventh generation:
1283 I. NELLIE M. (Johnson) born January 26, 1859.
1284 II. FREDERICK H. (Johnson) born June 17, 1868.

832. HENRIETTA DOUGLAS,[6] (Alfred.[5] Job,[4] Job,[3] Elijah,[2] John,[1]) daughter of Alfred and Frances E. (Nash) Douglas, was born in West Gardiner October 20, 1848; married (1) July 26, 1864, Jesse Stover of Bath, where they settled, then removed to Boston; married (2) September 19, 1872, by Rev. William C. Hart, James Jones, a native of England; he is a rigger and resides in Bath.

Children by first marriage:
1285 I. CLARA FRANCES (Stover) born in Bath December 27, 1867; died May 9, 1868.
1286 II. FRANCES SOPHIA (Stover) born in Boston June 23, 1871.

836. BENJAMIN FRANKLIN[6] DOUGLASS (Seth,[5] Job[4] Job[3] Elijah,[2] John,[1]) son of Seth and Mary Jane (Smith) Douglas, born in Brunswick September 17, 1855; married, June 15, 1878, Elizabeth B. Southard, born in Harpswell July 4, 1859; they reside in Brunswick.

Children born in Brunswick:
1287 I. ETHEL JANE[7] born March 1, 1879.
1288 II. ALICE IRENE[7] born June 6, 1881.
1289 III. ARCHIBALD PERRY[7] born December 2, 1883.
1290 IV. ARTHUR E.[7] born July 5, 1888.

842. Edwin Charles[6] Douglas (Charles,[5] Benjamin[4] Job,[3] Elijah,[2] John.[1]) oldest son of Charles and Eunice (Pratt) Douglass, born in Bowdoin March 6, 1841; married, April 11, 1863, Hattie R., daughter of Josiah and Clarissa (Richardson) Smith, born in Litchfield January 28, 1841. They settled in Winthrop, removed to Litchfield and from there to Lewiston, where he worked several years at his trade as house joiner. He worked on the city hall of Lewiston ; he at one time bought and occupied a farm in Webster ; he enlisted in the 15th Maine Regiment of the War of the Rebellion; served nine months and was discharged for sickness ; he now resides in Lewiston and is doing a thriving business in the grocery trade.

One child :

1291 I. Stilman Walter[7] born April 29, 1865; died December 19, 1881.

844. Warren P.[6] Douglas (Charles[5] Benjamin,[4] Job[3] Elijah,[2] John,[1]) son of Charles and Eunice (Pratt) Douglas born in Bowdoin October 5, 1845 ; married, July 15, 1866, Lois, daughter of Jedson and Laura Fisher of Lewiston, born November 17, 1844; she died October 8, 1880 He married, second, Ida F. Field ; they reside at Lewiston, where he is employed in the mill.

Children :

1292 I. Minnie Laura born in Lewiston May 6, 1867; died there 1877.
1293 II. Mabel M., born in Wisconsin September 28, 1877.
1294 III. Berten W., born in Gardiner April 27, 1879.

Children by second marriage :

1295 IV. Ina G., born in Great Falls, N. H., June 11, 1885.
1296 V. Harry W., born in Lewiston March 11, 1888.

846. Ella A.[6] Douglas (Charles,[5] Benjamin,[4] Job,[3] Elijah,[2] John,[1]) daughter of Charles and Eunice (Pratt)

Douglas, born in Bowdoin July 27, 1859; married, first, Isaiah Merrifield, son of Monsieus and Mariam (Lane) Merrifield of Wolfborough, N. H.; he died July, 1881; her second husband is J. Eben Butler; they reside at Springvale.

Children by first marriage, born in Springvale:

1297 I. EVERETT F. (Merrifield) born March 9, 1875.
1298 II. ARTHUR J. (Merrifield) born June 22, 1877.

848. DANIEL A.[6] DOUGLASS (William,[5] Benjamin,[4] Job,[3] Elijah,[2] John,[1]) son of William and Roxcellana (Rodic) Douglas, was born in Bowdoin April 22, 1847; married, August 13, 1865, Mary Elizabeth, daughter of Benjamin B. and Rachel J. (Bates) Douglas [850], he settled on his father's homestead in Bowdoin, where he died; she married Abizah Small of Bowdoin, where they reside.

Children born in Bowdoin:

1299 I. LAURA A.,[7] born February 8, 1867.
1300 II. ALBERT M.,[7] born May 18, 1868.

Child by second marriage:

1301 III. EMMA (Small)

851. JAMES ALEXANDER[6] DOUGLAS (Benjaman Booker,[5] Benjamin,[4] Job[3] Elijah John,[1]) son of Benjamin B. and Rachel (Bates) Douglas, was born in Richmond April 24, 1849; married, first, Sarah Davis, May 13, 1866; second, Georgia Lawrence. In his early manhood he worked in the mills and drove a team in Lewiston. In 1865 he enlisted and went into camp Coburn in Augusta, but the war being nearly over he only remained a few months and was discharged; he is now in Omaha, Neb., where he is a dealer in horses and a railroad contractor; his second wife died May 10, 1887.

Children:

1302 I. OREMANDAR,[7] born in Lewiston, July 31, 1867.

1303 II. EDWIN,⁷ born March, 1872.

Children by second marriage :

1304 III. JAMES ALEXANDER,⁷ JR., born in Mount Clemens, Mich., October 17, 1882.

1305 IV. VIOLET,⁷ born in Rochester, New York, November 10, 1885.

852. FREDERIC BATES⁶ DOUGLASS (Benjamin B.⁵ Benjamin⁴ Job,³ Elijah,² John,¹) married, June 22, 1877, at Chillicth, Ohio, Hester Robinson of Hillsborough, Ohio; they reside at Dayton, Ohio.

Children:

1306 I. MYRTIE,⁷ born in Nelsonville, Ohio, April 8, 1878.
1307 II. SOPHIE,⁷ born at Celina, Ohio, January 28, 1881.
1308 III. MINNIE,⁷ born in Dayton, Ohio, March 4, 1886.

854. BENJAMIN BOOKER⁶ DOUGLASS (Benjamin Booker,⁵ Benjamin,⁴ Job,³ Elijah,² John,¹) born in Bowdoin October 2, 1859; married, June 24, 1879, Minnie S. Buker, daughter of Rev. Alvah J. Buker of Bowdoin; he is a farmer and resides in his native town.

Children born in Bowdoin :

1309 I. RATHEUS A.,⁷ born June 13, 1880.
1310 II. FLORA F.,⁷ born July 25, 1883.
1311 III. ETHEL M.,⁷ born March 8, 1887.

927. ELIZA ELLEN⁶ DOUGLASS (Elijah W.,⁵ Ephraim,⁴ John,³ John,² John,¹) daughter of Elijah W. and Mehitable C. Douglass, born in Middleboro, Mass., August 5, 1852; married, January 16, 1866, Frederick Pratt.

Children :

1312 I. BERTHA EUGENA (Pratt) born August 5, 1871.
1313 II. WILLIAM A. (Pratt) born November 11, 1873.

930. LUTHER ANDERSON⁶ DOUGLAS (Luther,⁵ Ephriam,⁴ John,³ John,² John,¹) son of Luther and Lucy S.

(Gibbs) Douglas, born in Sandwich, Mass., July 25, 1847; married, June 1, 1878, Ella, daughter of Francis P. and Mary S. (Howes) Brewer, born in the town of Brewer February 18, 1853; Col. John Brewer, her great-grandfather, for whom the town was named, was one of the early settlers on the banks of the Penobscot River. Mr. Douglas, at the age of nine years, went to live on a farm with his grandfather Gibbs, where he remained until he was 17 years of age; he then resided at home most of the time for the next three years, at which time he went to Plymouth, Mass., and clerked in a hotel at that place for four years; he subsequently was employed as clerk or manager in hotels, in different towns for several years. In April, 1872, he went to Hingham, Mass. and was clerk in the Cushing House for four years; he then opened a clothing store, which business he continues to follow; his store is pleasantly situated in the village and he is doing a thriving business.

Their children:

1314 I. ALICE,[7] born in Hingham, Mass., October 17, 1878.

1315 II. DOROTHY FRANCES,[7] born in Hingham, February 4, 1890. The youngest person in this book.

933. FRANK M.[6] DOUGLAS (Luther,[5] Ephriam,[4] John[3] John,[2] John,[1]) son of Luther and Lucy S. (Gibbs, Douglass, was born in West Sandwich, Mass., July 25, 1851; married Josephine N., daughter of Thomas and Alice Foley, born June 17, 1850. They settled in Boston, removed to Portland and now reside in Lynn, Mass., where he is agent for a Sewing Machine Company.

Children:

1316 I. FRANK D.,[7] born in Cape Elizabeth, Maine, March 7, 1882.

1317 II. MARY J.,[7] born in Lynn, Mass., March 19, 1884.

1318　III.　LUCY S.,[7] born in Lynn, March 17, 1886.
1319　IV.　MABEL G.,[7] born in Lynn, October 11, 1888.

934.　CHARLES EVERETT[6] DOUGLAS (Luther,[5] Ephriam,[4] John,[3] John,[2] John,[1]) son of Luther and Lucy S. (Gibbs) born in Sandwich, Mass., September 27, 1853; married, November 28, 1877, Ella Gibbs, daughter of Capt. Bradford and Henrietta Maria (Bent) Gibbs, born in South Plymouth May 26, 1859; they reside at Sagamore, where he is engineer in a car manufactory.

Their children, born in Sagamore, Mass.:
1320　I.　LINDA L.,[7] born November 2, 1878.
1321　II.　CHARLES L.,[7] born October 15, 1880.
1322　III.　ELLA J.,[7] born November 18, 1882.
1323　IV.　ANNIE A.,[7] born January 14, 1888.

936.　MARY MARTHA[6] DOUGLAS (Luther,[5] Ephriam,[4] John,[3] John,[2] John,[1]) daughter of Luther and Lucy S. (Gibbs) Douglass, born in Sandwich, Mass., October 13, 1858; married, November 6, 1879, Charles Sherman, son of Henry and Lucy B. Sherman, born February 14, 1856; they settled in Plympton, Mass., removed to South Middleborough; they now reside in Rochester, Mass.

Their children :
1324　I.　ELLA MAY (Sherman) born in Plympton, September 12, 1880; died April 5, 1881.
1325　II.　GEORGE HENRY (Sherman) born in Plympton, January 18, 1882; died August 12, 1883.
1326　III.　FREDERIC WINSLOW (Sherman) born in Plympton, June 8, 1883.
1327　IV.　CHARLES WILLIAM (Sherman) born in Middleborough, April 1, 1885.
1328　V.　FRANCIS LESLIE (Sherman) born in Middleborough, September 5, 1886.

946.　ALONZO[6] DOUGLAS (John,[5] John,[4] John,[3] John,[2] John,[1]) son of John and Cynthia Adelia Douglas; was born in Hartland, Vt., November 29, 1844; married, October 11, 1865, Emma Evans of Annsvill, Oneida County, N. Y., where they reside on a farm.

Children, seventh generation, born in Annsvill, N.Y.:

1329　I.　CYNTHIA ETTA,[7] born January 25, 1867.
1330　II.　ALICE,[7] born September 1, 1873.

947.　NANCY AMANDA[6] DOUGLAS (John,[5] John,[4] John[3] John,[2] John,[1]) sister of the preceding, was born in Hartland, Vt., August 7, 1846; married (1) January 1, 1866, in her native town, Levi Bishop of Bridgwater, Vermont; (2) Stephen Bishop, a brother of her first husband, a farmer; he resides at Bridgwater, Vermont.

Children by first marriage:

1331　I.　CHARLES LEVI (Bishop) born January 25 ——
1332　II.　CYNTHIA ADELLA (Bishop) born August 3, 1868; died September 2, 1872.
1333　III.　LORA RUTH (Bishop) born in Guthrie Co., Iowa, January 19, 1871; died September, 1872.
1334　IV.　JOHN D. (Bishop) born in Nebraska, September, 1872, and died same day.

Children by second marriage:

1335　V.　JAMES WARREN (Bishop) born October 16, 1874; died January 5, 1878.
1336　VI.　JAMES STEPHEN (Bishop) born January 11, 1878.

949.　RHODA MEHITABLE[6] DOUGLAS (John,[5] John,[4] John,[3] John,[2] John,[1]) sister of the preceding, was born in Hartland, Vt., September 25, 1850; married Lyman B. Stoddard of Warren, Vt., where they live; he is a farmer.

Children seventh generation:

1337　I.　HARRY LYMAN (Stoddard) born in Woodstock, Vt., December 24, 1861.
1338　II.　LILLIE (Stoddard) born in Warren, Vt., March 6, 1874.
1339　III.　CLAYTON DOUGLAS (Stoddard) born in Warren, May 21, 1875.

1340 IV. PERLEY V. B. (Stoddard) born May 8, 1878.

950. ADDIE BETSEY[6] DOUGLAS (John,[5] John,[4] John,[3] John,[2] John,[1]) sister of the preceding, born in Northumberland, N. H., July 1, 1852; married, October 30, 18—, Franklin Stoddard of Warren, Vermont, where they reside on a farm.

Children, born in Warren, Vt.:

1341 I. HELEN ADELINE (Stoddard) born September 1, 1872.
1342 II. MINNIE ADELAID (Stoddard) born August 5, 1874.
1343 III. JOHN FRANKLIN (Stoddard) born July 10, 1876.
1344 IV. ——— (Stoddard) born October 10, 1877.

952. ANSEL MORRIS[6] DOUGLAS (John,[5] John,[4] John,[3] John,[2] John,[1]) son of John and Cynthia A. Douglas, born in Northumberland, N. H., July 1, 1856; married February 9, 1876, Arvilla Davis; resides in Moretown, Vt.

One child :

1345 I. JOHN WARREN,[7] born March 18, 1878.

958. JULIA MARIA[6] DOUGLAS (Reuben,[5] John,[4] John,[3] John,[2] John,[1]) daughter of Reuben and Catharine A. (Thomas) Douglas, born September 29, 1849; married, October 2, 1870, Pardon Augustus Whitney: he is a machinist; they reside in Southington, Conn.

Their children, born in Southington :

1346 I. FRANK AUGUSTUS (Whitney) born May 27, 1871; died August 19, 1871.
1347 II. JENNIE MARIA (Whitney) born June 10, 1872.
1348 III. LUCY MABEL (Whitney) born February 12, 1875.

962. MARIA A.[6] DOUGLAS (William,[5] John,[4] John,[3] John,[2] John,[1]) daughter of Warren Douglas, born May 17, 1852; married, February 5, 1879, Henry D. Underwood, born March 6, 1846; he died in his native town, Concord, Vt., March 30, 1884.

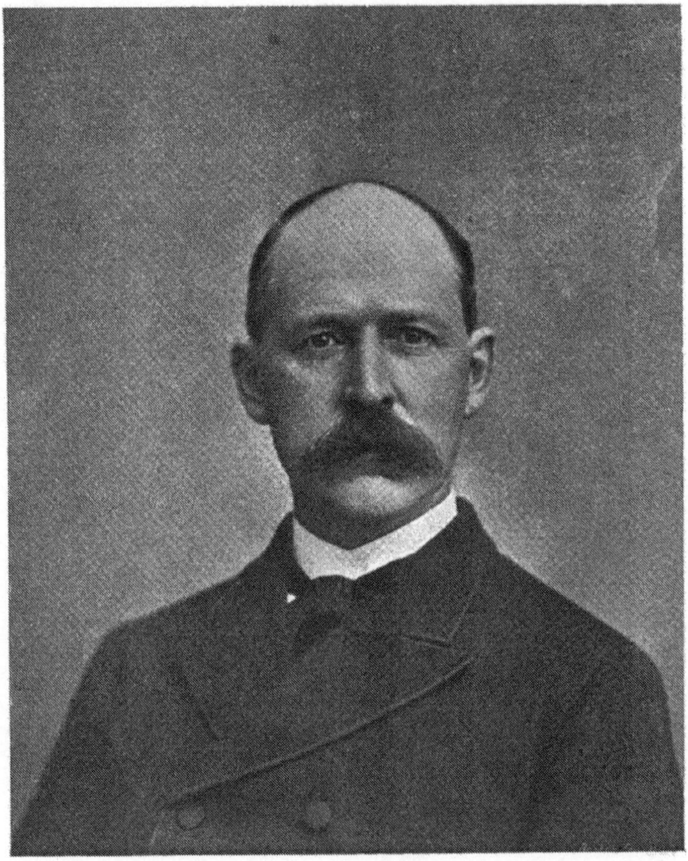

Children :

1349 I. JENNIE M. (Underwood) born December 18, 1879.
1350 II. MARY H. (Underwood) born December 8, 1883.

974. HON. WILLIAM LEWIS[6] DOUGLAS (William,[5] Earl[4] John,[3] John,[2] John,[1]) son of William and Mary C. Douglas, born in Plymouth, Mass., August 22, 1845; married, September 6, 1868, Naomi Augusta, daughter of Burgess P. and Naomi Terry, born December 4, 1848; His parents dying when he was young, he was left to gain a livelihood as best he could. During his minority he learned the shoemaker's trade; after his marriage they settled at North Bridgewater, Mass., now Brockton, where he worked at his trade and in a few years was promoted to foreman of the shop, which position he held until he went into business for himself; he is known all over the United States as the manufacturer of the celebrated Three Dollar Shoe and other grades of shoes.

Mr. Douglas is a man of noble character, energetic and alive to public interest. He represented his city in the legislature for the years 1883-4; he also represented the second Plymouth District in the State Senate in 1886. In 1889 he was elected Mayor of the city of Brockton.

Their children:

1351 I. ALICE AUGUSTA[7] born in Plymouth, Mass., June 3, 1869.
1352 II. MARION LEWIS,[7] born in North Bridgwater, now Brockton, Mass., April 29, 1872.
1353 III. AMY REYNOLDS,[7] born in Brockton September 5, 1874.

975. MARY ANNIE[6] DOUGLAS (William,[5] Earl,[4] John[3] John,[2] John,[1]) sister of the preceding and daughter of William and Mary C. (Vaughn) Douglas, was born in Plymouth, Mass., March 26, 1847; married Frank L. Hoar, born in Bristol, R. I., March 22, 1846; settled in his native town

where he has always resided; he is engaged in the manufactury of gum for the National Rubber Co., of Bristol.

Children seventh generation, born in Bristol, R. I.:

1354 I. Lillie Frances, (Hoar) born June 13, 1871.
1355 II. Jennie Ross (Hoar) born October 19, 1874.

982. Theodore Warren[5] Douglas (Luther,[5] Warren,[4] John,[3] John,[2] John,[1]) son of Luther Douglas, born in Taberg, Oneida County, N. Y., September 3, 1838; married, January 1, 1866, Mary Ann Wannastrand, born in Weyanverg, Wisconsin, April 1, 1851.

Children:

1356 I. Flora Ella[7] born in Parfreysville, Wisconsin, December 8, 1866.
1357 II. Luther Edward,[7] born in Almond, Wisconsin, July 1, 1868.
1358 III. Alice Maria,[7] born in Embarrase, Wisconsin, Feb. 28, 1870; died October 26, 1875.
1359 IV. Lydia Jane,[7] born in Almond, August 20, 1873.
1360 V. William,[7] born in Pine Grove July 26, 1875.

997. Harriet Amanda[6] Douglas (Warren,[5] Warren,[4] John,[3] John,[2] John,[1]) daughter of Warren and Sally (Storms) Douglas, born in Amesville, Oneida County, N. Y., December 2, 1843; married, July 1, 1861, Charles Wilson, son of John and Hepsehath Wilson, born in Eagle, Lincolnshire, England, March 23, 1839; he is a machinist; settled in Amesville, N. Y., where he still lives.

Their child:

1361 I. Charles Franklin (Wilson) born in Amesville, July 26, 1862; died October 2, 1862.

998. Albert Marion[6] Douglas (Warren,[5] Warren,[4] John,[3] John,[2] John,[1]) brother of the preceding, born in Amesville, N. Y., February 5, 1847, married, December 22, 1869, Clara Cordelia, daughter of Drius and Mary C.

Hale, born May 31, 1847. They settled in Amesville, N. Y., where he resides and is in company with Mr. Charles Wilson in the machine business.

Their children, born in Amesville, N. Y.:

1362　I.　EDDIE[7] born October 25, 1870; died there November 3, 1870.

1363　II.　MARION,[7] twin, born April 12, 1872; died April 13, 1872.

1364　III.　HATTIE MAY[7] twin, born April 12, 1872; died April 13, 1872.

1034. JESSE P.[6] DOUGLAS (Jesse P.[5] Joshua,[4] John,[3] John,[2] John,[1]) son of Jesse P. and Roxanna (Manter) Douglas; was born in Plymouth, Mass., December 5, 1845; married May 1, 1870.

Child, seventh generation:

1365　JOANNA F., born in Plymouth, Mass., June, 1871.

1038. EMILY S.[6] DOUGLAS (Elisha,[5] Joshua,[4] John,[3] John,[2] John,[1]) daughter of Elisha and Susan P. (King) Douglas, was born in Plymouth, Mass., November 14, 1843; married, March 14, 1863, Pelham Sampson, of Plymouth, where they reside; he is employed by the Robinson Iron Works of that place.

Children, born in Plymouth, Mass.:

1366　I.　FRED A. (Sampson) born January 19, 1864.
1367　II.　PELHAM F. (Sampson) born December 14, 1869.
1368　III.　LILIAN C. (Sampson) born May 5, 1872.

1040. ELISHA T.[6] DOUGLAS (Elisha,[5] Joshua,[4] John,[3] John[2] John,[1]) son of Elisha and Susan P. (King) Douglas, born in Plymouth, Mass., October 22, 1851; married, first, April 14, 1873, Evie A. Barrett; she died February 9, 1880; he married, second, November 8, 1881, Annie Reamy; Mr. Douglas is a machinist and resides at Plymouth Village.

One child by first marriage:

1369 I. Lena Mabel[7] born in Plymouth February, 1, 1874.

Children by second marriage born in Plymouth:

1370 II. Mertice May[7] born May 26, 1882.
1371 III. Alton Howard[7] born May 16, 1884.
1372 IV. Elisha Milton[7] born January 9, 1887; died February 2, 1889.
1373 V. Frances C.[7] born July 26, 1888.

1041. Clara F.[6] Douglas (William M.,[5] Joshua,[4] John,[3] John,[2] John,[1]) daughter of William M. and Sarepta (Pierce) Douglas. born in Rochester, Mass., April 23, 1851; married, July 24, 1869, Thomas W. Gault, born in Wareham, Mass. He runs a furnace in a mill at Freemont, Mass.

Children born in Wareham:

1374 I. William T. (Gault) born March 22, 1873; died April 4, 1878.
1375 II. Edgar T. (Gault) born April 6, 1877.
1376 III. Clara T. (Gault) born September 5, 1882.

1043. Maria L.[6] Douglas (William M.,[5] Joshua,[4] John,[3] John,[2] John,[1]) sister of the preceding, born January 31, 1857; married, first, Frank W. Ryan; married, second, Albert W. West, son of Henry and Rolinda (Foster) West.

Child by first marriage:

1377 I. Alice B. (Ryan) born September 24, 1875.

Children by second marriage:

1378 II. Albert W. (West) born December 26, 1883.
1379 III. Cora M. (West) born February 24, 1885.

COPY OF DEED GIVEN TO JOHN DOUGLAS.

The First Deed Granted JOHN DOUGLAS, of Middleborough, Mass., our earliest ancestor in America:

To all People to whom these presents shall come—GREETING:

Know ye that I John Bennett Junr. of the town of Middleborough in the County of Plymouth in New England for and in consideration of the sum of Thirty Pounds in Money to me already in hand paid by John Douglas of the town of Middleborough aforesaid. Wherewith I do acknowledge myself to be fully satisfied contented and paid. Have freely and absolutely Bargained and sold alienated enfeoffed and confirmed and by these presents do bargain sell alienate enfeoffed and confirm unto him the said John Douglas and his heirs and assigns forever a certain lot of land containing by estimation about thirty-seven acres be it more or less, being in number the one hundred thirty fourth Lot in the Third allotment in the purchase called the Sixteen Shilling Purchase in the Township of Middleborough aforesaid and did originally belong unto the Right of Frances Coombs the bounds hereof may at large appear upon the records of said purchase.

To Have and to Hold all the aforesaid lot of land lying and being as aforesaid with all and singular the profits privileges and appurtenances thereunto belonging from me the said John Bennett and my Heirs unto him the said John Douglas and his Heirs and assigns forever; with all my whole right title and interest of and unto the same and every part and parcel thereof to belong and appertain unto the only proper use and benefit & behoof of him the said John Douglas and his heirs and assigns forever. Warranting that at the time of the signing & sealing hereof I have good right full power and lawful authority in myself to dispose of ye above said premises with their appurtenances & every part and parcel thereof as is above expressed and do by these presents bind & oblige myself and my heirs forever to Warrant & Defend the title of the same against the lawful claims of all persons whatsoever. In witness whereof I the aforesaid John Bennett Junr have hereunto set my hand & seal this seventh day of May one thousand seven hundred thirty and nine.

JOHN BENNETT, Junr. [Seal.]

Plymouth ss, May ye 7th 1739. Then the above named John Bennett Junr personally appeared and acknowledged the above written instrument to be his act and deed.

Before me BENJ. WHITE Justice of Peace.

Signed sealed & del in
the presence of us
  SAMUEL TINKHAM JR.
  JACOB THOMPSON
    Received & recorded July 25th 1739.

pr JOSIAH COTTON Regt.

PLYMOUTH ss., April 30th, 1873.

The foregoing is a **true** copy from the Registry of Deeds, Book 33, Fol. 23.

WM. S. DANFORTH, Rg.

Copy of a Deed granted to CORNELIUS DOUGLAS, SR., by Belcher Noyes, Agent for the Pejepscot Proprietors.

To all Persons unto whom these Presents shall come Belcher Noyes of Boston in the County of Suffolk and Province of the Massachusetts Bay in New England, Esq., sends Greeting:—

Whereas the Proprietors of Land at Pejepscot, have laid out a New Township, to be called *Royalsborough, lying in the County of Cumberland, and Province aforesaid, described as follows, viz :—To begin at the Northeast corner of the Town of North Yarmouth, from thence to Androscoggin River, and down said river to the Northeast corner of the Township of Brunswick, and on the Northwest line of said Brunswick to extend to North Yarmouth line, and on said line on a Northwest course to the forementioned bounds, Including land granted to Jonathan Bagley Esq., and said Proprietors at their meeting duly warned according to Law, held at Boston aforesaid, by adjournment March 3d, 1768, did by vote appoint Messrs Jonathan Bagley, Belcher Noyes & Moses Little, a committee for this special purpose, to bring forward the settlement of said New Township and to procure Settlers agreable to the tenor of said Vote, and also impowered said Belcher Noyes to execute Deeds to the Settlers in behalf of said Proprietors, as by said Vote on their Records will more fully appear.

Know ye that I the said Belcher Noyes, pursuant to the aforementioned vote of said Proprietors, for and in consideration of the sum of Twenty-six Pounds thirteen shillings and four Pence lawfull money of said Province, received of Cornelius Douglas of said Royalsborough in the County of Cumberland & Province aforesaid, Yeoman in behalf of said Proprietors ; do by these Presents freely, fully and absolutely grant, bargain, sell, convey and confirm unto him, the said Cornelius Douglas his Heirs & assigns forever : A certain tract of Land, situate, lying and being in said New intended Township of Royalsborough, known in the Division of Lots by number Twenty Eight, described & bounded as follows, beginning about four rods from a Stake at the Southwest corner of Lot number Twenty Seven, thence Southwest one hundred and Sixty rods to the Southeast corner of Lot number Twenty Nine, thence Northwest one hundred rods, thence Northeast one hundred and sixty rods, thence Southeast one hundred rods, to the first mentioned bounds.

To Have and to Hold the above described lot of land, together with all & singular, the privileges, commodities and appurtenances to the same belonging or appertaining unto him the said Cornelius Douglas, his Heirs & assigns, as a free inheritance in fee simple forever : hereby covenanting in behalf of the said Proprietors, their respective Heirs, Executors and Administrators, to and with the said Cornelius Douglas, his Heirs and assigns, to warrant, confirm and defend him & them in the Possession of the said granted Premises against the lawfull claims of all Persons whatsoever.

In testimony that this Instrument shall be forever hereafter acknowledged by said Proprietors as their act and Deed, and be held good and valid by them, I the said Belcher Noyes, by virtue of the aforesaid vote, do hereto set my hand and seal this tenth day of December, Anno Domini, one thousand seven hundred and seventy-six.

BELCHER NOYES,   [SEAL]

Signed Sealed and Delivered
    in presence of us
ISAAC MERRILL,   JONATHAN BAYLEY.

ESSEX, ss. December 13, 1776. Then the above named Belcher Noyes Esq. acknowledged this instrument, executed by him in behalf of said Proprietors, as their act and deed.   Before
ISAAC MERRILL, *Justice of Peace.*

Rec'd 2d April, 1777 and recorded from the original.

Pr ENOCH FREEMAN, *Regr.*

---

* Now the town of Durham.

INDEX I.

DESCENDANTS OF JOHN DOUGLAS, BEARING HIS NAME.
CHRISTIAN NAMES OF THE DOUGLASES.

The figures before each name denote the year of birth; the figures after the name denote the consecutive number under which the birth is recorded. Names of those who are known to have died young are omitted.

A.

1802	Abner	180	1848	Albion L.	1051
1811	Abigail	320	1888	Annie A.	1323
1822	Abia	464	1869	Annie Vesty	1245
1796	Abijah	223	1874	Amy Reynolds	1353
1814	Abraham	293	1833	Alonzo Simeon	338
1851	Absalom	1079	1860	" C.	891
1795	Absalom	156	1844	"	945
1858	Albion	1089	1839	Amanda	642
1839	Absalom	504	1830	Amanda M.	458
1852	Addie Betsey	949	1842	Amanda Jane	763
1868	Albert M.	1300	1839	Ambros B.	411
1857	Albert	1059	1846	Ambros B.	414
1854	" L.	963	1827	Amos Bailey	220
1847	" M.	998	1825	Almira	639
1859	" H.	895	1859	Amy Cynthia	1010
1850	" Freeman	925	1852	Anna L.	833
1841	Albert	412	1863	Annie Julia	685
1852	Alfred Eugene	819	1864	Annie Belle	703
1871	Alfred N.	1065	1784	Annie	30
1881	Affie May	1212	1818	Annie Bailey	216
1865	Alice May	689	1792	Anna	38
1860	" G.	837	1835	Andrew Jackson	470
1861	" Frances	1175	1859	Annie M.	1169
1871	" Carrie	1182	1884	Alton Howard	1371
1869	" M.	1274	1859	Alvin W.	1220
1881	" Irene	1288	1849	Ansel Gibbs	931
1869	" Augusta	1351	1856	Ansel Morris	951
1878	Alice	1314	1857	Arthur B.	1219
1873	Alice	1330	1888	Arthur E.	1290
1799	Allen	172	1839	Arabine F.	762
1842	Albion C.	840	1883	Archibald Percy	1289
1858	Albion	1089	1834	Asa Albion	759

B.

1791	Barnabas Nye	167	1849	Betsey L.	1078
	Barton	340	1843	" Jane	595
18	Bathana	341	1802	"	289
1855	Benjamin F.	836	1812	"	448
1858	" Booker	854	1839	"	550
1789	Benjamin	60	1875	Blanch	972
1825	Benjamin Booker	336	1878	Berthie A.	973
1793	Betsey	168	1879	Berton W.	1294

C.

1843	Calbert Daniel	551	1855	Charles Everett	1055
1830	Caroline S	556	1843	" Albert	984
18	Caroline	576	1872	" Edward	1179
1820	Catharine A	217	1880	" Leonard	1211
1852	Calvin Howe	798	1855	" F	1218
1863	Carrie May	1077	1880	" L	1321
1863	Carrie Agnes	1176	1862	"	1081
1881	Carrie May	1267	1840	Cephes Henry	805
1869	Charles	1261	1857	Chloe A	694
1837	Caroline L	593	1869	Christina	699
1830	Charles	252	1837	Charlotte A	503
1816	"	332	1828	Christopher R	499
1853	" Albert	567	1799	Celia	158
1812	"	324	1803	Clarassa	364
1849	" R.	597	1830	Clarabel May	1030
1833	" Frances	652	1851	Clara F	1041
1872	" Bailey	704	1866	Cora Rebecca	1277
1854	"	731	1749	Cornelius	7
1847	" H	787	1780	Cornelius	28
1839	" Lyman	792	1798	Cornelius	42
1845	Charles Alfred	831	1819	Cynthia Adaline	452
1858	" Bishop	890	1839	Cynthia B	471
1853	" Everett	934	1850	Cynthia Addia	953
1863	" Lincoln	956	1867	Cynthia Etta	1329
1856	" Henry	964			

D.

1864	Daisy H	1157		David	179
1877	Dana C	904	1840	" Cornelius	262
1839	Daniel Berry	594	1816	"	371
1847	" A	848	1833	" Bennett	391
1857	" Franklin	701	1821	" C	495
1861	David	1090	1822	Dianna Dillingham	218
1747	Daniel	6	1813	Delight	368
1796	Daniel	33	1842	Dianna	421
1824	Daniel Robert	219	1810	Deborah	429
1830	Daniel K	408	18	Dulensin	339
1796	David	41	1890	Dorothy Frances	1315
1779	David	46	1856	Delia J	1256
1783	David	72			

E.

1784	Earl	123	1886	Estella Alice	1270
1832	Edwin	780	—	Emma Small	1301
1845	Edwin Weston	795	1760	Elizabeth	19
1845	Edward Berry	807	1786	"	48
1841	Edwin Charles	842	1782	"	56
1871	Edward A	1066	1804	"	105
1874	Edwin Allen	1135	1798	"	109
1872	Edwin	1303	1810	"	162
1770	Edward	35	—	"	281
1812	Edward Franklin	232		"	736
1845	Edwin Delas	564	1822	Eliza Jane	249
1879	Ethel Jane	1287	1827	Eliza H	388
1867	Edgar Emerson	1125	1826	Eliza	445
1839	Elbridge Thompson	655	1824	Eliza Ann	466
1720	Elijah	2	1828	Eliza Ann	580
1768	"	14	1833	Eliza	781
1775	"	45	1809	Elmira	107
1786	"	58	1832	Emily	501

INDEX. 215

1801	Elijah	130	1838	Edsell A		418
1809	"	319	1841	Ellen Augusta		656
1822	"	435	1854	Ellen Maria		680
1847	" Eliot	923	1845	Ellen Elizabeth		764
1792	Elias	169	1846	Ellen D		1039
1851	Elisha T. P.	1040	1838	Emily		783
1822	Elisha	300	1839	Emily		803
1771	Elisha	22	1843	Emily S.		1038
1816	Elisha	474	1871	Elmer Edward		1057
1820	Elisha	494	1849	Emma Jane		986
1862	Effie S.	1156	1869	Elsie Western		1181
1860	Ella Jane	687	1845	Esther Ann		816
1859	Ella A	846	1887	Ethel M		1311
1855	Ella Jane	935	1816	Elvira Jane		619
1882	Ella J	1322	1841	Elvira Nancy		643
1873	Elanora Bailey	1194				

F.

1859	Frank Pierce	881	1857	Franklin Porter		1014
1861	" R.	896	1863	Flora D		967
1851	" M.	933	1866	Flora Ella		1356
1856	" Leslie	961	1864	Flora		1276
1858	" L.	965	1883	Flora F		1310
1883	" Elwell	1213	1888	Frances C		1373
1862	" N.	1275	1851	Frederic B		852
1882	" D.	1316	1882	Fred Evans		903
1870	Frank Emery	1264	1879	Fred Wesley		1266
1854	Franklin Jay	988	1808	Freelove E		437

G.

1812	Gardiner, Rev	294	18—	George W		1278
1884	Gifford	1204	1762	"		24
1829	Gilman S	739	1787	"		77
1829	George	589	1792	"		126
1859	" Gifford	702	1796	"		171
1837	" Henry	741	1824	"		250
1840	" Henry	838	1816	"		331
1868	" Hinckley	882	1834	" P.		410
1872	" Alfred	1032	1850	" Emery		424
1868	" Weston	1063	1823	"		465
1859	" E.	1076	1844	" Washington		507
1870	" Christopher	1118	1834	"		559
1882	" Warren	1198	1837	"		561
1884	" Gifford	1204	1845	" Allen		582
1866	George	1128				

H.

1800	Hannah	66	1888	Harry W		1296
1790	"	78	1871	Harry A		1193
1794	"	222	1878	Harry R		1282
1822	"	256	1805	Harrison		365
1814	" Elizabeth	287	1871	Herbert		971
1818	" "	333	1851	"		1153
1814	"	370	1872	" Eugene		1188
1839	"	549	1865	"		1272
1832	"	581	1861	Henry		1091
1819	"	434	1812	Hiram Randall		163
1835	" M.	592	1809	"		183
1856	" Jane	598	1835	"		502
1835	" Elizabeth	753	1849	" William		553
1864	" Randall	893	1856	"		555

1831	Harriet Jane	641		1858	Hiram	1080
1833	" Ann	752		1845	Henry Clay	493
1839	"	995		1844	" Clay	664
1843	" Amanda	997		1866	" Howard	686
	"	577		1855	" Howard	928
18—	"	177		1868	" Lewis	1056
1836	" Graves	489		1848	Henrietta	832
1850	Hattie P	977		1876	Howard M	1066½
1857	" M	1168		1871	Hurbert	970
1864	Hattie E	1259		1796	Hugh	80
1872	" May	136		1800	Hugh	110
1853	Harriet Randall	888		1800	Huldah	227

I.

1855	Ida May	1167		1843	Isaac M	815
1848	Ida M	1216		1863	"	897
1858	Ida Affie	799		1806	"	106
1885	Ina G	1295		1811	"	114
1859	Isabel	1155		1832	" Henry	604
1867	Isabel	1273		1851	" H	420
1826	Ira Gifferson	456		1831	Irene	307
1835	Isaiah	722		1756	Israel	10
1856	"	732		1796	"	63
1886	" Willis	1214		1802	"	104
1823	"	335		1792	"	221
1843	Isaac Fisher	757		18—	"	343
1852	" Wesley	789		1828	Ivory Warren	640

J.

1780	James	55		1844	John A	419
1800	"	279		1858	" Franklin	426
1807	" S	312		1814	"	439
1850	" Howard	384		1821	" Edward	453
1845	" Madison	508		1826	"	467
1843	" Oscar	563		1824	" B	496
1849	" Alexander	851		1863	" F	505
1855	" Warren	1058		1835	" Edward	653
1882	" Alexander Jr	1304		1862	" Henry	682
1845	Jane Maria	758		1863	" Henry Jr	697
1813	Jane	322		1825	" W	735
1809	Jane	366		1830	" Albion	779
1785	Jenney	74		1837	" Henry	790
1797	Jenney	102		1860	" E	1080
1856	Jennie Elmer	425		1867	" Franklin	1177
1869	Jennie Blake	894		1876	" Weston	1184
1860	Jennie M	1000		1878	" Warren	1345
1814	Jesse P	473		1855	Joshua E	1042
1859	Jesse C	695		1753	Joseph	8
1845	Jessie P	1034		1774	"	37
1754	Job	9		1793	"	39
1787	Job	59		1776	"	53
1802	Job	280		1819	"	248
1805	Joanna	112		1817	"	278
1817	"	297		1809	"	284
1871	" F	1365		1812	"	431
1695	John	1		1861	" H	734
1722	"	3		1858	"	432
1774	"	15		1794	Joshua	40
1752	"	16		1794	"	127
1768	"	34		1833	" Lufkin	253
1792	"	100		1840	"	480
1803	"	111		1826	Joseph B	497

INDEX.   217

1782	John	122	18—	Joseph	578
1828	"	251	1888	" Nathan	1215
1826	" Henry	259	1770	Jotham	27
1832	" Henry	260	——	Jotham	178
1820	" Nichols	263	1821	Julia Ann	299
1814	"	295	1827	"	306
1803	" Banks	311	1823	" Ann	386
1821	"	383	1849	" Maria	958
1829	" William	407	1863	" E	1044

K.

| 1852 | Kate Meroa | 959 | —— | Kerziah | 176 |

L.

1867	Laura A	1299	1808	Lucy	161
1857	Lilla Ann	989	1860	Luella Clark	684
1865	Lillian Eliza	1031	1801	Lucy	310
1878	Linda L	1320	1830	Lucy E	500
1859	Lizzie Ann	670	1843	Lucy Jane	666
1850	" Freeman	566	1862	Lucy Elizabeth	1061
1877	" Maria	1195	1886	Lucy S	1318
1875	Leander M	1281	1847	Luther Anderson	930
1874	Lena Mabel	1369	1868	" Edward	1357
1873	Leonora Ardell	839	1826	"	436
1858	Leona May	768	1810	"	447
1812	Lemuel	185	1799	Lydia	43
1852	Lewis Morrill	679	1780	Lydia	121
1824	Lewis	444	1799	Lydia	129
1804	Levi	181	1820	Lydia	255
1839	Lodiac	983	1824	Lydia	264
1844	Lory Harmon	657	1817	Lydia	433
1835	Louisa	801	1818	Lydia	451
1812	Louisa	315	1873	Lydia Jane	1359
1850	Lucinda F	797	1840	Lydia M	813
1788	Lucy	125			

M.

1888	Mabel G	1319	1822	Mary	476
1877	Mabel M	1293	1847	Mary Emily	552
1881	Mabel F	1042½	1847	Mary A	565
1877	Mabel B	1134	1855	Mary	591
1870	Mabel F	1279	1845	Mary E. W	596
1848	Maggie P	967	1860	Mary Narcissa	709
1847	Maria	705	18	Mary L	738
1841	Maria Godwin	793	1838	Mary Stinson	754
1852	Maria A	962	1841	Mary Jane	804
1835	Maria S	980	1835	Mary Ellen	811
1834	Maria E	469	1847	Mary Augusta	845
1794	Mariam	62	1847	Mary Elizabeth	850
1797	Mariam	157	1862	Mary Pinkham	892
1819	Mariam	298	1858	Mary Martha	936
1817	Mahalah	166	1840	Maynard H	996
1819	Mahala	186	1844	Mary Jane	1011
1847	Margaret Emma	765	1857	Maria L	1043
1848	Margaret Jane	835	1850	Mary O	1075
1849	Marion	1152	1846	Mary Diantha	957
1863	Merrilla	1092	1865	Mary L	968
1868	Marrianna S	1178	1847	Mary Annie	975
1857	Martha	1009	1835	Mary S	980
1866	Martin Alonzo	1064	1744	Martin	5
1872	Marion Lewis	1352	1837	Martin V. B	479
1872	Marion	1363	1828	Martha P	468
1882	Mertice May	1370	1866	Maud M	1255

218   INDEX.

1844	Mary Jane		1011	1817	Mehitable C	440
1884	Mary J		1317	1784	Mercy	57
1862	Mary Etta		955	1808	Mercy	274
—	Mary E		1246	1809	Mercy	292
1763	Mary		13	1858	Mercy Jane	929
1757	Mary		18	1803	Melentha	427
1792	Mary		61	1886	Minnie	1308
1793	Mary		79	1861	Millie	696
1799	Mary		103	1874	Milton Herbert	692
—	Mary		173	1867	Minnie L	1292
1821	Mary A		187	1784	Moses	47
1835	Mary		265	1837	Moses Swift	560
1810	Mary		275	1876	Myra C	902
1810	Mary		285	1874	Myron Earle	1127
1811	Mary		286	1877	Myrtie Edna	1189
1840	Mary Jane		392	1878	Myrtie	1306
1843	Mary Ellen		413	1858	Melvin P	952

N.

1857	Nancy M		1036	1852	Nathan Winslow	1054
1855	Nancy		1008	1841	Nellie E	665
1846	Nancy A		946	1869	Nellie May	1187
1782	Nabby		29	1868	Nettie L	1263
—	Nancy		174	1814	Nehemiah Owen	316
1825	Nancy		302	1764	Noah	25
1816	Nancy Swift		450	1794	Noah	170
1812	Nathan		276	1841	Noah E	472
1824	Nathan King		477	—	Noah	575
1850	Nathan		728	1836	Noah H	782

O.

1848	Oliver A		415	1836	Oscar G	769
1846	Orlando Kellog		423	1849	Oscar Eaton	788
1867	Oremanda		1302	1877	Otis N	1265
1842	Otis H		785	1888	Oscar E	1271

P.

1840	Parmelia C		562	1807	Phebe	230
1761	Patience		12	1832	Phebe Nye	557
1803	Patience		44	1858	Phebe J	733
1781	Patience		71	1816	Philip Banks	317
1818	Pauline Jane		374	1823	Philanda	454
1798	Paul		226	1816	Peter	288
1767	Phebe		21	1797	Polley	108
1772	Phebe		36	1850	Polley Adaline	987
1792	Phebe		32	1760	Prudence	23
1814	Phebe		164	—	Prudence	175
1798	Phebe		224			

R.

1788	Rachel		49	1819	Rhoda	318
1806	Rachel		182	1828	Rhoda Harriet	457
1790	Rebecca		52	1834	Robert Walter	261
1830	Rachel R		737	1882	Robert E	1203
1853	Rachel Jane		853	1879	Robert Walter	1210
1880	Ratheur A		1309	1862	Rosa Harvey	688
1777	Rebecca		119	1870	Rosella	1093
1834	Rebecca Helen		740	1840	Roxanna F	1033
1821	Rhoda Coombs		621	1837	Rufus Collins	654
1820	Reuben		441	1802	Ruth	67
1853	Reuben Seth		950	1804	Ruth	160
1829	Richard O		389	1841	Ruth A	492
1800	Rhoda		225	1809	Rufus	231
1850	Rhoda Mehitable		948			

INDEX. 219

S.

Year	Name	Page
1885	Sadie G	1186
1887	Sadie Brown	1200
1789	Salvana	31
1814	Salley	115
1778	Samuel Dr	54
1788	Samuel	98
——	Samuel	301
1806	Samuel	291
1819	Samuel	375
1759	Sarah	11
1763	Sarah	20
1798	Sarah	64
1805	Sarah	131
1804	Sarah	282
——	Sarah B	296
1828	Sarah Jane	337
1818	Sarah	372
18—	Sarah M	417
1813	Sarah	438
1841	Sarah Ann	506
1854	Sarah Amanda	554
1852	Sarah M	730
1836	Sarah Ann	760
1843	Sarah Jane	843
1825	Sarah	587
1848	Sarah A	999
1882	Sarah E	1045
1767	Selah	26
1825	Seth	330
1823	Sewall	188
1826	Silas S	579
1823	Soloman	301½
1843	Sophia B	794
1881	Sophia	1307
1845	Stephen B	667
1848	Stephen Albert	678
1865	Stilman W	1291
1796	Southworth	128
1847	Stowers A	879
1790	Susana	99
1832	Stephen Sennett	390
18—	Susan	342
1839	Susan Fisher	755
1838	Susan O	761
1840	Susan T	770
1852	Susan F	1035
1841	Susan M	1037

T.

Year	Name	Page
1838	Theodore	982
1807	Theodates	283
1777	Thomas	69
——	Thomas	117
1804	Thomas	290
1849	Thomas Jackson	817
1855	Thomas Nash	834

V.

Year	Name	Page
1887	Vera	1205
1885	Violet	1305
1871	Viola E	1251

W.

Year	Name	Page
1818	Waitstell Webber	118
1786	Warren	124
1809	Warren	446
1814	Warren	449
1827	Warren S	478
1847	Warren O	796
1845	Warren P	844
1868	Walter Henry	683
1867	Walter	969
1874	Walter	1094
1869	Walter Franklin	1126
1868	Warren D	1250
1825	Washington	455
1837	Wilbur F	802
1784	William	73
1795	William	101
1837	William A	184
1847	William Henry	254
1833	William Booker	308
1809	William Booker	313
1821	William	334
1812	William	369
1824	William B	377
1825	William, Capt	387
18	William	416
1827	William	442
1820	William	443
1819	William Manter	475
1827	William	588
1819	William Estes	620
1854	William Harris	767
1845	William W	786
1832	William Sidney	800
1859	William Willis	849
1854	William Warren	880
1855	William Randall	889
1860	William Edward	966
1847	Warren O	796
1845	Warren P	844
1868	Walter Henry	683
1867	Walter	969
1874	Walter	1094
1869	Walter Franklin	1126
1861	Walter Scott	1257
1827	William	588
1845	William Lewis	974
1852	William Marcelous	1013
1859	William	1060
1875	William	1360
1837	Wilbur F	802
1867	William Henry	1260

INDEX II.

DESCENDANTS OF JOHN DOUGLAS BEARING OTHER NAMES.
FOR EXPLANATION SEE INDEX I.

ALLEN.

1817	Daniel D	202	1860	Josephine Chatman	1129
1814	Joseph B	201	1862	Sarah Jane	1130
1821	Levi D	204	1865	James Edwin	1131
1819	Mary	203	1872	Mellin Douglass	1132
1811	Phebe	200	1874	Leslie Chapman	1133

ALDRIDGE.

| 1879 | Vesta Ann | 1206 | 1884 | John Earnest | 1208 |
| 1881 | Henry Alton | 1207 | 1888 | Fred Lawrence | 1209 |

ARTHUR.

1863	Charles E	605	1853	Martha H	601
1855	George F	602	1862	Sarah H	604
1850	Mary F	600	1849	William H	599

AUSTEN.

1794	Anna	233	1803	Lydia	238
1801	Cornelius	237	1804	Phebe	239
1797	David	235	1811	Rebecca	242
1809	Esther	241	1807	Susanna	240
1795	John	234			

BAILEY.

| 1850 | Eben C | 710 | 1855 | Lydia Jane | 712 |
| 1852 | Phebe Anna | 711 | 1857 | John Herbert | 713 |

BATES.

1809	Benjamin	459	1813	Lucy	461
1815	Cynthia	462	1811	Lydia S	460
1816	Joseph	463			

BEAN.

1841	Marcia Ann	1141	1850	Harrison D	1146
1842	Abijah L	1142	1852	Lydia Emma	1147
1844	Mary A	1143	1855	Ella Jane	1148
1846	Rhoda Alice	1144	1857	Clara M	1149
1849	Phebe F	1145	1858	Eliza Small	1150

BEAL.

| 1885 | Mary Ann | 1191 | 1886 | Lizzie Ella | 1192 |

BIGELOW.

| 1870 | Harmon E | | | | 1190 |

INDEX.

BOOKER.

1794	Daniel	92	1789	Mary	90
1796	Elizabeth	93	1799	Mercy	94
1791	Hannah	91	1802	Patience	95
1809	Israel	97	1806	Miram	96
1783	James	88	1809	Israel	97

CAMPBELL.

—	Alfred	346	—	Octava	344
—	Alonzo	349	—	Rebecca	351
—	John	348	—	Warren	350
—	Lucretia	345	—	William	347

CHAPMAN.

1848	Israel Lewis	872	1860	Stephen Franklin	876
1854	George William	874	1864	Julia Rich	877
1857	Mary Sennett	875	1867	Ann Howard	878

CLARK.

1832	Mary R	909½	1842	Alice H	913
1837	Sarah R	910	1845	Helen M	914
1838	Deborah F	911	1847	Robert	915
1841	Hattie C	912			

COOMBS.

1822	Julia D	628	1836	Harriet A	634
1824	Mary Oliver	629	1837	Elvira J	635
1827	Huldah M	630	1839	Mary Olive	636
1829	Ellen	631	1842	Martha W	637
1831	Benjamin F	632	1844	Thomas A	638
1824	Rhoda E	633			

CURTIS.

1833	Samuel E	861	1844	George S	866
1835	Robert	862	1860	Mary Jane	1113
1838	Nehemiah	863	1862	Charles Nelson	1114
1841	David F	864	1864	Horace	1115
1843	Joseph P	865	1867	Hiram H	1116

CUSHMAN.

1853	Julia L	1121	1859	Henry	1123
1856	Carrie D	1122	1866	Emery	1124

DAY.

1841	Emeline	725	1847	George H	726

DAVIS.

1843	Benjamin F	273	1837	Lydia Ellen	271
1831	Dorcas W	268	1833	Margaret Snow	269
1835	Joseph Henry	270	1841	William Penn	272

EATON.

1817	Pauline	610	1826	Dorcas	614
1819	Anstress	611	1831	Alice I	616
1821	Caroline	612	1833	Maria S	617
1823	Hannah	613	1836	Abner H	618

ELLIS.

1858	Emily F	1025	1869	Rebecca H	1028
1859	Lizzie J	1026	1872	Franklin B	1029
1866	Winfield E	1027			

EVANS.

1835	Luther	990	1837	Danial F	1001
1836	Warren H	991	1840	Nathan	1002
1838	Rhoda J	992	1847	Eli Hugh	1004
1843	George W	993	1852	Charles W	1006
1848	Emma Jane	994			

EVEREST.

1857 Corelius 714

FANSWORTH.

1885 Annie L 1165

FREEMAN.

1865 Carrie May 1068

FIELD.

1835	Abagail G	399	1829	Mary Ann	396
1827	Elmira J	395	1837	Susan	400
1833	Eliza F	398			

FORBUS.

—	Axie	354	—	Martha	353
—	Amanda	356	—	Mercy	355
—	Mary	352			

FRENCH.

1847	Charles D	406	—	Jeremiah	405
1835	Elizabeth A	402	1837	Samuel D	403
1842	Fannie M	404	1833	William	401

GODDARD.

1826	Ira	243	1854	Lufkin Douglas	673
1830	Lydia Ann	245	1854	Abby Jane	674
1833	Patience Douglas	246	1856	Charles Winslow	675
1827	Silas	244	1859	Franklin Eli	676
1835	S. Jane	247	1861	Robert Henry	677
1851	James Emery	672			

GROVES.

1805	Lucy	195	1827	Isabel	213
1807	John	196	1830	George W	214
1810	Mary Ann	197	1817	Oliver	208
1812	Mikel	198	1824	Rufus	211
1813	Delenda	199	1812	Samuel	206
1827	Aurilla	212	1819	Sarah	209
1821	Henry W	210			

GAULT.

1873	William T	1374	1882	Clara T	1376
1877	Edgar T	1375			

HARMON.

1833	Sarah E	646	1839	George H	649
1835	Esther C	647	1841	Francis E	650
1837	Edward F	648	1843	Henrietta L	651

HALL.

1870	Hiram G	1119	1872	Eugene	1120

HOYT.

1851	Charles Thomas	606	1857	Sarah A	608
1853	Elbridge J	607	1861	George A	609

HUTCHINSON.

1867	Lillian A	1173	1869	Ernest E	1174

HOLMES.

——	Elisha	153	——	Samuel	155
——	Mary	154			

HORTON.

1846	Barbery	547	1844	Nathaniel	546
1833	Christopher	542	1839	Phebe	544
1848	Hiram	548	1842	Rube	545
1831	Lemuel C	541	1837	Eliza	543

JACKSON.

1871	Cora	706	1878	Gilbert E	706½

JOHNSON.

1859	Nellie M	1283	1868	Frederic H	1284

JORDAN.

1843	Charles H	525	1824	Russell	516
1826	Daniel R	517	1822	Salley	515
1836	Elizabeth	522	1827	Sarah A	518
1832	Hannah L	520	1839	Thursa M	523
1830	Isaac	519	1863	Charles E	1102
1834	James	521	1865	Alice	1103
1820	Mahala D	514	1871	Thursa L	1104
1841	Patience P	524	1874	Lillian L	1105

JEWELL.

1848	Julia	539	1844	Sarah Ann	538
1839	Louisa	536	1841	Thomas E	537
1851	Reuben R	540			

JONES.

1828	George	622	1834	John	625
1830	Amos	623	1836	Lemuel	626
1838	Ann	624	1841	Israel	627

KING.

1820	Betsey M	570	1824	Mary A	572
1815	Catherine C	568	1829	Nathaniel	573
1818	Charles F	569	1822	Patience	571
——	Lucy B	574			

KELLEY.

1857	Laura A	1095	1862	Amanda A	1099
1858	L. R	1096	1864	Viola A	1100
1860	Lucy A	1097	1867	Benjamin F	1101
1861	Mary E	1098			

LARRABEE.

1837	George H	660	1841	William F	662
1839	Lora H	661	1844	Charlotte M	663

LONGLEY.

1834	Thomas Henry	867	1841	George Earl	870
1837	Sarah Jane	868	1847	Esther	871
1839	William E	869			

MANTER.

1827	John D	484	1821	Preston, Capt.	481
1832	James L	487	1828	Rebecca	485
1823	Lydia	482	1830	Thomas B	486
1839	Lydia W	488	1824	William	483

MACE.

1829	Elizabeth	937	1846	Clarissa	939
1833	Nathan	938			

MARSH.

1846	Nellie G	907	1851	Isadora F	909
1849	George W	908			

MICHOLS.

—	Elias	509	—	Oliver	513
—	Irene	512	—	Rebecca	511
—	John	510			

MERRIMAN.

1830	Isabella	855	1836	Sarah J	858
1832	David D	856	1838	Frances	859
1837	Eli	857	1842	Susan	860

MORSE.

1835	Augustus F	267	1832	George N	266

McKINNEY.

1867	Leforest	1109	1869	Fanney	1111
1868	Hiram W	1110	1872	Thomas E	1112

PATCHER.

1848	Realfy	1082	1865	Thomas P	1086
1859	Almira	1083	1853	Sarah E	1087
1860	Emily	1084	1866	Hiram P	1088
1862	William A	1085			

PATTEE.

1830	Collins	528	1843	Ezra	534
1832	Caroline	529	1827	Henry	526
1836	Collins	531	1828	Hiram	527
1838	Caroline	532	1840	Mary Ann	533
1834	Emily	530	1845	Ruth	535

PIERCE.

1842	Mary Thomas	1016	1850	Laura A.		1049
1845	Caroline E	1017	1853	Sarah T.		1050
1848	Branch H	1018	1856	Charles M		1051
1846	Mary S	1047	1867	Nellie A. C.		1053
1848	Philip R. S.	1048				

PREBLE.

1824	Sarah E	742	1836	Betsey		748
1826	Abraham F	743	1837	Reuben		749
1828	Joseph	744	1839	Olivia		750
1830	Mary O	745	1841	Martha Ann		751
1834	Zelia	747				

RAYMOND.

1849	Sarah V	941	1854	Samuel T		943
1851	Dora A	942				

REYNOLDS.

18—	Daniel	145	—	Lydia		152
—	Ephriam	143	—	Mary		146
—	Elizabeth	144	1794	Phebe		148
1897	Hannah	149	1791	Roger		147
1802	Jacob	150	—	Tryphena		142
—	John	151				

ROBINSON.

1846	Jane K	916	1854	Colis C		920
1848	John Q	917	1856	Mary H		921
1850	William G	918	1857	Robert D		922
1852	Charles F	919				

RODICK.

1815	Daniel	358	1822	Mary		361
1820	Eliza Jane	360	1825	Roxilana		363
1805	Israel	357	1823	Sophrona		362
1817	Jane	359				

ROFF.

1840	Henrietta	772	1845	Henry		774
1842	Maria	773				

RYAN.

1875	Alice B		1377

SIMMONS.

—	Betsey	133	—	Lydia		141
—	Elijah	132	—	Mary		135
—	James	137	—	Persilla		136
—	Judith	139	—	Sarah		138
—	Libteth	140	—	Thaddeous		134

SIMPSON.

—	David	394	—	Lydia		393

SPINNEY.

1852	Elijah M		1222

STANTON.

| 1857 | John W . . . . 1071 | 1867 | Frederick . . . . 1073 |
| 1860 | William Wesley . . . . . 1072 | 1869 | Merritt . . . . 1074 |

SAMPSON.

| 1864 | Fred A . . . . 1366 | 1872 | Lillian C . . . . 1368 |
| 1869 | Pelham F . . . . 1367 | | |

STORER.

1871 Frances S 1286

SWIFT.

1846	Sarah Frances 1020	1852	Ruth B 1023
1848	Nehemiah G 1021	1854	Phineas 1024
1851	Ellen Maria 1022		

TARR.

1845	Abbie Jane 1158	1855	Marshal M 1162
1847	George 1159	1858	Leonard M 1163
1849	William A 1160	1861	Henry C 1164
1853	John F 1161		

TAYLOR.

| 1880 | Douglas . . . . 1201 | 1882 | Ethel . . . . 1202 |

WARD.

| 1844 | Charles Henry . . . . . . 775 | 1849 | Sarah E . . . . 777 |
| 1847 | James Alfred . . . . . . 776 | 1854 | Emma Jane . . . . . . 778 |

WILLIAMS.

| 1858 | Mary Ella . . . . 883 | 1862 | Mary Abby . . . . 885 |
| 1860 | William A . . . . 884 | 1864 | Hannah E . . . . 886 |

WHITE.

| —— | Amy Gifford . . . . . . 583 | —— | Alfred . . . . 585 |
| —— | Almira Frances . . . . . 584 | —— | Mary . . . . 586 |

WING.

| 1869 | Harold Clifton . . . . . . 1137 | 1875 | Alfred Boardman . . . . . 1139 |
| 1870 | Chester Brainard . . . . 1138 | | |

WINSHIP.

1851 Julia Ann 1019

WEST.

| 1883 | Albert W . . . . 1388 | 1885 | Cora M . . . . 1389 |

WELCH.

——	Esther 193	——	Nancy 189
——	John 190	——	Sarah Bailey 191
——	James 194	——	Salina Russell 192

WHEELER.

| 1819 | Daniel Perry . . . . 382 | 1814 | Lydia Buffum . . . . . . 380 |
| 1816 | John Douglas . . . . . . 381 | 1830 | William Henry . . . . . 383 |

NON - CIRCULATING

Lightning Source UK Ltd.
Milton Keynes UK
UKHW021840280621
386319UK00002B/352